# The 1st Cav in Vietnam

# The 1st Cav in Vietnam

## Anatomy of a Division

### Shelby L. Stanton

PRESIDIO

BALLANTINE BOOKS • NEW YORK

This book was originally published with the title:
# Anatomy of a Division

A Presidio Press Book
Published by The Ballantine Publishing Group

Presidio Press is a trademark of Random House, Inc.

www.ballantinebooks.com

**Library of Congress Cataloging-in-Publication Data**

Stanton, Shelby L., 1948–
  Anatomy of a division.

  Bibliography: p. 260
  Includes index.
  ISBN 0-89141-642-0
  1. Vietnamese Conflict, 1961–1975—Regimental histories.
  2. United States. Army. Cavalry Division, 1st—History. I. Title.
  DS558.4.S73  1987    959.704'34    86-25425
  ISBN: 0-89141-686-2 (paperback)
  ISBN: 0-89141-259-X (hardcover)

Printed in the United States of America

First Ballantine Books edition: February 2003

*To the memory of my father,*
*Samuel Shelton Stanton*
*1914–1986*

# Contents

## Maps

# Preface

Historically, the majority of U.S. cavalry served as dragoons. They rode into battle but fought on foot. The airmobile 1st Cavalry Division continued this cavalry tradition by riding helicopters into battle. The division cavalrymen employed automatic weapons, and were supported by aerial rocket artillery—the airmobile equivalent of the famed horse artillery—but dismounted to fight.

This book is a critical analysis of the mechanism and composition of the airmobile cavalry division, from its inception through the end of the Vietnam conflict (when its airmobile status was terminated). How the airmobile cavalry division was raised, managed, functioned, performed, and was supported are the important themes of this work. The book compares the division's utilization of helicopters which gave vertical dimension to such cavalry missions as reconnaissance, pursuit, raids, screening, exploitation, and the flexible shock action of mounted attack.

The book is not intended as a conventional division history, and therefore does not attempt to recount every divisional encounter of the Vietnam war. Although the main course of the division's service in Vietnam is given as a necessary prelude to understanding its unique combat role, specific actions were chosen to represent certain cavalry techniques as applied in an airmobile environment. Since the book is arranged chronologically, with special topics treated last, the missions and organization of the division's various components are not addressed until Chapter 10. However, the reader is encouraged to read this chapter preparatory to the battle sections, if more clarity is desired in intradivisional unit relationships.

Throughout this volume's treatment of division performance in Vietnam, the reader should remember that the airmobile division was still being developed when thrust into combat. The tactical and operational warfare parameters which determined the airmobile division's employment were also in the experimental stage. The division was sent into a remote, geographically hostile environment, burdened with many political restrictions in an increasingly unpopular war against a strong and cunning enemy, and was expected to demonstrate the value of combat airmobility by securing battlefield victory. It reflects great credit upon the personnel of the 1st Cavalry Division that this airmobile doctrine was implemented successfully under such circumstances.

The author received encouragement and assistance from several people in the writing of this book. Of these, the author is especially grateful for the excellent guidance of Colonel Rod Paschall, Director of the U.S. Army Military History Institute, and he outstanding professional resources which this important facility offered. Special thanks are owed to my editor, Adele Horwitz, and my wife, Kathryn, for their dedicated support. The author must also pay tribute to the government military historians of the Vietnam era, who insured that a valuable record of the Army's role and internal action was available for future scholars.

Shelby L. Stanton
Captain, U.S. Army, Retired
Bethesda, Maryland

# Anatomy of a Division

# "Cavalry, and I Don't Mean Horses!"

## *Aerial Cavalry Evolution*

The 1st Cavalry Division's arrival on the battlefields of Vietnam was not presaged by the sound of trumpets or thundering hooves, but rather by the close suppressive fires of aerial gunships and fighter-bombers escorting waves of assault helicopters. After being transported over miles of normally inaccessible jungle terrain, the airmobile cavalrymen were inserted into their remote landing zones by dismounting from their troopship skids into the midst of enemy positions below. For the first time in military history, a combat organization was designed and structured to rely on the shock and fury of vertical helicopter attack to deliver its frontline soldiers. However, these bold airmobile strikes represented only the mailed fists of a larger Army machine. How this machine was conceived and created, the interrelationship of its component parts, and how it functioned and performed are the substance of this book.

The air assault itself represented the very *raison d'être* of the airmobile cavalry division and the culminated focus of its resources toward battlefield domination. The dangerous art of infantry attack from the sky demanded a carefully conceived and synchronized orchestration of all division elements of the greater body. Scout and reconnaissance aircraft and pathfinders served as the eyes which found and marked the landing fields and their approaches. Airlifted artillery howitzers and cannon, the muscle power manned by artillerymen but supplied and maintained by ammunition and ordnance teams, fired the necessary preparatory barrages.

The assault helicopter formations were an integral part of division aviation, the legs of the division, and the troops they carried were the hardened workhands with the essential tools of war. Fire support was continued during final helicopter descents by shifting artillery to one side, conducting simultaneous airstrikes with napalm, bombs, and 20-mm cannon strafing on the opposite flank, and using armed helicopters with rockets, miniguns, and automatic grenade launchers to cover the rest of the target area. Navigation for the airmobile columns had to be precise and tightly controlled in order to avoid Air Force flight paths and artillery shell trajectories. This rigid fire control was insured by commanders and observation officers, the directing brains, in control helicopters linked by signalmen with sophisticated radio and communications equipment.

Once on the ground, the air assaulted troops relied on the integrated efficiency of all other organizational segments for their survival and replenishment. If the hands were cut off and eliminated, the remainder of the divisional body was denuded of its main protection and directly threatened with destruction. The successful conduct of the air assault was the responsibility of the primary and special staffs, the heart of the division, which planned and coordinated offensive action with all constituent segments. Engineers provided the building muscle required to clear the ground, construct airstrips and helipads, and furnish defensive positions. Their skilled enterprise could cover body parts with a shell of protection or shield of defense. Discipline within the body of troops was enforced and regulated by an organic military police corps. The entire divisional structure was nourished by a host of supply troops, serviced by support technicians, and repaired by maintenance personnel.

Together, these diverse but integral elements composed the total division fighting machine. Without them the division lacked the fabric of life; without the fusion of their combined energy the division was crippled in its performance; without the direction offered by aggressive leadership the division remained blinded and handicapped in its ability. When properly led and interconnected, these components forged a powerful division that became a major instrument of national will.

Divisions are a recent development in the history of organized warfare, being initially employed by France in the late 1700s. They became an accepted part of peacetime European military establishments during the next century. In the United States, divisions were temporarily raised during the Civil War, but did not become primary formations within the army structure until the passage of the National Defense Act of 1916, just prior to America's entry into World War I. Divisions now constitute the basic framework of most world armies.

The division is essentially the modern equivalent of the ancient Roman legion. In both cases, infantry, engineer, artillery, signal, and service troops are combined into permanent organizations capable of independent and sustained combat operations. Divisions, like legions, are self-sufficient combat commands capable of influencing direction of battle with only normal support. As Rome safeguarded her empire with a vanguard of fighting legions, the modern United States protected its global interests with a number of combat divisions. In the post–World War II era, the United States usually fielded an average of sixteen Army and two Marine divisions.

In the mid-twentieth century, divisions were still landbound. Although marine divisions had amphibious ability, and airborne divisions could enter desired territory by parachute descent, actual battlefield maneuver was restricted to the timeless pace and terrain limitations of marching infantry. Mechanized and armored divisions were faster, but were confined by terrain restrictions. In the 1950 Korean War even vehicular speed, which promised to reset the clockwork of modern battle during previous lightning war campaigns, was effectively slowed by rugged landscape and improved antitank weapons to the step of escorting foot soldiers. Aerial transport of divisions was rare, since airlift was expensive and required assembly in secure airport staging areas at either end of the trip.

At the same time, helicopter technology was producing machines of increasing size and dependability. In the immediate post-Korean decade, the technical basis was built for a series of helicopters which could deliver hovering firepower and vertical lift dimensions to the battlefield. These newly introduced designs were improved and utilized to create an organization destined to radically alter forever both the mode and rate of ground combat.

Under the farsighted guidance of a few select leaders, the United States Army engineered a novel set of tactics based on newly developed weaponry and air assault principles. This effort was initiated during the summer of 1962, when a board of officers headed by Gen. Hamilton H. Howze studied the promise of tactical airmobility with a few trial units at the infantry school post of Fort Benning, Georgia. Following their recommendations for further formal testing, the Army raised the 11th Air Assault Division and its associated 10th Air Transport Brigade. After three years of testing, an entirely new type of division was created. This unit, the 1st Cavalry Division (Airmobile), represented the first airmobile combat force in history and "a landmark in the evolution of U.S. Army organization."[1]

In 1965 the 1st Cavalry Division was deployed to the war-torn highlands and jungles of Vietnam. There for the next seven years, this highly mobile and aggressive formation proved the validity of the airmobile concept. The division contained more than twenty thousand men at peak combat strength, but its real firepower was forged by fusing its manpower, weapons, and transportation with cavalry doctrine. Maximum shockpower was maintained by joining the division's light infantrymen and supporting artillery with an aerial armada of helicopters. A host of command ships following a vanguard of scout helicopters led the troop-filled utility helicopters into battle. They were escorted by waves of attack gunships and rocket helicopters, while medical evacuation and resupply helicopters stood ready to assist. From the smallest scout helicopters brazenly circling over enemy targets to the largest crane and cargo helicopters whirling howitzers and supplies into forward positions, the 1st Cavalry Division (Airmobile) represented the essence of modern, mobile Army striking power. From the field its wartime commander Maj. Gen. Harry W. O. Kinnard declared to *Newsweek* that he was "freed from the tyranny of terrain."[2]

The 1st Cavalry Division (Airmobile) was one of the most powerful war machines ever fielded, and certainly one of the best-trained and best-equipped American units sent into combat. The division successfully merged the infant doctrine of vertical aerial assault with traditional cavalry functions to produce a revolutionary new style of warfare. Its actual genesis, however, was conceived a decade earlier in the frozen hills of Korea as a result of one of the worst battlefield defeats suffered by American arms, a loss occasioned by the lack of cavalry.

1. Virgil Ney, *Evolution of the U.S. Army Division, 1939–1968*, CORG Memorandum M-365, Headquarters, United States Army Combat Developments Command, Fort Belvoir, Virginia, 1969, p. 92.
2. *Newsweek*, 13 December 1965, p. 28.

In the American tradition, cavalry had always signified the fast light cavalry: horse troopers capable of covering the wilderness distances of a vast continent. Light cavalry excelled in scouting and reconnaissance, providing a mobile screen for the slower infantry, and riding dispatches as messengers. Mounted militia volunteers, rangers, and light dragoons served a vital role in frontier warfare, tracking down and pursuing Indian marauders. During the Mexican War, horse soldiers performed important reconnaissance and pursuit missions. Later mass migration west into unexplored territory brought the need for mobile protection of the settlers, and mounted riflemen answered the call.

In the United States, cavalry became a force to be reckoned with during the Civil War. Cavalry activity often closely conformed to traditional experience. For instance, mounted riders gathered information about opposing forces, destroyed bridges and engaged in other harassing actions, and provided general messenger and mobile guard details. The dash and cunning of a few imaginative cavalry leaders also gave a new, expanded dimension to cavalry service. Their names rang like rattling sabers across the pages of history: Jeb Stuart, Custer, Sheridan, and Forrest. They grouped cavalrymen into independent formations equally capable of executing swift attacks or decisive delaying actions and sent reinforced units of riders patrolling through the broken eastern woodlands to cover the flanks of entire armies marching on campaign.

One of the most important tactical results of this heightened cavalry emphasis was the cavalry raid. Cavalry raids overran outposts and disrupted lines of communication, created havoc and confusion in the opponent's camp, captured or destroyed supplies, secured reliable long-range information about enemy dispositions, and shielded larger troop movements.

After the Civil War, cavalry was again fragmented as a result of the fluid warfare required in securing the Far West. Cavalry regiments were dispersed across the thinly garrisoned frontier. The end of the Indian Wars and the reduced need to police the western interior spelled the doom of the traditional American cavalry, although several later Mexican border incidents temporarily created a need for cavalry on mounted patrol duty. In the next few conflicts preceding World War II, American cavalry troops were generally limited to courier service or fighting as dismounted infantry.

Renewed bandit and other illegal activity along the desolate boundary between Mexico and the United States necessitated continuous patrolling of the region by horse soldiers. Under the new National Defense Act, the 1st Cavalry Division was formed on 12 September 1921 to safeguard the southwestern borders and to prevent gunrunning, cattle rustling, and the smuggling of narcotics, liquor, and other high-duty items. The economic depression of the 1930s spawned the Civilian Conservation Corps, and the division was soon relegated to providing logistical and administrative cadre for CCC companies in the Arizona–New Mexico district.

Prior to and during the Second World War, there was little agreement on the proper employment and function of Army cavalry on the armored-infantry battlefield, so the cavalry compromised, adopting a little of both. The basic problem was the advent of improved motorization in the scheme of modern warfare, and the resulting demise of the horse on which the cavalry was largely reliant and traditionally attached to. Cavalry adopted new doctrines premised on light mechanized reconnaissance, converted into infantry, or perished. This led to a postwar consensus that cavalry had either been misused altogether or lacked enough combat striking power to properly fulfill its assigned reconnaissance roles.

In 1941 the entire 1st Cavalry Division was assembled at Fort Bliss, Texas, for extensive field training. Its authorized personnel strength jumped from 3,575 to 10,110 troops. News of the Japanese attack on Pearl Harbor, which thrust the United States into active hostilities, found many members of the division on furlough or back in civilian life, but men poured into Fort Bliss from all over the country to rejoin their units. The cavalry troopers remained horse soldiers until February 1943, when the division received orders assigning it overseas. The changeover from horses to jeeps commenced. Since the division was intended for amphibious assault duty in the southwest Pacific, it was transformed by special equipment allowances and its cavalrymen retrained as foot soldiers. Finally, on 20 July 1945, in the Philippines, the division was completely reorganized as an infantry formation. At that point the division's only association with its proud cavalry heritage was the honorary retention of its cavalry designators.

While the 1st Cavalry Division fought as infantry, other smaller cavalry units struggled across Europe in armored cars and light tanks. Their tactical reconnaissance functions were lost in a war where big armored divisions were relied upon to punch through enemy lines, and strategic cavalry functions were replaced by aircraft. Even Lt. Gen. George S. Patton, Jr.'s, own Third Army "Household Cavalry," the 6th Cavalry Group, was relegated to messenger service between his speeding armored divisions; he officially redesignated the group as his Army Information Service.

Armor emerged from the conclusion of World War II as the decisive ground arm of mobility. The eminence of armor was sealed by the Army Organization Act of 1950, which combined armor and cavalry into one branch, designated as armor. The armor branch was technically to be a continuation of cavalry, but actual cavalry functions were quickly eroded by the mainstream armor philosophy that massed tank formations would dominate the atomic battlefield of the future. Many armor officers believed that future wars would witness the mailed fists of armored giants hammering each other into capitulation under a rain of nuclear warheads and held little regard for the traditional American cavalry mode of fast raids, light reconnaissance, and mobile security. In the immediate postwar years the only cavalry that existed was the U.S. Constabulary in occupied Europe and the 1st Cavalry Division, an infantry outfit stationed in Japan.

Cavalry was conceptually a different arm of mobility from armor. The cavalry mobility differential was based on shock effect through firepower, which also screened both time and information. Cavalry existed to deny the enemy that talisman of success—surprise—while providing friendly forces with the means to achieve the same result. Cavalry had ceased to be associated with horses, crossed sabres, crumpled wide-brimmed campaign hats, and carbines slung from the hip, but no one seemed to know where modern cavalry fitted. "Fighting Joe" Hooker's famous Civil War adage, "Who ever saw a dead cavalryman?" had been sadly shortened to simply "Who ever saw cavalry?" By June 1950, when invading North Korean armies surged over the 38th parallel into the south, the United States military had lost its real cavalry ability. The gallant arm of decision which Forrest had once described as arriving "fustest with the mostest" was now, in terms of mobility and firepower, "lastest with the leastest."

On 18 July 1950, fifteen years before entering Vietnam, the 1st Cavalry Division was sent to the rugged peninsula of South Korea to reinforce Lt. Gen. Walton H. Walker's Eighth Army. The division was one-third understrength and infantry in all but name. It was committed to the rapidly shrinking Pusan perimeter as Walker's allied contingents retreated farther south. Obviously, the tactical situation called for a cavalry force to be committed at once, to screen and delay while the heavier infantry and armored forces built up a more substantial defense. Neither Walker, United Nations Command General Douglas MacArthur, nor the United States military had any true cavalry available. In many cases Walker's infantry was outpaced by North Korean armored columns. The Eighth Army fell back with wide-open flanks, desperately trading space, weapons, and even lives for time. On Walker's left a gap of a hundred miles extending to the sea could have been readily penetrated, a situation begging for cavalry, but none was around. The "cavalry" division on hand was composed of foot soldiers in foxholes grimly defending the main road from Seoul to Pusan.

By mid-September Walker's army was compressed into a dangerously small pocket in the extreme southeastern portion of the Korean peninsula. General MacArthur broke this stalemate on 15 September with a daring amphibious assault behind North Korean lines at Inchon, just west of Seoul. The successful surprise landing left the North Korean army stunned and cut off. The return to fluid warfare on American terms of mobility promised both a rapid breakthrough to the north and a fast linkup between the invading X Corps and Walker's army advancing from the south. The situation was ripe for highly mobile cavalry forces which could exploit the opening, but none was forthcoming. The rear of the Naktong River line could have been seized in hours by daring cavalry, but instead nearly two weeks elapsed before the American forces linked up.

The move north to destroy the remnants of the North Korean army was not preceded by "flying columns" of swift cavalry, but advanced at the tortuous road-bound pace of a mechanized column twisting through the jagged Korean mountains. This column was composed of mixed tanks and trucks, all moving forward at the pace of foot soldiers groping blindly from road bend to road bend and from hill to hill. In October the entire Korean peninsula was wide open, but Walker's divisions were forced by the lack of adequate long-range cavalry reconnaissance to advance in ignorance of enemy dispositions.

The lack of cavalry prevented the scouting of likely enemy assembly areas throughout the advance. In late October the 6th Republic of Korea Division was surprised and broken by a sudden attack east of Unsan. On 1 November a battalion of the 1st Cavalry Division's 8th Cavalry Regiment was suddenly surrounded and smashed by another carefully prepared trap, leaving the Americans bewildered as the enemy melted into the mist-shrouded mountains. T. R. Fehrenbach aptly described the situation in his classic treatise on the Korean conflict, *This Kind of War:* "In the frightful terrain such patrolling was dangerous. It could not be supported by wheels, and where wheels could not go, neither could sizable units of Americans. And in such horrendous terrain a vast army could be—and was—hidden in a very small area, observing perfect camouflage discipline, waiting."[3]

During the last week of October, the Americans reached the Yalu River, but the absence of any properly balanced cavalry force continued to invite disaster. Adequate ground surveillance of the Yalu River crossings was manifestly impossible. The American divisions were struck with complete and overwhelming surprise by thirty Chinese divisions on 26 November 1950. Without cavalry to patrol or cover the steep maze of mountain peaks and razorback ridges, Walker was doomed to a crushing piecemeal defeat as unit after unit stumbled into Chinese ambush.

The question "Where was Walker's cavalry?" was answered bluntly four years later by Maj. Gen. James M. Gavin (West Point, 1929), an enthusiastic cavalry supporter and highly respected commander of the crack 82d Airborne Division during World War II, in his landmark *Armor* article, "Cavalry, and I Don't Mean Horses!" Gavin found that Walker simply had no adequate cavalry, since real cavalry had ceased to exist throughout the Army, and offered a startling but technically feasible solution to the tragic Yalu debacle. He stated, "Where was the cavalry? . . . and I don't mean horses. I mean helicopters and light aircraft, to lift soldiers armed with automatic weapons and hand-carried light antitank weapons, and also lightweight reconnaissance vehicles, mounting antitank weapons the equal of or better than the Russian T-34s [tanks]. . . . If ever in the history of our armed forces there was a need for the cavalry arm—airlifted in light planes, helicopters, and assault-type aircraft—this was it."[4]

3. T. R. Fehrenbach, *This Kind of War* (New York: Macmillan Company, 1963) p. 296.
4. Maj. Gen. James M. Gavin, "Cavalry, and I Don't Mean Horses!" *Armor*, Volume LXIII, No. 3, p. 18.

General Gavin was a paratrooper, a light infantryman well acquainted with the mobility potential of aircraft. Like many hardy World War II army parachute volunteers, he felt paratroopers were the modern heirs to the bold cavalrymen of yesteryear, since the emphasis on heavy armor excluded most tankers from the fast raiding and slashing agility of the old light dragoons. In the 1943 invasion of Sicily, Gavin's 505th Parachute Regimental Combat Team drew the tough assignment of parachuting between the German reserves and the allied assault beaches. Although their method of entry called for parachutes instead of saddles, their actual missions were all historically typical of cavalry—to screen larger troop movements (the landings), to delay enemy use of critical terrain, and to secure several crossroads.

Gavin considered most parachutist missions conducted during the war to be cavalry-style operations. For example, a battalion of the 509th Parachute Infantry jumped into Avellino, Italy, to secure a key road center leading to the allied landing site at Salerno. In the invasion of France, the 82d and 101st Airborne Divisions were directed to block all enemy attempts to reinforce the beaches and to attack from the rear, another classic cavalry mission. Gavin was convinced that "what we needed next was a closer integration with the inheritors of the cavalry role, the armored forces, without loss to the highly mobile and aggressive character of the airborne forces, the 'lean and mean' philosophy."[5]

Gavin felt that the armor branch was unresponsive. Instead of reducing the weight of mechanized equipment so that aircraft could be developed and produced to carry the new light armored forces into battle, vehicles got only heavier. He refused to give up, and when promoted to Army Assistant Chief of Staff for Operations, Gavin walked the halls of the Pentagon, pleading for the cause of airmobility. He had several staff studies prepared on the subject and summarized these in his article which first appeared in *Harper's* magazine, but it did not receive widespread professional military attention until reprinted in the May-June issue of *Armor* magazine, itself the retitled continuation of the older esteemed *Cavalry Journal*. Gavin wrote urgently, "Cavalry-type screening missions will have to be conducted at much greater distances, and with much greater rapidity, than have hitherto

---

5. Ibid., p. 21.

been considered acceptable. The mobility differential to make this possible *must* be achieved. It is within our grasp, fortunately, in the air vehicles now being developed—assault transports, light utility planes, helicopters, and convertaplanes. Forces so organized and equipped will have a predominant influence on future warfare."[6]

Gavin's article reflected the vision of a few cavalry and helicopter enthusiasts and proved to be the catalyst which sparked the imagination of several other forward-thinking officers. These capable men represented diverse backgrounds, ranging from old horsemen-turned-armor-commanders to light infantrymen who doubled as aviators, but they all shared Gavin's conviction that modern aerial cavalry was necessary. They eventually implemented the revolutionary air assault philosophy, but the realization of airmobility still faced the prospects of a long, uphill struggle through the restrained Army bureaucracy.

After the Korean War, in the mid-1950s, the Army was axed by budget cuts. Big bombs and massive retaliation were the rage in military thought. Maj. Edwin L. "Spec" Powell, who would later become the Director of Army Aviation, listened to many analysts proclaiming, "Well, the only purpose for an army in the future is to defend strategic air bases."[7] Within the Army there was widespread sentiment that the Korean War was the cause of current disfavor and that the conflict had been "fought on Asian soil on Asiatic terms," where restricted combat in the hellish mountain ranges forced the Army to trade rifleman for rifleman, without benefit of America's technical edge in mobility and supporting firepower.

The Army possessed airplanes and primitive helicopters, but had no conception of their true value. Many officers with Korean experience under their belts vividly remembered the fragile light observation helicopters darting up and down sheer mountainsides carrying litter patients and emergency supplies. Only a very few foresaw the future possibility of waves of sturdier helicopters ferrying whole battalions across such ranges. The natural inertia of the military

---

6. Ibid., p. 22. Emphasis cited in the original article.
7. U.S. Army Military History Institute, *Senior Officers Debriefing Program*, conversations between Brig. Gen. Edwin L. Powell and Col. Bryce R. Kramer and Col. Ralph J. Powell, Carlisle Barracks, Pennsylvania, 1978, p. 31. Hereafter cited as USAMHI, Powell Debriefing.

institution confined embryonic aviation development to practices everyone was used to, such as spotting artillery fire with light Cub observation planes.

The Director of Army Aviation in 1955 was a distinguished ex–horse cavalryman, Gen. Hamilton H. Howze, who became one of the driving forces in airmobile development. A West Point graduate who was qualified as both an airplane and helicopter pilot, Howze had seen World War II action with the 1st Armored Division in North Africa and Italy. He recalled that the "army hadn't grasped at all, from its experience in Korea, the real utility of the light aircraft and what could be done by really integrating them into the tactics and combat support of the army. There was really very little knowledge in the army that the Marines, during one very small operation in Korea, had lifted a small party of Marines to the top of an unoccupied mountain, and had found this to be a useful thing to do."[8] Still, the Korean conflict had produced a general awareness of the need to strengthen Army aviation.

In the absence of formal Army policy, officers in several scattered posts began experimenting with whatever material was available. They often worked without official guidance and in spite of high-echelon disapproval and even ridicule. In June 1956 Col. Jay D. Vanderpool, the energetic chief of the Army aviation school's combat development office at Fort Rucker, Alabama, assembled an armed helicopter platoon, mounting weapons and other hardware scrounged, borrowed, or stolen from junkyards and other units. Jay's "Sky-Cav" platoon soon gained a notorious reputation for jerry-rigged rockets and hair-raising treetop-level aerial firing demonstrations. Two years later this unlikely outfit was legitimized as the Army's provisional 7292d Aerial Combat Reconnaissance Company, but Vanderpool was already conceiving "armair" formations up to division in size. Col. John J. Tolson took over the Army infantry school's airborne department at Fort Benning, Georgia, and created an airmo-

8. U.S. Army Military History Institute Research Collection, *Senior Officer Debriefing Program: History of Army Aviation*, conversations between Gen. Hamilton Howze and Col. Glenn A. Smith and Lt. Col. August M. Cianciolo, Carlisle Barracks, Pennsylvania, p. 8. Hereafter cited as USAMHI, Howze Debriefing.

bility section which included a field experiment helicopter company.[9] This formative stage of airmobility reflected the continuing disjointed nature of the Army aviation effort. In October 1959 the Army Chief of Research and Development, Lt. Gen. Arthur G. Trudeau, initiated the Army aircraft development plan to seek firm guidance in bridging the gap between Army and Air Force responsibilities and to permit aircraft development in harmony with projected Army requirements. Although Trudeau felt that light observation aircraft remained the "bread-and-butter" mission of Army aviation, Army expectation studies in two other areas (manned surveillance and tactical transport) were also presented to industry at Fort Monroe, Virginia, on 1 December 1959. These studies allowed exploration of technical approaches by the aircraft manufacturers, and two months later forty-five companies submitted 119 design concepts in response.[10]

The Army Chief of Staff, Gen. Lyman L. Lemnitzer, established a board of officers on 15 January 1960 to consider the Army aircraft development plan and to receive the industry proposals. The board was chaired by Lt. Gen. Gordon B. Rogers, the deputy commanding general of the Continental Army Command, and included several airmobility enthusiasts. The guiding genius behind the board was its secretary, Col. Robert R. "Bob" Williams, who was the first pilot to be designated Master Army Aviator. The Rogers Board advocated immediate development of a new helicopter capable of observation, target acquisition, reconnaissance, and command and control functions. Although the Rogers Board was primarily interested in deciding on aircraft types, it also recommended that a study be prepared "to determine whether the concept of air fighting units was practical and if an experimental unit should be activated to test feasibility and develop material requirements."[11]

The Rogers Board review was almost completely confined to development in aviation material. The board still suggested the possible

---

9. Lt. Gen. John J. Tolson, *Vietnam Studies: Airmobility, 1961–1971* (Washington, D.C.: Department of the Army, 1973), pp. 5–6.

10. Army Aircraft Requirements Review Board booklet, Fort Monroe, Virginia, dtd 29 February 1960.

11. Ltr, Army Aircraft Requirements Review Board to CofSA, dtd 10 March 1960. Subj: AACFT Rqr Rev Bd, commonly referred to as the Rogers Board Report.

aviation means needed to reposition fighting forces on the battlefield using aerial lift instead of relying solely on ground maneuver. The board was soon outpaced by events which gripped the Army and altered its aviation outlook after 1960: the reorganization of Army divisions (ROAD), the Berlin and Cuban emergencies and the reserve call-up, the rapid unit expansion in response to a multitude of international crises, and Military Advisory Group Army aircraft requirements in many countries—including the prospect of combat needs in Laos, Thailand, and Vietnam. Cols. John Norton, the chief of the Continental Army's aviation section, and Alexander J. Rankin of the aviation board at Fort Rucker, clearly recognized that a fresh approach was needed.

When Robert S. McNamara became Secretary of Defense in 1961, he ushered in sweeping changes aimed at completely reorganizing the Department of the Army and its methods of warfare. He was highly displeased with Army Secretary Elvis J. Stahr, Jr.'s, report on the status of Army aviation plans. McNamara realized that the current Army procurement program was hopelessly inadequate in every category of aircraft and considered it dangerously conservative. Furthermore, McNamara felt that the Army failed to exert any strong, unified aviation effort and was plagued by reticence and budgetary restraint which were blocking the adaptation of necessary aircraft and equipment. Most important, he believed that officers with progressive ideas about airmobility were not being heard.

McNamara's team of civilian experts in the Systems Analysis Office was determined to allow modern ideas to get to the secretary without being stifled by reactionary bureaucratic resistance. Several officials of that office arranged for McNamara to consult privately with Brig. Gen. Clifton F. von Kann, the Director of Army Aviation (who was a parachutist as well as a pilot and former Rogers Board member), and another Army airmobility enthusiast, Maj. James J. Brockmyer, the Army Aviation Action Officer, who was one of the original Cub pilots. McNamara was convinced that a breakthrough in airmobility was possible with the new Bell helicopter models. He was given a list of officers who also believed that Army aviation needed new direction, and the substance for letters which he sent to the Secretary of the Army.[12]

12. Alain C. Enthoven and K. Wayne Smith, *How Much Is Enough? Shaping the Defense Program, 1961–1969* (New York: Harper & Row) p. 100.

Defense Secretary McNamara sent two strong directives to Stahr on 19 April 1962, summarizing his extreme dissatisfaction with Army aviation posture. Furthermore, McNamara took the radical step of directly naming Lt. Gen. Hamilton H. Howze and other pro-airmobility officers to a task force to re-examine the Army's posture. In effect, McNamara ordered the Army to implement airmobility, told the Army how to do it, and who should run it. While both memorandums opened new horizons, the second proved to be the birthright of the new airmobile division, and is reproduced here in its entirety:[13]

THE SECRETARY OF DEFENSE
Washington, D.C.
April 19, 1962

MEMORANDUM FOR MR. STAHR

I have not been satisfied with Army program submissions for tactical mobility. I do not believe that the Army has fully explored the opportunities offered by aeronautical technology for making a revolutionary break with traditional surface mobility means. Air vehicles operating close to, but above, the ground appear to me to offer the possibility of a quantum increase in effectiveness. I think that every possibility in this area should be explored.

We have found that air transportation is cheaper than rail or ship transportation even in peacetime. The urgency of wartime operation makes air transportation even more important. By exploiting aeronautical potential, we should be able to achieve a major increase in effectiveness while spending on air mobility systems no more than we have been spending on systems oriented for ground transportation.

I therefore believe that the Army's re-examination of its aviation requirements should be a bold "new look" at land warfare mobility. It should be conducted in an atmosphere divorced from traditional viewpoints and past policies. The only objective the actual task force should be given is that of acquiring the maximum attainable mobility within alternative funding levels and technology. This necessitates a readiness to substitute air

13. Memo, SECDEF for SA, 19 Apr 62, Subj: AAVN, w/Incl, with comments from USAMHI; Powell Debriefing.

mobility systems for traditional ground systems wherever analysis shows the substitution to improve our capabilities or effectiveness. It also requires that bold, new ideas which the task force may recommend be protected from veto or dilution by conservative staff review.

In order to ensure the success of the re-examination I am requesting in my official memorandum, I urge you to give its implementation your close personal attention. More specifically, I suggest that you establish a managing group of selected individuals to direct the review and keep you advised of its progress. If you choose to appoint such a committee, I suggest the following individuals be considered as appropriate for service thereon: Lt. Gen. Hamilton H. Howze, Brig. Gen. Delk M. Oden, Brig. Gen. Walter B. Richardson, Col. Robert R. Williams, Col. John Norton, Col. A. J. Rankin, Mr. Frank A. Parker, Dr. Edwin W. Paxson, and Mr. Edward H. Heinemann.

Existing Army activities such as Fort Rucker, RAC, STAG (Strategic and Tactics Analysis Group, Washington, D.C.), CDEC (Combat Development Experimental Center, Ft. Ord), and CORG (Combat Operations Research Group, Ft. Monroe), combined with the troop units and military study headquarters of CONARC, and in cooperation with Air Force troop carrier elements, appear to provide the required capabilities to conduct the analyses, field tests and exercises, provided their efforts are properly directed.

The studies already made by the Army of air mobile divisions and their subordinate air mobile units, of air mobile reconnaissance regiments, and of aerial artillery indicate the type of doctrinal concepts which could be evolved, although there has been no action to carry these concepts into effect. Parallel studies are also needed to provide air vehicles of improved capabilities and to eliminate ground-surface equipment and forces whose duplicate but less effective capabilities can no longer be justified economically. Improved V/STOL (Vertical/Short Takeoff or Landing) air vehicles may also be required as optimized weapons platforms, command and communications vehicles, and as short-range prime movers of heavy loads up to 40 or 50 tons.

I shall be disappointed if the Army's re-examination merely produces logistics-oriented recommendations to procure more of the same, rather than a plan for implementing fresh and perhaps unorthodox concepts which will give us a significant increase in mobility.

(Signed) ROBERT S. McNAMARA

Gen. George H. Decker, the Army Chief of Staff, was infuriated that inside insurgents had circumvented proper channels. The memorandums caused consternation in the military staff, sending shock waves throughout the upper echelons of the Army establishment, but they allowed recommendations to reach the top without being watered down. Within a week Lieutenant General Howze, commander of the XVIII Airborne Corps at Fort Bragg, was directed to head the task force, formally called the U.S. Army Tactical Mobility Requirements Board. The Army accorded the undertaking the highest possible priority, second only to operations in active combat areas. The Army's new Director of Aviation, Brig. Gen. Delk M. Oden, a 2d Armored Division war-hero-turned-pilot, was very pleased, while Howze called McNamara's memorandum the "best directive ever written."[14]

McNamara was handing the Secretary of the Army deadlines so fast that there was little time to do anything but say yes. The Howze Board was instructed to submit its final report within four months of actual working time, and its dynamic officers were determined to make it a success. Some, like chairman of the security committee Brig. Gen. Frederic W. Boye, Jr., the assistant commandant of the armor school, had distinguished themselves as armor leaders in World War II and were sons of horse cavalry officers. Many, like Brig. Gen. Edward L. Rowny, who headed the critical field test committee, were paratrooper graduates of the Army airborne school. The administrative workhorse of the Howze Board was the Secretariat, composed of rising stars of airmobility such as Cols. Norton, Putnam, Rankin, and Beatty.

The board was headquartered in Fort Bragg's Erwin School building, since it was empty during summer vacation, where the lights

14. USAMHI, Howze Debriefing. It is important to remember that the Army's Combat Developments Command, which would normally conduct such a study, was not organized until June 1962; thus the need for a special board under Howze.

burned past midnight every night as officers argued, wrote, and struggled through files and reports. They worked at a feverish pace as committee members constantly shuttled all over the country, and brainstorming sessions lasted until all hours. One recalled, "Many of us just ran ourselves into the ground; we worked so darned hard we almost couldn't think straight." The documents were "roughly knee deep on the floor" of one large room, and staff sections had to be limited in generating paperwork. Even so, by September more than six hundred footlocker loads of paperwork were produced.[15]

There were precious few aviation assets to work with, and a dispute arose between staffs at Fort Rucker and Fort Knox concerning the constitution of the provisional 17th Air Cavalry Group, since General Howze insisted on having the best-qualified personnel and best equipment available. However, some units, like the 1st Aviation Company (Caribou transport), were already being sent overseas, where Army Secretary Stahr believed it could still be part of the study "in the operational laboratory of Vietnam." This proved impossible. A smattering of other units, like the 8305th Aerial Combat Reconnaissance Unit (Provisional) at Fort Rucker, were employed.[16]

The Howze Board studied the application of Army aircraft to the traditional cavalry role of mounted combat, especially in reconnaissance, security, and target acquisition. They examined possible Army operations in Southeast Asia, Europe, Northeast Asia, and the Middle East. One of the board's most innovative concepts was the proposal for an Air Cavalry Combat Brigade (ACCB) to fight from an aerial-mounted position and perform the historical role of cavalry in exploitation, pursuit, counterattack, delay, and flank protection. This brigade was designed for the offense, seeking out and destroying the enemy while carrying out traditional cavalry missions. An even larger Combined Arms Air Brigade was envisioned to "flesh out" the ACCB and provide the commander with a decisive combat tool.[17]

15. Frederic A. Bergerson, *The Army Gets an Air Force* (Baltimore and London: The Johns Hopkins University Press, 1980), p. 112.
16. U.S. Army Combat Developments Command, *The Origins, Deliberations, and Recommendations of the U.S. Army Tactical Mobility Requirements Board*, Fort Leavenworth, Kansas, 1969, pp. 19, 47, 60.
17. Ibid., pp. 50–51.

For divisional purposes the committees began with the simplest, lightest, and most airmobile force they could develop, looking first at Southeast Asia. For this purpose an Army Reorganized Airmobile Division (RAID) was proposed along with a corps task force, which was actually a small airmobile field army supported by a special support brigade. The RAID could provide enough aircraft to sustain combat by aerial reconnaissance and fire support, simultaneously airlifting one-third of itself for distances of more than sixty miles. Since three RAID divisions were claimed to be as effective in Southeast Asia as four Army and two Marine divisions combined, they needed to be fielded as quickly as possible. For European fighting the board developed an aviation-enhanced armored division, which was termed the Reorganized Universal Division.

General Howze felt that completely new organizations such as RAID were unrealistic, but in keeping with his directive to implement "bold, new ideas" had the board redesign the standard infantry division, replacing wheels with aviation wherever possible. This resulted in an airmobile division with slightly less manpower than a standard division, but with 2,751 fewer vehicles and some four hundred aircraft.[18] The board agreed that fast, hard-hitting troops were needed to destroy an enemy quickly, to seize an objective, and then to deploy to areas from which they could make the most of their gains. The organization needed to be light, but effective, in firepower, communications, and mobility.

The test force at the board's disposal included one battle group, engineers, and artillery from the 82d Airborne Division and 150 aircraft of the 6th Aviation Group (Provisional).[19] Forty field tests were

18. The Howze Board proposed airmobile division contained 14,678 personnel compared to the standard 15,799; 920 vehicles compared to 3,671; and 400 aircraft compared to 103 in the standard infantry division.
19. The 6th Aviation Group was board-generated and built around the 3d Transportation and the 82d Aviation Battalions, reinforced by the 31st Transportation Company (Light Helicopter), 61st Aviation Company (Light Fixed Wing), 123d Medical Company (Helicopter), 82d and 101st Aviation Companies (Airmobile), 54th Transportation Company (Medium Helicopter), 22d Special Warfare Aviation Detachment, and Troop C of the 17th Cavalry (Air). The 138th, 154th, 544th Transportation Detachments (Field Maintenance), 6th Aviation Operating Detachment, 25th Transportation

conducted, but only three were of week-long duration, pitting air-mobile troops against mock irregulars in the Appalachian Mountains (which simulated Laotian territory), Fort Bragg, and Fort Stewart. The board finally proposed several new organizations: an air assault division, a division with increased mobility through its 459 aircraft; an air cavalry combat brigade totaling 316 helicopters to destroy or neutralize mechanized enemy forces by aerial firepower; a corps aviation brigade (207 aircraft) to allow rapid movement of reserves; an air transport brigade (134 aircraft) to support the air assault division logistically; and a special warfare aviation brigade of 125 aircraft to render immediate aviation support to units in combat. The board also considered the future, where the air cavalry combat brigade would be succeeded by the armair brigade, a self-sustaining unit of all arms smaller than a division, which could be used for rapid strike, economy of force, mobile reserve, and fire brigade actions. A more lethal airmobile division was foreseen as the outgrowth of the air assault division.

The board recommended that the mix of forces best suited to modernize the Army would, within six years, give four infantry, four mechanized, and three armored divisions; five air assault divisions with their five associated air transport brigades; and three air cavalry combat brigades. One air assault division was to be based in Korea; another stationed in Hawaii with a brigade forward on Okinawa; and of the three envisioned for United States assignment, two would be additionally paratrooper-qualified. One air cavalry combat brigade was to be sent to Europe for availability in the Middle East or North Africa, and two brigades placed in the United States were to replace the armored cavalry regiments there. The special warfare brigade, which the board urgently recommended be activated the following year at Fort Bragg, would have five operational squadrons—four of them organized for Southeast Asia, the Middle East, Africa, and Latin America. Over $5.4 billion (in 1962 dollars) would have to be spent to procure the 10,565 total aircraft required.

General Howze knew that the Army would probably react nega-

---

Company (Direct Support), and Simmons Army Air Field Command were also involved. USATMRB, Annex O—Field Tests, and Howze Board correspondence.

tively toward the increased cost of airmobile units over conventional forces. The initial investment for more complex aircraft, as well as the higher costs for operation and maintenance, was quite high. The estimated $987 million cost of an air assault division was somewhat offset by its favorable ratio of effectiveness over a standard division, priced at $742 million. The frightfully expensive $366 million air cavalry combat brigade was considered absolutely necessary for Laotian and Vietnam duty, where indigenous troops could not secure overland supply routes. The board recommendations that the Army terminate development of both the main battle tank and rough-terrain vehicle, to allow financing of airmobility programs, were bound to cause hostility.[20]

Dr. Stockfisch, the Defense Secretary's representative, was very pleased with the way the Howze Board studies were progressing. He was particularly enthusiastic over the board's concept of the final presentation, which would include a two-page letter, a twenty-page summary, a two-inch-thick report, and a two-foot-thick backup in a foot locker. He believed Secretary McNamara should be furnished everything, including the footlocker.[21] In keeping with the 1 September 1962 deadline imposed by the Secretary of Defense, the board submitted its report to the Department of the Army on 20 August. General Howze's conclusion was direct and simple: "Adoption of the Army of the airmobile concept—however imperfectly it may be described and justified in this report—is necessary and desirable. In some respects the transition is inevitable, just as was that from animal mobility to motor."

The Howze Board was in operation from May through August 1962, working in five different U.S. locations. Consisting of 199 officers, 41 enlisted men, and 53 civilians, it involved more than 3,500

---

20. USCONARC/USARSTRIKE, *Annual Historical Summary, 1 July 1962–30 June 1963*, p.99. Costs are cited from U.S. Army Combat Developments Command, *The Origins, Deliberations, and Recommendations of the U.S. Army Tactical Mobility Requirements Board*, Fort Leavenworth, Kansas, 1969, p. 104. Comparative costs of other proposed organizations were the corps aviation brigade, $329 million; air transport brigade, $464 million; and the special warfare brigade, $149 million.

21. MFR, COL A. J. Rankin, 7 Jun 62, Subj: FONECON Between Mr. Fred Wolcott and COL Rankin, 7 June 62, 0930 hours. AJCG-AB.

personnel in direct support. The eight working committees had one purpose: to free the ground soldier from the restrictions of battlefield movement by replacing conventional ground transportation with aircraft. The study was conducted on a high-priority basis in an atmosphere divorced as far as possible from current viewpoints and doctrine.

Many of the board's conclusions were never acted upon. The Army never fielded a special warfare or corps aviation brigade. Only one air transport brigade was formed, to support one experimental, understrength air assault division. The Army formed only two airmobile divisions, both to fight in Vietnam, one—the 1st Cavalry—an outgrowth of the test air assault division in July 1965; the other—the 101st Airborne Division—three years later. No air cavalry combat brigade was officially organized, although an ad hoc formation was created temporarily on the Cambodian front during the Vietnam War by a former Howze Board officer.

The Howze Board charted new horizons in airmobility and represented the turning point in providing the Army with aerial cavalry. The board's recommendations led to further experimentation with the raising of the 11th Air Assault Division, but its ultimate legacy became the 1st Cavalry Division (Airmobile). This division was the major outcome of the board's hard work and deliberations. When the division was dispatched to Vietnam in 1965, it would ultimately change the conduct of land warfare. The division's bold air assault and sustained pursuit operations made it, six months after arriving in Vietnam, in Defense Secretary McNamara's words, "unique in the history of the American Army": there was "no other division in the world like it."

# CHAPTER 2

# From Test to Battle

*Progression from Air Assault to Cavalry Division*

The new Secretary of the Army, Cyrus R. Vance, agreed with the Howze Board that helicoptered infantry offered unprecedented combat striking potential and that the Army should test airmobility at the earliest opportunity. He forwarded these recommendations to Defense Secretary McNamara on 15 September 1962. The Air Force was opposed to rapidly expanding Army aircraft utilization, especially in the armed helicopter and larger transport categories. However, McNamara wholeheartedly agreed that the Army required internal helicopter assets to make airmobility work and endorsed immediate field testing of the concept.[1]

When the final Howze report reached McNamara in September, the Army was escalating overseas operations and reorganizing its internal structure. Beginning that same month, Special Forces teams from the United States arrived in Vietnam to reinforce contingents from Okinawa. These increasing "Green Beret" troop commitments were at the forefront of additional aviation, combat support, and advisory elements. The situation in Vietnam was not the only factor causing the Army to endorse more flexible response. On 1 October racial troubles in the South required General Howze to leave his airmobile testing considerations and command ten paratrooper battle groups

---

1. Memo, SA to SECDEF, 15 Sep 62, Subj: Preliminary Army Review of the Report of the Army Tactical Mobility Requirements Board.

rapidly deployed to Mississippi and Tennessee. Just fifteen days later, major Army forces were alerted for a possible invasion of Cuba.

The Army ordered the new airmobile test force and evaluation group to be formed at the infantry school post of Fort Benning, Georgia, in the beginning of 1963. Although the project was given top priority, competing demands for aviation and personnel resources interfered with the trial airmobile unit throughout its existence. The programmed assembly and testing of the experimental unit continued to be affected adversely by Vietnam developments, domestic disturbances, and Cuban emergency contingencies, as well as the high level of activity at Fort Benning. The 2d Infantry Division stationed on post was planned for conversion to the new ROAD (Reorganization Objective Army Divisions) structure in January because of its planned rotation to Europe that April. The division's reorganization was already a year behind schedule because of the Berlin crisis.[2]

In accordance with McNamara's desires to commence airmobile testing in early 1963, Army Chief of Staff, Gen. Earle K. Wheeler, approved the activation of a reduced-strength air assault division and supporting air transport brigade just before the end of December. Maj. Gen. Harry W. O. Kinnard was handpicked to command the airmobile unit and summoned to the Pentagon. Kinnard was a vigorous and athletic paratroop commander, who served with particular esteem during World War II under Gen. Maxwell D. Taylor. Taylor later became President Kennedy's military advisor and was the current Chairman of the Joint Chiefs of Staff. Wheeler's guidance to Kinnard was straightforward: reconfigure the division so that all material could be flown by air, replacing as many wheels with helicopters as possible. Kinnard would have completely free reign, even in the selection of key personnel. Wheeler's final instructions were equally succinct: "You are going to run the organization. I want you to find out how far and fast the Army can go, and should go in the direction of air mobility."[3]

2. USCONARC/USARSTRIKE, *Annual Historical Summary, 1 July 1962–30 June 1963*, Fort Monroe, Virginia, dtd 1 Jan 65.

3. DCSUTR Avn Div, *Semiannual Hist Rept, 1 Jul–31 Jul 62*, pp. 1–3, and USAMHI, *Senior Officer Debriefing Program*, Lt. Gen. H. W. O. Kinnard, by Col. Glenn A. Smith and Lt. Col. August M. Cianciolo, Carlisle

Harry William Osborn Kinnard was born into an Army family on 7 May 1915 at Dallas, Texas. An avid sportsman and the captain of the fencing team at West Point, he graduated as an infantry lieutenant in 1939. Kinnard served initially with the Hawaiian Division and was sent to Fort Benning after America entered World War II. He completed jump school in late 1942 and joined the 501st Parachute Infantry Regiment, which was sent to Europe as part of the 101st Airborne Division. He parachuted into Normandy during the 6 June 1944 invasion of France and took over the regiment's 1st Battalion six days later. During the September 1944 airdrop into Holland, the division operations officer was severely wounded, and Major General Taylor promoted Kinnard to the job. At twenty-nine Kinnard was a full colonel. During the Battle of the Bulge, he served in the division's heroic defense of Bastogne. After the war, Kinnard held a succession of posts which included command of the 1st Airborne Battle Group, 501st Infantry (101st Airborne Division), and executive to the Secretary of the Army just prior to the assembly of the Howze Board. On 21 July 1962 he became assistant division commander of the 101st Airborne Division at Fort Campbell, Kentucky. In accordance with Wheeler's directive, Kinnard arrived at Fort Benning to take over the newly created 11th Air Assault Division (Test) on 1 February 1963 and received his aviator wings that July.

Kinnard knew that he faced a tough job. Part of the training scheme required joint testing with the Air Force, including long-range airlift support. The fact that the Air Force expressed open displeasure over "airmobility," which it considered an Army intrusion into the skies, was only one of his problems. The Army staff remained unconvinced that the frightfully expensive air assault division was actually worth the extra cost over a regular division. From that aspect alone Kinnard faced an uphill fight, since the military budget was being rapidly depleted by the global tempo of increased Army operations. Fortunately, for testing purposes at least, McNamara's blessing insured that enough money was available. As Col. George P. Seneff, who commanded the division's 11th Aviation Group, later summed up the situation, "For the first time in the history of the Army, a bunch of

---

Barracks, Pennsylvania: 1977, p. 12. Hereafter cited as USAMHI, Kinnard Debriefing.

people had been turned loose with high priority on personnel and equipment, given their own budget, and told, O.K., here's the dough, we'll get the people and equipment; [you] come up with a concept and prove it."[4]

General Kinnard was an infantryman with a solid airborne background who firmly believed that the airmobile division should conform to the light paratrooper infantry mold. He felt that the innovative science of airmobility must be linked to the flexible, tough airborne spirit rather than to the "old" Army aviation mentality, which he considered typified by Army aircraft liaison and cargo transport duty. Kinnard believed "air mobile parachute people were ideally suited to bring in the air mobile concept" since "airmobility required a frame of mind that paratroopers best adapted to," and emphasized that all combat arms of the test unit should be parachutist-qualified. As a result, the new formation was redesignated from the 11th Airborne Division, "The Blue Angels" of World War II fame in the Pacific.[5]

One of Major General Kinnard's first selections for his division staff was Col. John M. Wright, Jr., a distinguished soldier captured on Corregidor Island and held as a prisoner by the Japanese during World War II. Wright was assigned to Seventh Army at Stuttgart, Germany, when he received orders to the newly forming 11th Air Assault Division at Fort Benning, and remembered his assignment as a "bolt out of the blue." When Wright asked for information about the unit from his fellow operations officers, only a handful had even heard of it, and they guessed that it was some type of aviation outfit. The Seventh Army Chief of Staff told Wright, "It's an experimental division at Fort Benning, and you're lucky to be assigned there rather than anywhere else, because nobody knows anything about it, which means that you should know very quickly as much about it as anybody!"[6] Brigadier General Wright was appointed as Kinnard's Assis-

4. USAMHI, *Senior Officers Debriefing Program*, Lt. Gen. George P. Seneff, by Lt. Col. Ronald K. Anderson, Carlisle Barracks, Pennsylvania. Hereafter cited as USAMHI, Seneff Debriefing.
5. USAMHI, Kinnard Debriefing, p. 11.
6. USAMHI, *Senior Officers Oral History Program*, Project 83-5, Lt. Gen. John M. Wright, Jr., USA, Ret., interviewed by Lt. Col. David M. Fishback, Carlisle Barracks, Pennsylvania: 1983, p. 364. Hereafter cited as USAMHI, Wright Interview.

tant Division Commander-B responsible for the logistics and aviation side of the division. After repeated requests for the aviator training that he deemed necessary, Wright was finally permitted to attend aviation school.

Kinnard chose Brig. Gen. Richard "Dick" T. Knowles as Assistant Division Commander-A to control tactical employment and field operations. Kinnard's chief of staff was Col. Elvy B. Roberts, who commanded the 1st Cavalry Division in Vietnam six years later. In the meantime the Army nominated Brig. Gen. Robert R. "Bob" Williams tö head the Test and Evaluation Group at Fort Benning, which was responsible for developing tests and for submitting progress reports. Williams's group reported directly to Lt. Gen. Charles W. G. Rich, who became overall test director for Project TEAM (Test and Evaluation of Air Mobility) on 1 August 1964 at Third Army headquarters, Fort McPherson. TEAM attempts to get hard data from Kinnard often led to acrimonious sessions, since the concept's rapid development often blurred distinctions between critical system flaws and simple training headaches. Kinnard was more interested in making the division go than in collecting statistics.

On 18 January 1963 the Army formally announced a three-phase testing program. Phase I would begin with Kinnard's infant air assault "division" at one-fourth strength, as available resources limited the force to one reinforced battalion and an equivalent small air transport "brigade" to support it. These elements would intensively train in airmobile operations and serve as a nucleus for progressive expansion in November. In Phase II, projected to last through most of 1964, the initial test unit would be expanded to a full brigade, still one-third the actual size of a division. Further training would culminate in a joint Army–Air Force testing program. During Phase III, starting in October 1964, the division would be brought up to full strength and undergo one year of advanced training. This phase would focus on the division's feasibility in all three levels of warfare; limited, medium, and all-out nuclear conflict. This final phase was never actually completed because of the need to expedite an airmobile force to Vietnam.[7]

7. Ltr OPS CDDC, DA dtd 7 Jan 63, Subj: Plans for the Initial Organization, Training, and Testing of Air Mobile Units.

Major General Kinnard's 11th Air Assault Division (Test) was activated along with its associated 10th Air Transport Brigade under Col. Delbert L. Bristol at Harmony Church, Fort Benning, Georgia, on 7 February 1963. The Phase I test force was initially authorized 291 officers, 187 warrant officers, and 3,114 enlisted men. The 1st Brigade under Col. George S. Beatty, Jr., consisted of a single battalion, Lt. Col. John T. "Jack" Hennessey's 3d Battalion, 187th Infantry, which was formed by levying officers and sergeants throughout the service and filling the ranks with soldiers from the 2d Infantry Division and paratrooper school on post. The 2d Battalion, 42d Artillery, was gathered from Fort Bragg, North Carolina, and Fort Sill, Oklahoma, and contained a battery each of howitzers, Little John missiles, and aerial rocket helicopters. Support, engineer, and maintenance units were created by gutting the 3d Missile Command at Fort Bragg. The aviation resources were created by stripping units scattered across the country from Fort Benning, Georgia, and Fort Riley, Kansas, to Fort Lewis, Washington. Factory production was stepped up in an effort to meet helicopter shortfalls.[8]

Fleshed out by this crusading cadre, who collectively referred to themselves as "Skysoldiers," the unit entered the field almost immediately in a series of grueling training and experimental exercises. Both ground troops and air crews forged a close-knit bond in their common zeal to prove that airmobility could work. Only limited heliports and training areas existed at Fort Benning, and the unit frequently went to Fort Stewart for more maneuver room. In September the reinforced infantry battalion moved there and began initial testing in Exercise AIR ASSAULT I. The command emphasis and continual observation that typified test force operations were already evident.

8. The 11th Air Assault Division (-) was initially composed of the 11th Aviation Group (Cos A and B of the 226th Avn Bn; Cos A and B of the 227th Avn Bn; Co A, 228th Avn Bn; 11th Avn Co; Co A, 611th Aircraft Maint & Support Bn; Tp B, 3d Sqdn, 17th Cav); 2d Bn of the 42d Artillery; 3d Bn of the 187th Infantry; Co A, 127th Engineer Bn; Co A, 511th Signal Bn; and the nucleus of the division general staff and support command (408th Supply & Service Co; Co A, 11th Medical Bn; and part of the 711th Maintenance Bn). On 1 October 1963 the 1st Bn, 187th Inf; Co A, 127th Eng Bn; and Co B, 6th Bn, 81st Arty, were officially designated as airborne units.

The scrutiny became so intense that Major General Kinnard retorted by punning Churchill's famous Battle of Britain tribute and quipped, "Never have so few been observed by so many so often." By October, when the exercise was completed, the bulk of personnel for the unit's Phase II expansion had been received.

The 11th Air Assault Division (Test) faced several serious problems, ranging from inadequate signal equipment to insufficient manning tables, but the most critical always remained aviation. Each aircraft type presented unique difficulties. The Air Force was very displeased about the Army's use of larger fixed-wing Caribou transport and Mohawk reconnaissance aircraft, which the division and air transport brigade considered essential. Kinnard's attempts to put machine guns on the OV1 Mohawk, a high-performance aircraft designed to seek out and provide immediate intelligence on the enemy regardless of terrain or weather conditions, caused a major interservice dispute. General Johnson finally withdrew the division's twenty-four armed Mohawks as "a sacrifice on the altar of accord with the Air Force." Later the Army was also forced to give up its valuable support CV2 Caribou transport planes.[9]

The UH-series Iroquois helicopters, popularly called Hueys by the soldiers, provided the majority of the unit's helicopter transport and gunship capability. The Huey carried eight combat-equipped soldiers along with a crew of two to four personnel, hauled equipment and supplies, and could be upgunned as an aerial weapons platform. Several production varieties insured better performance throughout the Vietnam era, and the Huey became the legendary mainstay of both the air assault test unit and its descendant, the 1st Cavalry Division.

The airmobile division depended on the twin-rotor CH47 Chinook helicopter, the principal Army air cargo transporter, to airlift its essential artillery and heavier supplies forward. Capable of carrying either forty-four troops or ten thousand pounds of cargo, the Chinook's importance was reflected in the division motto, "If you can't carry it in a Chinook, you're better off without it." Unfortunately, the Chinook was proving to be a first-rate disaster. Its producer, Vertol, had just sold out to Boeing, and extreme quality control and management problems plagued the entire Chinook program. The Chinook battalion

9. USAMHI, Kinnard Debriefing, p. 16.

skipper, Lt. Col. Benjamin S. Silver, considered it a sterling day if only half of his helicopters were flying. The Chinook was not only unreliable, but the division could not get spare parts. Rotor blades that spun off in flight caused an increasing number of fatal crashes. Colonel Seneff, the flight boss of the 11th Air Assault Division, considered the aircraft a nightmare.

The disastrous Chinook situation became so alarming that it endangered the entire test program, forcing Brigadier General Wright to meet face-to-face with Bob Tharrington of Boeing Company and its Vertol Division. Both agreed to do everything possible to correct the situation. Working in close cooperation, both division maintenance personnel and manufacturing employees struggled determinedly to improve CH47 helicopter performance. Finally, every Chinook could be put into the air at once, enabling Lieutenant Colonel Silver to begin formation exercises. Although the Chinook still faced problems, the division began to rely on this essential medium-size helicopter which served throughout the Vietnam War.

The Pentagon realigned the entire airmobility program in March 1964 to accelerate testing of the 11th Air Assault Division, so that separate Army and Air Force evaluations could be completed by the end of the year. The division continued to build as the training effort was redoubled. Aviation was stabilized at one aerial surveillance and escort (226th Avn) battalion, one Chinook assault support helicopter (228th Avn) battalion, and two Huey assault helicopter (227th, 229th Avn) battalions. The infantry brigade contained three battalions (1st Battalions of the 187th, 188th, and 511th Infantry), but Kinnard needed more riflemen and cannoneers. The following month Col. William R. Lynch's reinforced 2d Brigade of the Fort Benning–based 2d Infantry Division (2d Bn, 23d Inf, and 1st and 2d Bns, 38th Inf) was attached, allowing Kinnard to reorganize his division into three miniature brigades of two infantry battalions each, supported by one aerial rocket battalion (3d Bn, 377th Arty), one Little John missile battalion (2d Bn, 42d Arty), and three howitzer battalions (1st Bn, 15th Arty; 5th Bn, 38th Arty; and 6th Bn, 81st Arty). The division expanded its support components proportionately as preparation intensified for the important fall testing.

The main arguments brought against the Army's air assault unit were the supposed vulnerability of its helicopters in actual combat, under adverse weather conditions, and at night. To disprove these contentions, division flight operations needed to be as realistic as possible. Stateside safety considerations threatened to preclude the required experience, since night flying and aerial gunnery were severely restricted, and low-level, nap-of-the-earth helicopter techniques were only taught instead of practiced. Col. Jack Norton, the head aviator of Continental Army Command (CONARC), and Seneff threw away the book and "relaxed" safety standards.

Under such strenuous training, aircraft losses resulting from new-model teething problems or pilot error or plain bad luck were inevitable. On 22 April 1964 a low-flying 226th Aviation Battalion observation plane hit wires and crashed into Fort Benning's Juniper Lake, killing both pilot and copilot despite parachute-equipped ejection seats. One of the most frightful incidents, which transpired during a parachute jump, miraculously produced no injuries. On 21 July a light OH13 Sioux helicopter of the 3d Squadron, 17th Cavalry, became entangled with a descending canopy ten feet off the ground, immediately slamming both paratrooper and aircraft into the earth.

The division constantly rehearsed formation flying regardless of time or weather as it learned to deliver troops over long distances. Improved searchlights were used for group movements at night. Formation flight was emphasized to the point that the aviators began joking, "If two of you need to go to the can, be sure to fly in formation!" During one exercise, Lt. Col. John B. Stockton's 227th Aviation Battalion (Assault Helicopter) went from Camp Blanding, Florida, to Fort Benning despite a wall of thunderstorms. The massed helicopters pushed forward in the driving rain, but the formation was inevitably broken apart by the weather front. The whole battalion was forced to sit down its craft in ones, twos, and threes, scattered over four Georgia counties, where the hapless crews spent the night with their helicopters mired in muddy fields or along sandy farm lanes.

The continuous formation training, night flying, and weather flight practice demanded hard work, but produced promising results. At the same time, incessant Army demands for pilots and advisors in Vietnam threatened much of the progress. Priority activation of aviation units kept stripping elements out of Kinnard's command, and temporary-duty replacements could not make up for the loss of some of his best aircraft and well-trained people. Throughout the test period the division suffered from an acute shortage of helicopters and experienced pilots.

Major General Kinnard believed that the testing program was being severely jeopardized by the turbulence and tight scheduling, but the Pentagon insisted on staging the fall testing as planned. In September 1964 the division moved into North and South Carolina on Exercise HAWK BLADE, actually a dress rehearsal for the big test, Exercise AIR ASSAULT II, to be conducted 14 October to 12 November across the same two states. The Joint Chiefs of Staff agreed to allow the Air Force to field-test its own alternate concept, GOLDFIRE I, at the same time (29 October to 13 November), using the 1st Infantry Division with the Ninth and Twelfth Air Forces in the Fort Leonard Wood, Missouri, area under the U.S. STRIKE Command. The requirement for additional joint testing would be determined after comparing results. Kinnard was keenly aware that the case for Army airmobility had to be successfully proven at this juncture.[10]

On the morning of 14 October 1964, the 11th Air Assault Division was scheduled to lift off in a massed 120-helicopter flight at 9:00 A.M. and assault objectives one hundred nautical miles away (the range of the Chinook). Hurricane Isbell offshore in the Atlantic blanketed the entire eastern seaboard with storms and low cloud ceilings, and the Air Force had already grounded most of its planes in that portion of the United States. Many distinguished visitors, in addition to the usual crowd of test observers, were present to witness the exercise. Those who wanted to see air cavalry defeated once and for all were rubbing their hands in anticipation.

Kinnard sent three aerial reconnaissance forces aloft, probing for holes in clouds laden with fierce winds and heavy rainstorms. John Stockton's assault helicopter battalion on the coast was flat on the ground, his Hueys awash in torrential rain, gusts snapping at the rotor blade tie-down ropes. The 229th Aviation Battalion (Assault Helicopter) under Earl Buchanan struggled through the middle route, while Seneff led his helicopters high on the hilltops. Skirting through towering thunderheads, the 120 troop-carrying helicopters followed his lead and planted a full battalion on the landing zones only one hour behind schedule.

---

10. ODSUTR Avn Div, *Semiannual Hist Rept, July–Dec 64*, pp. 2–3, and Hq TEC Gp, Fort Benning, *Final Report, Project Team*, dtd 15 Jan 65, Volume I, p. ix.

The rash of predicted accidents failed to materialize during the next four weeks, although foul weather, pilot fatigue, and mechanical difficulties downed a number of aircraft. One of the worst losses occurred when two 10th Air Transport Brigade Caribou transports crashed head-on twelve miles from Fort Gordon over Hephzibah, Georgia, on the last day of October, killing all aboard. On 5 and 6 November two armed Hueys of the 3d Battalion, 377th Artillery, suffered engine compressor failures near Cheraw, South Carolina, resulting in either death or crippling vertebral fractures among all crew members. Power lines, terrain miscalculations, and futile attempts to switch over to instruments in sudden cloudbursts littered still more helicopters across the Carolina backcountry, but fortunately most injuries were not serious.

In one month the test division conclusively demonstrated that its elements could seek out the enemy over a wide area despite unfavorable weather conditions, find him, and then rapidly bring together the necessary firepower and troops to destroy him. Army airmobility passed its most crucial test. A month after AIR ASSAULT II was concluded, test director Lieutenant General Rich presented his final evaluation to Army Combat Developments Command, which forwarded it on 5 January 1965 with favorable comments to Army Chief of Staff Harold K. Johnson. Johnson recommended to the Joint Chiefs of Staff that no aspect of the Army airmobility concept warranted further joint testing by U.S. STRIKE Command.[11]

The Army's success with its test air assault division was a direct result of the innovative manner in which the unit was created and allowed to operate. Kinnard was given great latitude in making necessary changes in doctrine, techniques, and organization. In this manner the revolutionary airmobile concepts advanced by the Howze Board received continued vitality. Brigadier General Wright considered the experiment a brilliant exception to the usual bureaucratic path to Army modernization and adaptation. He later stated, "If you want to get someplace in a hurry with a new concept, new developments, or new ideas, then find a responsible individual, give him a mission, turn

---

11. USCONARC/USARSTRIKE, *Annual Historical Summary, 1 July 1964 to 30 June 1965*, Fort Monroe, Virginia.

him loose, leave him alone, and let him report back when he is ready. And that's just what General Kinnard was permitted to do."[12]

Kinnard was immensely proud of his men and rewarded their hard training and sacrifice with a special air assault badge, designed to duplicate the esprit that the paratrooper and aviator wings achieved. The Army turned down all his attempts to make the badge official, but the test unit awarded it to all 1st Brigade members. On 3 December 1964 the badge was presented to the men of the 2d Brigade, formerly of the 2d Infantry Division, as a result of their performance in AIR ASSAULT II. Although the badge was terminated when the test unit was discontinued, it finally gained official sanction fifteen years later when revived for the airmobile infantrymen of the modern post-Vietnam Army.

In the spring of 1965, the general atmosphere within the 11th Air Assault Division was one of rueful resignation to expected disbandment rather than wartime preparation. No one visualized that in a few short months the division would be cranked up to combat strength and sent over to Vietnam. Most airmobile doctrinists actually predicted a dull period in Army aviation while reports of the test division were reviewed and torn apart, only to be ripped up again at Army and Defense Department level, all to be followed by a couple of years of debate.

The division originators felt there was ample evidence to support this gloomy conclusion, even though Lieutenant General Rich's report strongly recommended against losing two years of test effort experience and equipment by dissipating the personnel or fragmenting the tested units. Division members considered actual Army interest in the unit fairly low. Overall support for the test unit was spotty as a result of competing demands, and many important outsiders were still vocally adamant in their opposition to the airmobile force. Kinnard's division had been formed only for trial purposes in the first place and remained at cadre status.

Officially, of course, the 11th Air Assault Division was never specifically intended for the war that was heating up in Vietnam. The airmobility test was designed to cover the tactical usefulness of the

12. USAMHI, Wright Interview, p. 373.

unit in any region.  In Vietnam the difficult terrain and elusive enemy presented a perfect opportunity for employing a division with rapid, integrated helicopter transport and firepower, but the Army budget and contingency plans were not programmed for an airmobile division.  Brigadier General Powell recalled the general consensus of opinion as "we did what McNamara told us to do and tested the division, now we'd send people off to other assignments and file the reports."  A confluence of several events joined to send the division to Vietnam instead of disbandment.  Foremost was the worsening military situation inside South Vietnam, where coups and battlefield defeats were giving the communist insurgency an upper hand against the Army of the Republic of Vietnam (ARVN).  The United States decided to intervene with regular forces to prevent communist takeover of this allied country, but lacked light divisions capable of operating efficiently in the tropical wilderness and mountain hinterland.  Both 82d and 101st Airborne Divisions had limited mobility once on the ground; normal infantry divisions were either mechanized or very reliant on motorized equipment; and armor divisions were too heavy.  Another strategic consideration favored airmobile conversion.  One of the most threatened areas in South Vietnam was its rugged central highlands, dominated by the politically important highland city of Pleiku.  The road leading inland (Highway 19) to Pleiku had been closed for years, preventing the expeditious arrival of any conventional division.

After the Marines landed to safeguard South Vietnam's northernmost airfield, followed by an Army paratrooper brigade to secure the southern airfield near the capital, the decision was made to send the new helicopter formation into the central section of South Vietnam.  Gen. Creighton W. Abrams, the Vice Chief of Staff, presided over a particularly bitter March Army policy council meeting concerning the deployment feasibility of such a move.  Abrams, a staunch armor officer, had had initial misgivings about the airmobility concept, but these had been erased during an earlier visit to Kinnard's outfit at Fort Benning.  Major General Kinnard had personally flown Abrams around in his helicopter, touring the dispersed, fast-paced test maneuvers and had shown him "exactly what the hell was going on."  At the conclusion of the heliborne command briefing, Abrams had confided to him, "I have to say, I'm considerably impressed."  After much discussion at the council meeting, Abrams flatly stated, "I feel it is extremely propitious that we happen to have this organization in existence at this point in time, and we will deploy it to Vietnam."[13]

Because of programming considerations, the 11th Air Assault Division (Test) would be inactivated and its assets merged into an already-budgeted regular Army division, which would be converted to airmobile status. Major General Kinnard felt that his own 101st Airborne Division should be the first converted to airmobile status and that another parachute division be used next. However, Army Chief of Staff General Johnson was a former 1st Cavalry Division trooper and had greater affinity for his own unit currently serving on border duty in Korea. General Johnson also believed that the cavalry title fitted better with swift, airmobile pursuit and was more suitable for counterinsurgency operations. The cavalry term appealed to many government officials who felt it very appropriate for an anti-insurgent campaign in Vietnam.

For low- to mid-intensity warfare operations, such as Vietnam, the new division was designed to provide stability and area control for both population and crop resources through the increased military advantages of aerial reconnaissance and heliborne security. After feverish preparation, the Army Combat Developments Command rushed brand-new test airmobile division tables of organization and equipment (TOE 67T) to Department of the Army (DA) headquarters on 1 May 1965, where they were approved before the end of the month. Out of respect for Kinnard's heartfelt desire for paratroopers, the Army Vice Chief of Staff directed that the 1st Brigade remain parachute-qualified.[14]

As a result of these recommendations, on 15 June 1965 Defense Secretary McNamara approved the incorporation of an airmobile division into the Army force structure with the designation of the 1st Cavalry Division (Airmobile). Since the present 1st Cavalry Division was serving as a standard ROAD infantry division at Tonggu, Korea, its assets were used to form a new Korea-based 2d Infantry Division. The cavalry colors were flown to Georgia for conversion beginning 1 July 1965. This swap of flags permitted the new division to draw

13. USAMHI, Kinnard Debriefing, p. 16, and Seneff Debriefing, p. 37.
14. Because of the nature of combat operations, paratrooper replacement difficulties, and the presence of other airborne units in Vietnam, the airborne capability of the 1st Cavalry Division was officially terminated on 1 September 1967.

on all resources at Fort Benning, but these provided only partial troop fill and material. Yet the newly formed division was ordered to be ready for combatant deployment, at full personnel manning and equipment levels, by 28 July 1965.[15] Airmobile cavalry would be sent to war after years of conceptual and field testing. However, General Kinnard still faced one last seemingly impossible hurdle: to raise his air assault unit nucleus to wartime division status in less than one month. The deadline appeared especially unreasonable since it ignored the extent of needed reorganization and training. A minimum of three months' preparation was mandated if a division required major restructuring prior to movement into a combat zone. Resulting short-fuse time pressures, major equipment shortages, and personnel problems threatened to cripple the airmobile enterprise even before it departed the United States. The lack of firm national policy direction toward Vietnam was primarily responsible for such an arbitrary deadline, but the Army also deliberately disregarded the most elementary time allowances involved in accomplishing such a major task.

Organizationally, the division was authorized eight airmobile infantry cavalry battalions, three light artillery battalions, one aerial rocket artillery battalion, a cavalry reconnaissance squadron, an engineer battalion, and supporting units. Several battalions had to be raised from scratch. Additional equipment procurement in excess of $28 million was estimated to outfit the new division. All stateside depots and supply points were frantically combed to locate and deliver thousands of required major and secondary items in the compressed time remaining. The logistical burden and high cost of displacing emergency equipment resources throughout the country created great waste and multiplied expenditures. Fortunately, sufficient prewar stockage and material shortcuts, such as helicopter depot rebuilds, enabled the division to reach projected levels.

The division was authorized 15,890 men upon activation. Only 9,489 were assigned, and more than 50 percent of this original complement was ineligible for overseas deployment under peacetime service criteria. Replacements were brought into the division around the

---

15. USCONARC/USARSTRIKE, *Annual Historical Summary, 1 July 1965 to 30 June 1965*, p. 187.

clock, immediately fed a hot meal, processed, assigned, and transported to their units. Continual personnel turbulence effectively shut down most unit training, since indoctrination and basic soldiering consumed the limited time available. The impending division move to Vietnam was secret, and many reporting soldiers arrived at Fort Benning with their families. Civilian dependents were turned away, creating severe individual financial and dislocation hardships which further disrupted troop programming.[16]

There was an acute shortage of aviators, paratroopers, and support personnel. Entire aviation companies were sent to Fort Benning from other commands, but more than three hundred newly assigned aviators (most of whom arrived after 15 July) still required transition on entirely new models of aircraft. The division training capacity was hopelessly swamped and, despite the full help of the aviation school, more than fifty division pilots still sailed without completing transition. The division initially contained 900 paratroopers, but needed 3,470. To secure manpower, the airborne-designated 1st and 2d Battalions of the 8th Cavalry resorted to "extreme pressure for volunteers" and a flurry of abbreviated jump courses. Support components never received their proper allocation of maintenance and supply experts.[17]

The most serious problem remained the large number of troops ineligible for overseas duty. Both DA and CONARC anticipated an emergency presidential announcement permitting the Vietnam-bound division to retain all essential troops. Divisional strength might even be supplemented by calling up selected reserve components. CONARC received word of the "no call-up" decision during Saturday afternoon, 24 July. Four days later President Johnson publicly an-

16. 1st Cavalry Division, *Quarterly Command Report*, OACSFOR-OT-RD 6501101, 1 Dec 65. Until 31 December 1965 personnel deploying with a unit to Vietnam had to have sixty days remaining on active duty from the date of departure from the port of embarkation, in addition to other peacetime criteria.
17. 1st Cavalry Division, *Quarterly Command Report*, OACSFOR-OT-RD 650110, 1 Dec 65, pp. 8, 9. Aviation companies attached to the division included the 110th Avn Co; Co A, 4th Avn Bn; Co A, 5th Avn Bn; 6th SFG Avn Co; and 7th SFG Avn Co. See also Shelby L. Stanton, *Vietnam Order of Battle*, rev. ed. (Millwood, N.Y.: Kraus Reprints, 1986), p. 72.

nounced that he was sending the 1st Cavalry Division to Vietnam, but chose not to issue the emergency decree. Major General Kinnard was "glued to the television set" during the national broadcast and was horrified to realize that his division would lose hundreds of highly skilled pilots, crew chiefs, mechanics, and other essential people at the worst possible time.[18]

Major General Kinnard departed Fort Benning on 16 August 1965 to be briefed by Gen. William C. Westmoreland, the commander of Military Assistance Command Vietnam (MACV). Kinnard was fearful that Westmoreland, who was in Vietnam during the 11th Air Assault tests at Fort Benning, might be out of touch with airmobility developments. These fears were confirmed as General Westmoreland announced a new plan of divisional utilization and moved to a large wall map. Pointing to widely scattered areas of the chart, he stated that he was breaking up the 1st Cavalry Division into three brigades: "I am going to put one here, and one here, and all over the country." Kinnard was aghast that his division, which depended upon massing fire- and shockpower, might be scattered all over the nation. He responded, "Please, can't I discuss that?" and countered that the Army Chief of Staff had specified the division's main task was prevention of a military split of South Vietnam by an NVA/VC thrust across critical east-west Highway 19 from Pleiku to Qui Nhon. Kinnard added that he needed the greatest concentrated mobility to insure this goal and concluded, "If you penny pocket them all over the country, you've lost it."[19]

General Kinnard actually wanted to base his division in Thailand and operate up and down Laos and Cambodia, breaking into the North Vietnamese Ho Chi Minh Trail—logistical and reinforcement lifeline into South Vietnam—at will. While this course of action would have caused maximum disruption and destruction of enemy forces, the United States politically limited the war's boundaries to operations inside South Vietnam only. Under the circumstances, Kinnard felt the next best thing was to keep the division together with a definite objective.

18. USAMHI, *Senior Officers Oral History Program,* Interview of LTG Harry W. O. Kinnard by LTC Jacob B. Couch, Jr., 1983; USACONARC/USARSTRIKE, *Annual Historical Summary, 1 Jul 65–30 Jun 66,* Fort Monroe, Virginia, pp. 79–81, 136–37.

19. USAMHI, Kinnard Debriefing, p. 34.

Westmoreland relented, and the division was assigned intact to secure the main line of communications into the western highlands.

Brigadier General Wright was already at Qui Nhon with a small thirty-one-man contingent, acquainting the MACV staff with division support needs and scouting a site for the future main base camp. He wanted enough space for a sizable rectangular heliport and the protective infantry and artillery which would be positioned around it, all on terrain suitable for a strong perimeter barrier. Since the cavalry division helicopters were its most vital resource, Wright was very concerned about a possible North Vietnamese or Chinese fighter-bomber attack on such a lucrative target. The MACV operations officer, Maj. Gen. William "Bill" DePuy, assured him, "Don't worry about an air attack on your base. If you should get that, we'll just wipe Peking off the map!"[20] Enemy airstrikes against the airmobile division's sprawling airfield complex represented the primary threat, but true to DePuy's word this vulnerability was never exposed during the Vietnam War.

Wright's contingent wore civilian clothes and traveled across the highlands, visiting Special Forces camps, regional outposts, and valley hamlets. They finally selected a centrally located area with good flying weather along Highway 19 at An Khe, a Green Beret campsite near two critical mountain passes. The French lost an entire mobile group along this strategic stretch of winding road in 1954, and devastating Viet Cong ambushes still interdicted the route. The An Khe Special Forces garrison had been defeated in a bloody contest for control of the road near Mang Yang Pass in February.

The 1,030-man division advance element was airlifted from Robbins Air Force Base, Georgia, to Cam Ranh Bay beginning 14 August 1965. On 27 August they were flown by C130 aircraft to the Special Forces An Khe camp airstrip, where they pitched pup tents along the runway. Brigadier General Wright did not want heavy earth-moving machinery clearing the airfield site, since the scraped ground would create severe dust and wreak havoc on helicopter operations. He walked over to the tents, machete in hand, and selected twenty-five senior officers and sergeants to follow him into the adjacent scrub brush. Wright's experience as a Japanese prisoner had taught him that a lot

20. USAMHI, Wright Interview, p. 389.

could be accomplished if enough men worked with their bare hands. As the assembled group watched curiously, Wright cut a twenty-foot circle of short-cropped, green grass out of the foliage with his machete and stated, "If each of us swung a machete enough times, and if we cleared enough of those twenty- to twenty-five-foot circles, then they would all finally fit together, and we would have a rectangle two kilometers by three kilometers where there would be nothing but this beautiful green grass . . . like a fine golf course."[21]

Not long afterward, a staff officer trying to find Col. Allen M. Burdett, Jr., was told that the colonel was out working on the "Golf Course." The name stuck, and the airfield's title became official for the duration of American presence in Vietnam. Over the next few weeks, the division base camp slowly took shape. Several deep gullies and boulder-strewn outcrops crisscrossed the landscape, but the longest sections of the new runway were laid out perfectly straight to enable better gunship firing passes against attacking infantry. Although initial base camp construction commenced without the division engineer battalion, the determined work of the advance element and borrowed construction troops made An Khe's Golf Course the world's largest helipad by the end of September.

While the division's advance party staked out and cleared the main camp, the majority of the division outloaded at Mobile, Alabama, and Jacksonville, Florida. The division embarkation was complicated by overcrowding problems and last-minute accommodation transfers at dockside. Several vessels, such as the poorly rehabilitated MSTS *Kula Gulf* and *Card*, were rapidly pressed into service for the journey. Steam pipes were leaking, machinery was broken, and conditions aboard were extremely uncomfortable. When Kinnard insisted on moving his aviators from the hottest bowels of the vessels to unused portions of the shiphand billeting area, the uncooperative Military Sea Transportation crews refused to sail. After some last-minute high command intervention, he secured better quarters and the threatened strike was averted. On 28 July 1965 the 1st Cavalry Division began its main overseas movement.

The task of moving the division across the Pacific was almost as momentous as getting it combat-ready in the first place. Six passenger vessels, eleven cargo ships, and four aircraft carriers were required to move more than 15,000 soldiers, 3,100 vehicles, 470 aircraft, and 19,000 long tons of cargo to Vietnam. The division continued training hundreds of new recruits even as it sailed. For example, the soldiers conducted familiarization and marksmanship training with new M16 automatic rifles by firing at apple crates pitched over vessel fantails into the ocean.

The undeveloped midcountry port of Qui Nhon was chosen as the division's destination because of its relative proximity to An Khe. However, Qui Nhon's unsophisticated facilities and shortage of service personnel led to predictions of a tedious over-the-beach unloading process lasting more than a month. One brigade was originally slated for offloading at Cam Ranh Bay, but directives changing it to Qui Nhon were received en route. Amendatory instructions were received throughout the voyage. Consequently, the arrival of cargo, personnel, and aircraft was disjointed.

The unloading process was complicated and backbreaking as cargo was lightered ashore from a distance of two to five miles at sea, Viet Cong attacks interrupted traffic on the access road to the final delivery area, and bad weather intervened, but the actual debarkation of the division (including the forty-mile inland move to An Khe) was completed in a mere fifteen days. However, the logistical inefficiency surrounding division support arrangements incountry led the Army to abandon properly conceived airmobile supply channels and simply adopt the "dumping ground" resource conditions of Qui Nhon and An Khe. This not only led to chronic supply mismanagement, but also created a crucial aviation gasoline shortage in the division's fall Ia Drang Valley campaign. Strategically the mobile 1st Cavalry Division became pinned to base security of the "An Khe logistical hub."[22]

The supply and medical difficulties were secondary to the fact that a powerful, reinforced division capable of aerial assault was emplaced in Vietnam ready to assist the allied cause. Westmoreland had the flying cavalry that Walker lacked, and it was located along a vital

22. I Field Force Vietnam, *Operational Report: Lessons Learned, 1 Oct–31 Dec 65*, p. 24. Some of these problems are also highlighted in Lt. Gen. John J. Tolson, *Vietnam Studies: Airmobility, 1961–1971* (Washington, D.C.: Dept. of the Army, 1973), pp. 67–73.

communications zone in one of the most threatened and remote regions of the country. Despite all the obstacles to the rapid assembly of the 1st Cavalry Division and the massive scope of its cross-Pacific move, the first elements of the division were engaged in combat on 18 September 1965—just ninety-five days after the reorganization of the 11th Air Assault Division into the 1st Cavalry Division had been approved.[23]

In retrospect the formation and testing of the initial air assault division concept were successful because most normal bureaucratic service obstacles were removed at the insistence of Defense Secretary McNamara. However, even with the highest national priorities attached to the airmobile program, competing requirements almost defeated the project. Only the diligence and sustained faith of the testing cadre, coupled with all-out industrial support, enabled Kinnard's experimental unit to flourish. The upgrading of this formation to a full-fledged division and its movement to Vietnam were nothing short of miraculous in view of last-minute deployment decisions and actions.

Every Army command, from the top at DA through STRIKE Command down to the local Fort Benning post garrison, contributed to the extraordinary effort which succeeded in making the 1st Cavalry Division (Airmobile) a battlefield reality. The division enjoyed the great advantages of an adequate continental manpower base, a sufficiently experienced NCO cadre, and the necessary supply stockage that existed at this early stage of the Vietnam buildup. Even so, in the final analysis the mission was accomplished because the high morale, well-drilled cooperation, extremely good training, and leadership of the pre-Vietnam Army allowed the division to surmount the worst difficulties. The prevailing soldiers' attitude was that, regardless of the drastic time, manpower, and material limitations, they were going to make the division work. The spirit of the First Team began to take hold. In less than one month, the small band of air assault Skysoldiers was turned into an entire division of airmobile Skytroopers.

23. 1st Cavalry Division, *Quarterly Command Report*, dtd 1 Dec 1965, pp. 11–14.

# CHAPTER 3

# Air Assault

## *Techniques, Ia Drang Valley Campaign*

The arrival of the 1st Cavalry Division (Airmobile) in South Vietnam was part of an increasing American combat role in the Second Indochina War. During the Vietnam era, the official mission of an airmobile division was to provide reconnaissance for larger field force commands, participate in stability operations short of all-out nuclear war ("low- and mid-intensity operations"), and provide security and control over the population and resources of an assigned area. In accordance with this general mission statement, the 1st Cavalry Division was assigned the responsibility of protecting its own base, Camp Radcliff at An Khe, reopening Highway 19 from the coast to Pleiku and safeguarding its traffic, and guarding specific coastal lowland rice harvests from Viet Cong disruption. These represented extremely limited geographical objectives of a static security nature.

The 1st Cavalry Division, however, was designed and destined for offensive action. Airmobility offered such great vertical maneuver and firepower advantages that events soon thrust the division into a predominate mode of aerial attack. The airmobile division entered the acrid crucible of combat in the Ia Drang Valley of Vietnam's western border, where it marshaled its air assault assets to locate and battle North Vietnamese Army regulars. There were grave blunders in the execution of this campaign, some of which led to decimation of entire cavalry companies and battalions, but the airmobility concept was still new and needed refinement. The basic air cavalry combination was sound and proved so during the next ten years of battlefield application in Vietnam. No single engagement demonstrated the basic validity of air assault as strikingly as the 1st Cavalry Division's Ia Drang Valley campaign.

To an Army largely ground oriented, the rapid and flexible response inherent in airmobile operations over the wide expanse of the Ia Drang Valley was almost beyond comprehension. In the thirty-seven-day period beginning late in October, divisional helicopters conducted twenty-two infantry battalion moves and sixty-six artillery battery displacements across distances as great as seventy-five miles at a time. While this new style of airmobile warfare used modern helicopters to overfly difficult terrain and leap beyond enemy defenses to strike deep into targeted objectives, its most successful application was in the traditional cavalry mode. The division excelled in assignments to reconnoiter, screen, delay, and conduct raids over wide fronts. By December 1965 division operations extended from the South China Sea to the Cambodian border along the axis of Highway 19, and from Bong Son to Tuy Hoa along the Vietnamese coast.[1]

The air assault reigned supreme in the attack phase of airmobility. Once contact was made, troops could be flexibly extracted by helicopter from less critical situations and quickly concentrated at the point of battle. Instant radio communications enabled commanders, who themselves were often aloft in helicopters, to monitor scoutship transmissions and to direct responsive airlandings in the midst of the most fluid situations. As the infantrymen poured out of helicopters with rifles and machine guns blazing, hovering gunships rendered immediate, close-in covering fire with rockets and other weapons. Rapid helicopter airlift of howitzers and ordnance assured that sustained artillery support was available for infantry fighting for remote and isolated landing zones. The NVA opposition was stunned and overwhelmed by this swiftly executed initial aerial onslaught, gaining the division an immediate reputation for tactical success.

When the North Vietnamese attacked the small Special Forces Plei Me camp near Cambodia on 19 October 1965, they were not anticipating any American airmobile response. Even from the allied standpoint, the encounter seemed to be an unlikely prelude for the most famous divisional airmobile retaliation in history. Camp Plei Me was located along the western highland border, an area outside direct 1st Cavalry Division responsibility, and the attack was disregarded as

1. 1st Cavalry Division, *Quarterly Command Report for Second Fiscal Quarter FY 66*, dtd 30 Nov 65, p. 1.

a mere regimental baptism-of-fire "shakedown" exercise. Such attacks of opportunity were not unusual as North Vietnamese formations traveled to permanent base areas inside South Vietnam. However, three days after Plei Me was besieged, allied intelligence estimated that at least two freshly infiltrated NVA regiments, spearheaded by VC shock troops, were involved in a determined bid to overrun the campsite. Since Plei Me guarded the southwestern approach to Pleiku, an enemy victory was a direct menace to Pleiku, which the 1st Cavalry Division had been sent to Vietnam to protect.[2]

The South Vietnamese II Corps commander gathered his available mechanized reserves within Pleiku City and began a road march to relieve Camp Plei Me. Usually NVA/VC attack plans included elaborate measures to entrap and destroy forces attempting to reach a besieged garrison, and the 1st Cavalry Division was requested to render artillery support in case of ambush. Col. Elvy B. Roberts's 1st Brigade was flown into the Pleiku vicinity on 23 October. The next day the South Vietnamese relief column was mauled by a major ambush which threatened to block further road movement. A divisional artillery control team was sent on one of the medical evacuation helicopters to the stranded convoy. The forward observers scrambled into the lead vehicles, and the advance resumed behind a rolling curtain of massed artillery fire.

The relief force reached Plei Me under this umbrella of shellfire at dusk on 25 October, breaking the siege. General Westmoreland believed that regimental-size NVA formations still endangered South Vietnam's entire central region. The intensity of the attack on Plei Me verified that the North Vietnamese might contest other critical locations, storm Pleiku, or even attempt to militarily slice the country across the middle. Westmoreland helicoptered to the 1st Brigade's forward command post at LZ (Landing Zone) Homecoming, where the howitzers of the 2d Battalion, 19th Artillery, were still shelling the jungles around Plei Me. The division already forestalled the NVA drive by helping to turn back enemy elements committed against Plei Me, but Westmoreland wanted the North Vietnamese decisively defeated. He ordered that the division "must now do more than merely

2. DA AGM-P(M) ACSFOR Report, *Operations Report 3-66—The Pleiku Campaign*, dtd 10 May 66, p. 10.

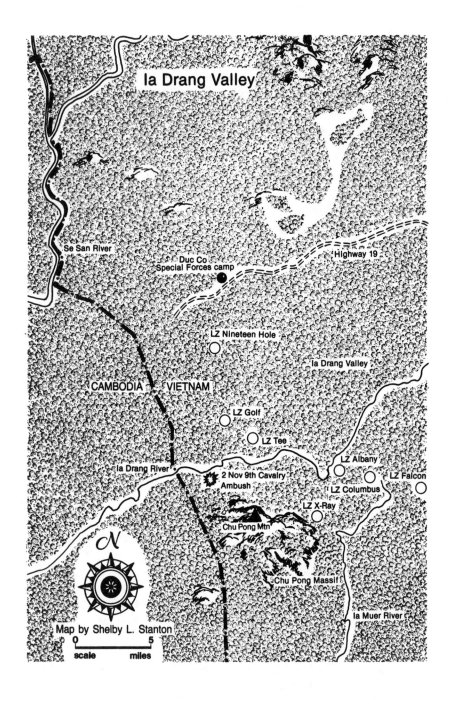

Ia Drang Valley

Se San River

Highway 19

Duc Co
Special Forces camp

LZ Nineteen Hole

Ia Drang Valley

CAMBODIA    VIETNAM

LZ Golf

LZ Tee

LZ Albany

Ia Drang River

LZ Falcon

2 Nov 9th Cavalry
Ambush

LZ Columbus

LZ X-Ray

Chu Pong Mtn

Chu Pong Massif

Ia Muer River

Map by Shelby L. Stanton

0          5
scale     miles

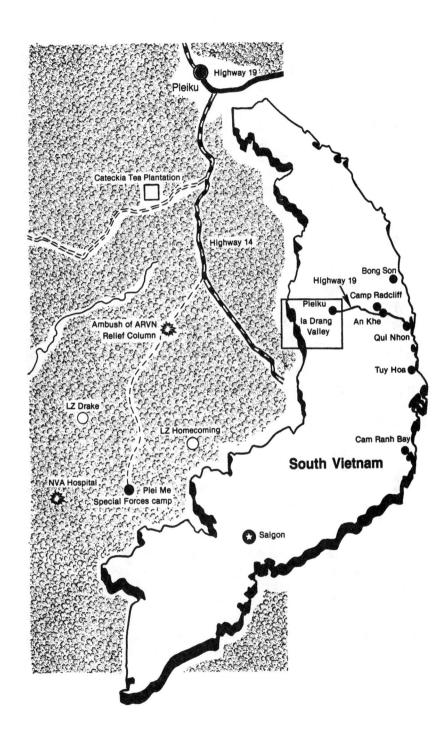

Highway 19

Pleiku

Cateckia Tea Plantation

Highway 14

Bong Son

Highway 19

Camp Radcliff

Pleiku

Ia Drang Valley

An Khe

Qui Nhon

Ambush of ARVN Relief Column

Tuy Hoa

LZ Drake

LZ Homecoming

Cam Ranh Bay

South Vietnam

NVA Hospital

Plei Me Special Forces camp

Saigon

contain the enemy; he must be sought out aggressively and destroyed."[3]

The NVA units which had participated in the Plei Me action were suspected to be regrouping in a 2,500-square kilometer area of rolling flatland between Plei Me and Cambodia. General Kinnard was confident that bold orchestration of his division's combined resources with air assault tactics would result in absolute domination of such a large battle arena. The region was not well mapped and contained few roads. The existing maze of trails could easily confuse normal ground orientation, but aerial observation promised accurate direction regardless. While a conventional division might be ineffective in seeking out and closing with the enemy in this vast and unfamiliar wilderness, the territory was ideal for long-range airmobile cavalry thrusts and flight operations.

Weather and terrain conditions were almost perfect. Only a few clouds were scattered high in the skies; night humidity was low; and temperatures ranged comfortably between 76 and 86 degrees Fahrenheit. Months of unrelenting heat had baked the red clay throughout the valleys and ridgelines into suitably hard earth for helicopter landings. Rivers and streams were seasonally dry. Only lush tropical vegetation and giant anthills protruded above the high elephant grass. The most thickly jungled sector existed on and around the prominent Chu Pong massif, which straddled the Cambodian border and loomed over the southwestern portion of the region's Ia Drang Valley.

The campaign, which existed under a series of operational code words (LONG REACH, SILVER BAYONET, GREEN HOUSE), but became historically designated after the main Ia Drang Valley west of Plei Me, began on 27 October 1965. The 1st Brigade—consisting of four infantry battalions, one light artillery battalion, most of the divisional cavalry reconnaissance squadron, and one aerial rocket artillery battery of gunship helicopters—fanned west of Pleiku toward Cambodia in classic cavalry pursuit of the enemy. Somewhere in the grasslands and forests below, bands of elusive *33d NVA Regiment* infantrymen were traveling back to their assembly areas. They were packing only light bedrolls, minimal personal gear, and sidearms as they dodged through woods and man-high grass.

---

3. Ibid., p. 42.

Lt. Col. John B. Stockton's reconnaissance 1st Squadron, 9th Cavalry, led the aerial drive. The small scoutships and armed gunships darted over the landscape, spotting and strafing small groups of fleeing North Vietnamese riflemen. The line battalions followed in dozens of Huey helicopters crammed with men and equipment. The first mission was to find the enemy. To effect the widest search as rapidly as possible, infantry battalions were fragmented into company-size increments. The troops were deposited over a multitude of selected landing sites; they cut their way out of the fields and into surrounding woodlines with machetes and axes and began patrolling their assigned sectors in the blistering sun. Fortunately, light leafy forests predominated, and foot movement was not unduly hampered by dense vegetation. Individual companies were deliberately placed in danger of clashing with larger enemy units, but the brigade was depending on its helicopters to speedily react and reinforce any contact which developed.

The brigade was soon dispersed over the entire area northwest of Plei Me, but the North Vietnamese had seemingly disappeared like phantoms. Nightly ambush positions and daily cloverleaf patrolling were exhausting and disappointing. Over the next few days Stockton's helicopters were reporting more fire passes and return automatic rifle fire, but there was no way to assess results. The various cavalry companies roaming the bush were inevitably trapping a few prisoners. These revealed that the North Vietnamese were growing tired and afraid of this unexpected helicopter harassment, but the main North Vietnamese contingents were still unlocated.

A band of enemy soldiers was observed by aerial scouts midway between Plei Me and Chu Pong mountain on the morning of 1 November. One of the reconnaissance squadron's three ground platoons, the Troop B Rifles, was already in flight and diverted to the scene. They skirmished across a small streambed and uncovered a fully stocked regimental hospital. The sweating cavalrymen spent most of the day dumping heaps of captured medical supplies aboard outgoing helicopters. Another squadron rifle platoon landed to help destroy the rest of the site. The squadron maintained a screen of scoutships overhead looking for more enemy soldiers, and that afternoon they detected hundreds of North Vietnamese soldiers approaching from the northeast. Gunships roared down to blast the advancing enemy with rockets and automatic weapons fire, but failed to slow down the counterattack on the hospital position. While aerial firepower rated high test scores with its appearance of utter devastation, the explosions and bullets seemed only to be tearing off tree limbs and killing a few clusters of men. The defending ground cavalry force at the hospital was quickly compressed into a very small perimeter. The last rifle platoon was inserted at the height of this intense firefight and was forced to leave the bullet-riddled helicopters under a hailstorm of gunfire. The hospital was beyond the range of division artillery, and close-quarters combat soon rendered aerial support impractical. The North Vietnamese assault faltered under the volume of return automatic and grenade fire and was discontinued when additional reinforcements of the 2d Battalion, 12th Cavalry, were airlanded later that day. The cavalry scored an opening success in its first confrontation with the NVA, although the enemy had not pressed its counterattack once it became evident that the hospital's condition was no longer worth fighting for.

Two days later Stockton's squadron probed deeper into the Ia Drang River Valley, where numerous trails leading into Cambodia were disclosed by aircraft reconnaissance. The squadron's same trio of rifle platoons established a hasty overnight patrol point south of the river and set up ambushes along a major east-west trail. Troop C Rifles at the southernmost ambush position sighted a full NVA company carrying supplies down the trail at 7:30 that evening. The North Vietnamese were talking and laughing loudly. Just before they entered the actual ambush site, the enemy commander decided to take a rest break. The Americans froze into their positions, not making a sound. This ordeal lasted an hour and a half, during which time various unaware NVA soldiers strayed close to the hidden cavalrymen, but failed to detect them.

Finally, the North Vietnamese re-formed into a single file and resumed marching down the trail. The cavalrymen breathlessly waited until the lead platoon passed the prepared kill zone and sprung the trap against the following weapons carriers. A deafening explosion of claymore-mine and automatic-rifle fire ripped through the main portage party, which was carrying machine guns, mortars, and recoilless rifles. The lead enemy platoon, which had been allowed to pass the main ambush, was simultaneously annihilated by cross fire from the cavalry ambush flank security element and another string of preset claymore mines. The firing lasted only two minutes and was executed with such violence and precision that every enemy soldier was cut down without firing a shot in return.

The cavalry platoon leader wisely decided that the destroyed company might be the vanguard of a larger force. The Troop C Rifles immediately returned to the main patrol base without counting bodies or collecting captured equipment. The base was set up just inside the treeline which surrounded the landing zone and was occupied by the other two 9th Cavalry rifle platoons and a mortar section. Within an hour the entire *8th Battalion* of the *66th NVA Regiment* surrounded the cavalry perimeter. The first mass attack against the patrol base was shattered by concentrated defensive fire. Numerous NVA snipers climbed into the trees and began to pick off cavalrymen exposed by the bright moonlight flooding the forest.

The North Vietnamese mounted another major assault against the weakening American lines at 11:15 P.M. For the first time in division history, aerial rocket artillery was employed at night in a close support role. Gunships hovering overhead responded with volleys of rocket salvos which careened through the foliage and detonated with lethal precision a scant fifty yards from friendly positions. The situation was becoming desperate, and urgent calls were made for reinforcements and medical evacuation craft. Incoming helicopters were buffeted by NVA gunfire during their descent; seriously wounded troopers were rushed aboard, and the helicopters pulled away. One crashed just beyond the landing zone, but another helicopter quickly dipped down to rescue its crew and radios before the North Vietnamese could reach the wreckage. One helicopter was so riddled by shrapnel and bullets that it almost disintegrated upon touching down with its load of wounded at the Special Forces Duc Co camp airstrip.

Twenty minutes after midnight reinforcements began to arrive at the patrol perimeter, marking the first time that divisional heliborne infantry reinforced a nocturnal military engagement. The available landing field was so small that only thirty men at a time could be inserted, but Company A of the 1st Battalion, 8th Cavalry, was emplaced alongside the squadron riflemen when the third major North Vietnamese assault smashed into the American lines at 3:30 A.M. The cavalry grimly held their positions. Just before dawn they repulsed the final and most determined NVA attack. One of the most gallant heroes of the firefight was Troop C Rifles Platoon Sgt. Florendo S. Pascual, who was killed at his post during the thick of combat.

During the entire firefight an attached Special Forces–led Rhade tribal reaction platoon had manned a separate ambush position just outside the main patrol perimeter. However, this added support could not be effectively utilized during the night action. The Troop B Rifles commander was hesitant about recalling them from their ambush position to reinforce, lest they be caught in NVA cross fires or become mistaken by their own troops for the enemy. He radioed the Special Forces–led Rhade platoon to move carefully and slowly toward the fight and to prepare to infiltrate into the defensive perimeter before dawn. Throughout the war, such elementary difficulties as native and Special Forces attire (causing uniform complications), language problems, and different tactical methods often precluded effective teamwork between regular Army and irregular troops.

The last brigade clash in the Ia Drang campaign's opening rounds occurred on 6 November near LZ Wing. Company B of the 2d Battalion, 8th Cavalry, stumbled across trenchlines containing North Vietnamese infantry and immediately attacked with two platoons. The entrenched *6th Battalion, 33d NVA Regiment,* not only pinned both platoons, but countered by moving to surround the entire company. The battalion's Company C hacked through dense jungle to reach its stranded sister unit and smashed into the rear of the North Vietnamese force at a stream crossing. As the new company tried to press a flanking attack, it also became locked in heavy combat and stalled.

Although a profuse amount of supporting air and artillery strikes was delivered, the two companies were unable to crack the NVA positions. After dark the companies linked up to establish one defensive perimeter, which was raked by NVA automatic weapons fire for the remainder of the night. During darkness the North Vietnamese withdrew, leaving snipers behind to mask their departure. The firefight was the bloodiest division confrontation in Vietnam to date, costing the cavalry twenty-six dead and fifty-three wounded. More ominous to division staff was the disheartening realization that the North Vietnamese were excellent jungle fighters and masters of light infantry tactics. They maintained their aggressive spirit despite battlefield losses or sudden shifts in local advantage because of airmobile response.

For the next three days the 1st Brigade conducted company sweeps which netted only stragglers and evidence that the *33d NVA Regiment* had been split apart and chased from the area. By 9 November the region west of Plei Me was considered largely clear of enemy troops since the missing *32d NVA Regiment,* which had not been encountered, was now suspected of having slipped east of Plei Me. Col. Thomas W. Brown's 3d Brigade took over the 1st Brigade's search mission, but intended to move east toward the central highlands instead. However, field force command believed that the NVA were still concentrating along the western Cambodian border. Since Roberts's brigade had just completed twelve days of airmobile hopping through mostly empty territory, Brown decided to reinvestigate a sector where previous combat had flared up but no follow-up ground sweep was conducted: the heavily jungled Ia Drang Valley. Although, "having drawn a blank up to this point, I wasn't sure what we would find or even if we'd find anything."[4] Colonel Brown possessed intelligence that an enemy base camp might exist there and thus give opportunity for decisive battle.

The North Vietnamese conveniently confirmed their continued presence west of Plei Me by mortaring Brown's 3d Brigade headquarters at the Cateckia Tea Plantation (southwest of Pleiku) just before midnight on 12 November. The brigade maneuvered its three fresh infantry and two artillery battalions westward, spearheaded by Stockton's ubiquitous 1st Squadron, 9th Cavalry. Lt. Col. Harold G. Moore's 1st Battalion of the 7th Cavalry was directed to begin searching the area around the Ia Drang near Chu Pong mountain on 14 November.

Lieutenant Colonel Moore was confident of NVA activity in the Ia Drang Valley. Suspecting possible trouble, Moore wanted his initial airlanded company to rapidly consolidate and the entire battalion landing expedited. He needed a field big enough to hold ten helicopters at once, and he personally conducted a reconnaissance flight over the rain forest canopy early on the designated morning of the air assault. Only two fields of that size existed, and one was full of jagged tree stumps. Moore quickly selected the other grassy clearing, coded LZ X-Ray, at the base of Chu Pong massif, and alerted supporting howitzers at nearby LZ Falcon to commence bombarding it.

Part of standard airmobile doctrine was breaking up possible enemy defenses around landing zones by firing artillery preparations on

4. Ltr, Col. Brown, Chief, CINCPAC J3 Current Ground Ops Branch, to Cpt Cash, DA Office of the Chief of Mil History, dtd 8 Aug 67, p. 2.

the chosen locations. To maintain a heavy volume of fire against the target, attack helicopters made rocket and machine gun runs across the LZ as the artillery fire was stopped or shifted. Troopships whirled in to land the infantry as the gunships made their final passes. Captain John Herren's Company B was air assaulted onto LZ X-Ray at 10:50 A.M. The cavalrymen did not meet immediate resistance as they moved through the grass and around the six-foot-high anthills to enter the woodline beyond. However, Lt. Al Deveny's 1st Platoon came under intense NVA fire in the scrub brush just after it crossed a dry creek.

Lt. Henry Herrick's 2d Platoon tried to link up with Deveny's pinned men, but was suddenly engulfed by intense fire from all sides and cut off. One four-man American machine gun team was wiped out, and North Vietnamese quickly turned the M60 weapon against the surrounded cavalrymen. Bullets clipped at grass-high level and slammed into the crumpled heaps of dead and wounded troops. The platoon survivors returned fire with their rifles flat against the dirt. Lieutenant Herrick and his platoon NCO, Sergeant First Class Palmer, were killed. By midafternoon, when squad leader Sgt. Clyde E. Savage assumed command after the other NCOs had been either killed or disabled, the original twenty-seven-man platoon had been reduced to only seven unwounded soldiers.

Within minutes after the Battle for LZ X-Ray began with the decimation of Herrick's platoon, it was apparent that Moore's battalion had tripped a hornet's nest. The majority of both *33d and 66th NVA Regiments* was located on the Chu Pong. Artillery and airstrikes pummeled the jungle with smoke-filled explosions, but failed to check the North Vietnamese infantrymen surging down the mountain slopes toward Company B's two platoons on the ridge. A steady rain of North Vietnamese mortar fires sent geysers of red dirt across the landing zone, and the thick pall of dust and smoke hindered fire support direction. Lieutenant Deal's reserve platoon was ordered to try to reach the trapped soldiers, even as Captain Herren heaved grenades at advancing NVA appearing in the high grass and streambeds on and around LZ X-Ray itself.

Lieutenant Colonel Moore set up his command post next to the emergency aid station at a large anthill in the center of the LZ and immediately called for the rest of his battalion. Helicopters darted in with Company C, doubling the number of Americans on the ground. When Capt. Ramon A. Nadal's Company A arrived next, Moore used them to reinforce the escalating firefight at the creekbed. Unfortunately, the situation deteriorated too fast to permit airlanding of Capt. Louis R. "Ray" Lefebvre's Company D. Accurate NVA automatic weapons fire swept the entire landing zone and even peppered the command anthill. Several Company D troopers were killed or wounded before their helicopters touched down, and Moore was forced to wave off further troopships.

Company B was embroiled in the most desperate fighting on the high ground just beyond the stream. Captain Nadal of Company A sent one of his platoons under Lt. Walter J. "Joe" Marm, Jr., to assist the breakthrough attempt by Deal's platoon of Company B, which was already advancing toward its isolated comrades. Lieutenant Marm formed his men in a line of skirmish to catch up, but the gap between him and Deal's platoon proved most fortuitous. By following behind Company B in the dense tropical vegetation, Marm's troops were able to mow down scores of fresh NVA soldiers who were moving around Company B's rear and unaware his platoon was closing the gap.

The North Vietnamese turned to charge Marm's platoon and flank his unit by scrambling past them into the creekbed, but succeeded only in running into the rest of Nadal's Company A, which was taking up positions in the gully. The sudden clash surprised both sides, and firing erupted at extremely close range. Lt. Bob Taft of the forward platoon was killed instantly, and radio communications silenced. The cavalrymen in the creekbed shoot-out reeled from the shock of the firefight, leaving Taft's body and a wounded trooper behind. Captain Nadal and his radioman, Sergeant Gill, jumped into the creek channel and pulled out the fallen men.

Farther uphill the violence of the North Vietnamese attack defeated all attempts to reach the shattered 2d Platoon. Increasing numbers of NVA reinforcements used frontal assaults and encircling movements to force the rest of Company B to fall back on Marm's platoon and retreat toward the creek. Both Companies A and B combined to form a defensive line facing the Chu Pong mountain, employing the waist-high creekbed as a trench. With these two depleted companies tied in to cover the LZ's western perimeter, Moore sent Capt. Robert H. Edward's Company C to defend the southern sector. His men had just assumed positions when they were charged by massed North Vietnamese infantry attempting to overrun the landing zone from a new direction. This attack was broken up, but another NVA group tried to penetrate between the two companies at the creek. Moore sent in his last reserves, the few troops of Company D under Captain LeFebvre, who had managed to land before the other helicopter insertions had been canceled. The NVA were blocked, but American losses were high. S. Sgt. George Gonzales took over the company remnants after LeFebvre was severely wounded.

Lieutenant Colonel Moore took advantage of a midafternoon respite to airland the rest of his battalion with the loss of only two helicopters. He reconstituted the emergency reserve and parceled out replacements throughout the perimeter. At the creek bottom Companies A and B took advantage of the slackening combat level to launch another counterattack aimed at reaching the isolated 2d Platoon. The cavalrymen surged forward at 4:20 P.M., but were fiercely opposed by well-camouflaged NVA soldiers occupying spider holes dug into the slope's dense tangle of shrubbery and bamboo thickets. Many troops were hit at point-blank range as they continued to struggle uphill.

Lieutenant Marm inspired his men forward by personal example, valiantly destroying one NVA machine gun nest with grenades (an act which earned him the first Medal of Honor awarded the division in Vietnam), but he was shot through the head and critically wounded. Several key forward observers were killed, and soon the entire artillery liaison radio frequency was swamped by undisciplined and frantic calls for urgent fire support. With crucial artillery direction hampered and casualties mounting in the face of more NVA crew-served weapons pits, the momentum of attack was lost. Lieutenant Colonel Moore resorted to an old Korean War trick, calling in white phosphorus rounds on top of the leading cavalrymen to enable the companies to break contact and regroup at the creek before twilight.

One of the foremost dangers of air assaulting infantry into unknown territory was the chance that units would be projected too close to larger enemy formations under unfavorable circumstances. This concern was counterbalanced by the division's need to force combat against an enemy reluctant to engage on other than his own terms. Therefore, airmobile commanders were trained to act boldly, even if such action meant risking adverse battle situations. Airmobile doctrine was to strike hard and fast, and reserves were counted on to redress the inevitable lack of proper but time-consuming battleground preparation. The trouble at LZ X-Ray resulted from the fact that Colonel Brown had insufficient reserves available to assist Moore's beleaguered battalion.

The rest of Colonel Brown's brigade was widely scattered in other ongoing sweep operations, and only one company was ready for rapid commitment to LZ X-Ray. This was the brigade's own base security element—Company B, 2d Battalion, 7th Cavalry, under Capt. Myron Diduryk. The company was airlifted to bolster Moore's battalion that evening, but this move only provided some extra manpower if battalion survival was jeopardized during the night. To provide enough strength to reverse the North Vietnamese battlefield initiative, other battalions were required. Beginning that afternoon, the rest of Lt. Col. Robert A. McDade's 2d Battalion, 7th Cavalry, was airmobiled west to LZ Macon, closer to X-Ray, but marshy ground there forced the helicopters to land on more-distant LZ Columbus instead.

In the meantime Lt. Col. Robert B. Tully's 2d Battalion of the 5th Cavalry was put back together at LZ Victor, but the assembly required time and led to other complications. The lack of helicopters, impending nightfall, and Brown's desire to avoid landing troops on a small LZ under fire after dark delayed Tully's departure until the next morning. The battalion was ordered to march overland to LZ X-Ray at first light, instead of using helicopter movement, because Brown "didn't relish the idea of moving a steady stream of helicopters into an LZ as hot as X-Ray," and he "was sure a foot move would be unobserved and the battalion might come in behind the enemy."[5]

Company C of Tully's battalion, under Capt. Edward A. Boyt, was searching through dense forest late that afternoon when word was received to cease operations and prepare the company for immediate helicopter extraction. Boyt was told they would be shuttled to LZ Victor overnight and form part of the relief expedition to X-Ray. His attached engineers frantically cleared a small landing zone out of the woods before sunset, using thirty pounds of explosives and breaking seventeen entrenching tools in the process. As the company was lifted out by helicopter, Boyt glimpsed the ongoing Battle of LZ X-Ray in the distance. It resembled a heavy ground fog with dancing splotches

5. Ibid., p. 3.

of colors, which he knew were produced by the discharge of dyed smoke grenades. He recalled thinking, "Oh hell, this is it!"[6]

Moore's men endured a restless but uneventful night on LZ X-Ray, and at dawn on 15 November patrols were sent forward beyond the foxholes. On the perimeter's southern side these cavalrymen were suddenly struck and overwhelmed by an NVA human-wave assault. The North Vietnamese soldiers charged across the elephant grass and through a series of multiple explosions as final defensive artillery shells and rockets pounded the earth. Cavalry grenadier and automatic rifle fire joined in hammering the NVA ranks, but the attack closed too fast to be defeated in front of the foxholes. The screaming North Vietnamese infantrymen bounded into the cavalry lines with bayonets fixed to their AK47 rifles. The melee of hand-to-hand combat was punctuated by rifle bursts fired from the hip. Individual struggles sometimes ended in mutual death as soldiers of both sides were sent spinning into the dirt. Captain Edwards was struck down as he radioed urgently for help.

A heavy cross fire ripped across the entire landing zone. Sergeant First Class McCawley led Company A's 2d Platoon out of the creekbed and tried to cross over the field to reinforce the southern side. His counterattack was stalled by a hail of gunfire near an anthill midway there. The North Vietnamese stormed the extended frontage held by Company D, an attack which threatened to overrun the nearby battalion mortars. Several perimeter sectors were under simultaneous attack, and the entire situation became chaotic. Supporting fires and airstrikes were brought in as close as possible and ordnance spilled into friendly lines. In many instances combatants were intermixed and any distinguishable edge of battle ceased to exist. The array of colored marking smoke mixed with thick clouds of powder and haze drifting over the battlefield.

Lieutenant Colonel Moore exerted a forceful, professional coolness in the midst of the confusion and near panic. One A1E Skyraider misdropped napalm close by his central command post, setting all the stacked rifle ammunition and grenade reserves on fire. Air Force F4C Phantoms and F100 fighter-bombers streaked in low over the horizon to hurl bomb clusters into the midst of massing North Vietnamese

6. Ltr, Capt. Boyt, Co D, USAINTS, dtd 20 Nov 67, p. 1.

infantry. The NVA attack waves disintegrated under this prompt air support, enabling the fatigued and hard-pressed cavalrymen to hold their positions during the most critical hours.

Just a mile and a half away, at LZ Victor, Tully's relief battalion began marching toward the din of battle at 8:00 A.M. Captain Boyt's company led one of the two columns as they advanced over a small ridgeline and brushed past a few sniper teams. Effective support fire was kept close by, and artillery rounds were lobbed into the woods around them. Tully's troops reached LZ X-Ray at noon. Although the movement failed in Brown's optimistic desire to trap NVA units between Moore's defending battalion and Tully's advancing one, the linkup relieved much of the danger. The North Vietnamese pulled back shortly after the reinforcing battalion arrived.

Lieutenant Colonel Moore's first task was to rescue the isolated platoon. The decimated unit was charged three times during the night, but each assault was defeated by the close-in shellfire directed by Sergeant Savage. The platoon position was reached and the wounded survivors and dead evacuated downslope. The rest of the day was spent consolidating positions, while Major General Kinnard dispatched another battalion, Lt. Col. Frederic Ackerson's 1st Battalion of the 5th Cavalry, to Colonel Brown's brigade base.

During the night, the NVA made two probes against LZ X-Ray positions. On the morning of 16 November, Diduryk's company became engaged in a firefight while searching the broken ground outside the perimeter. The company broke contact under covering artillery fire and called in airstrikes. A later sweep of the battlefield satisfied one of Moore's last major concerns, when the bodies of three missing battalion members were discovered. Although pesky North Vietnamese sniper fire continued, the Battle for LZ X-Ray was over. No attempt was made to go into the Chu Pong after the North Vietnamese, because B52 bombing strikes were now planned against the mountain. The men of Moore's battalion were airlifted to Pleiku for rest and reorganization. LZ X-Ray was occupied by both Tully's and McDade's battalions for another night and then abandoned on 17 November.[7]

---

7. U.S. units present at the Battle for LZ X-Ray were 1st Battalion, 7th Cavalry; Company A and B, 2d Battalion, 7th Cavalry; Company C, 8th

Tully's battalion went back to LZ Columbus while McDade's battalion moved overland to meet helicopters at a field coded LZ Albany, six miles away. McDade's order of march was led by Company A, followed by the battalion reconnaissance platoon, Company C, Company D, the battalion command group, and Company A from Ackerson's recently arrived battalion (this final company replaced McDade's own Company B, which fought hard at LZ X-Ray and was airlifted to Pleiku with Moore's personnel). The long, winding column pushed northwest through the tropical forest and high elephant grass.

The first elements had already reached LZ Albany when the *8th Battalion, 66th NVA Regiment,* attacked the length of the column. The ferocity and scale of the ambush split the battalion in two. Machine gun, grenade, and automatic rifle fire raked the cavalry ranks as snipers shot down leaders and radiomen. The middle of the column caved in under the force of the attack as North Vietnamese soldiers charged completely through the cavalry lines in several places. As the column was shattered, the battle disintegrated into a largely leaderless gel of individual melees and skirmishes between splintered groups.

Some soldiers were in a state of shock, running and firing at everything. Others were locked in a vortex of close-quarters fighting. Arriving North Vietnamese reinforcements were sent straight into battle without discarding their heavy combat packs. Dead and wounded men were strewn across fields littered with military accoutrements and smashed brushwood. There were hardly any field dressings, water, or transmission of orders. To many, it seemed that the air was filled with a sleet of bullets.

Throughout the action, groups of cavalrymen rushed toward nearby patches of open grassland, mistaking them for the landing zone and thereby actually running deeper into the ambush. The terrified troops were either frozen to the ground or crawled on their elbows, pistols and rifles propped up in wildly shaking hands. Slithering along the grass, they pushed aside clumps of foliage to fire directly into the

Engineer Battalion, and three demolitions teams; 229th Pathfinder Team (Provisional), 11th Aviation Group; artillery liaison and forward observer sections of the 1st Battalion, 21st Artillery. Losses were KIA: 79, WIA: 121. NVA killed by body count were 634 with more than 1,000 more casualties estimated; 6 were captured.

faces of enemy soldiers also wriggling through the same singed and cratered earth. Grenade explosions and the incessant rattle of small arms fire never drowned out the shrill cries for medics and the chilling screams of death. One veteran remembered the battle only as "a massacre."[8]

For hours the amorphous battle prevented artillery and tactical air support, but by midafternoon two large, ragged pockets of American resistance had formed. The stunned remnants of Company C joined McDade's command group, which combined to fight west toward the clearing where both Company A and the recon platoon were making their stands. Company D and the 5th Cavalry's Company A were separated and pushed to the east by the flow of battle. This gave enough semblance to the battlefield to enable rocket-firing helicopters to sweep across the front, followed by close-range napalm bombing. The roaring fireballs spewed across the burning grass and through onrushing NVA riflemen, although some Americans trapped outside the treeline were also burned to death.

Once again brigade reinforcing options were found wanting. Colonel Brown at the brigade's tea plantation base possessed only a single company available for immediate deployment. This was Company B of McDade's original command, already depleted at X-Ray and recuperating at Pleiku. At dusk the unit was flown into the main LZ Albany pocket of resistance. The tempo of fighting tapered off at nightfall, and Company B of Ackerson's battalion marched from LZ Columbus toward the other defensive pocket. The company reached the eastern perimeter, which was held by sister Company A (at the tail of McDade's original column), at 10:00 P.M. A continuous ring of artillery shellfire and aircraft flare illumination around the surrounded perimeters discouraged further mass NVA attacks.

The killing continued outside the perimeters as NVA soldiers combed the woods seeking out lost or wounded Americans. Automatic gunfire lashed through the forests, sending rounds ricocheting off darkened trees. Shadows crossed and wobbled under parachuted flares sinking to earth. Volunteers made repeated forays beyond the main lines into this eerie, artificial half-light to bring in wounded

8. Sp4 Jack P. Smith, "Death in the Ia Drang Valley," *Saturday Evening Post*.

comrades from the open. Sometimes the cavalry rescue parties and stretcher teams encountered so many wounded that only a few could be carried back. The wounded dragged themselves after full litters until they collapsed or lost consciousness.

The North Vietnamese retreated as daylight approached, and McDade's battalion was assembled around LZ Albany on 18 November. The other main pocket of soldiers, consisting mostly of 5th Cavalry troops, withdrew to LZ Columbus under Ackerson's control. McDade's troops spent the rest of the day searching the battlefield to find the wounded and missing, recover the dead, and collect equipment. Although an NVA attack was made against LZ Columbus that evening, the sanguinary Battle of LZ Albany was the last major action of the Ia Drang Valley campaign.[9]

On 20 November Col. William R. Lynch's 2d Brigade relieved Brown's brigade, but the fresh airmobile battalions made only meager contacts as the NVA retreated into Cambodia. North Vietnamese cohesion and battlefield staying power had been destroyed by weeks of unrelenting division air assault pressure and heavy losses. Below the division's wide-ranging Huey helicopters, the fields and patches of woodland were finally clear of North Vietnamese troops. A 9th Cavalry scoutship rescued Pfc. Toby Braveboy (Co A, 2d Bn, 7th Cavalry), who had been twice wounded in the LZ Albany battle on 17 November, when he was sighted waving his T-shirt from a jungle clearing on 24 November. Two days later Operation SILVER BAYONET was officially terminated. The Ia Drang Valley campaign was over.

During a month of sustained action, the 1st Cavalry Division (Airmobile) sought out, located, and met the regular NVA on the field of battle and won some of its fiercest Vietnam encounters. Helicopter-delivered infantry dominated the zone of operations, setting the future pace of wartime airmobility and validating the revolutionary role of aerial cavalry as originally perceived by General Gavin. Many suspected doctrinal truths about airmobility were verified. Airmobile operations had to be characterized by careful planning and followed by

---

9. Casualties in the Battle of LZ Albany on 17 November 1965 were KIA: 151, WIA: 121, and MIA: 4. NVA losses were 403 killed and confirmed by body count with many more losses suspected.

deliberate, bold, and violent execution. While the division could helicopter its troops throughout the battle zone, regardless of terrain restrictions, faster than any other organization and decisively engage distant enemy units by vertical air assault, this flexible striking power placed a very high premium on thorough preparation and the availability of sufficient reserves.

Numerous problems arose in the course of the bitterly fought campaign. Unexpected levels of combat outstripped division capability to reinforce adverse situations, especially in the Battles of LZs X-Ray and Albany, where the lack of properly assembled reserves almost resulted in disaster. The inability of aerial firepower alone to effectively stop NVA close assaults was manifested in the Battle of LZ Albany and a number of other firefights. The October division logistical crises produced severe shortages of essential supply stocks, such as aviation fuel, during the entire period. There were initial difficulties maintaining radio communications over the long distances involved, although orbiting CV2 radio relay aircraft offered a partial solution. The division spent the month of December rebuilding its logistical posture, extensively overhauling its overworked helicopters and equipment, and replacing personnel.

The frightful casualty levels seriously eroded division strength. In the two months of October and November the division suffered 334 killed, 736 wounded, 364 nonbattle injuries, and 2,828 cases of malaria, scrub typhus, and other serious diseases. This total represented more than 25 percent of the division's authorized strength (15,955). Even though many men were eventually returned to their units, the division used 5,211 replacements to complete rebuilding by the end of the year. Division assigned strength thus stood at 16,732 in December, but nearly a third (31 percent) were newly assigned. Such a high turnover rate invariably created turmoil and reduced overall efficiency.[10]

Despite the significant problems and high cost, the division's Ia Drang Valley campaign remained a magnificent military accomplishment. An initial North Vietnamese victory over Camp Plei Me was prevented by the 1st Cavalry Division's presence in the region. The

10. Personnel statistics from 1st Cavalry Division, *Quarterly Command Report for Second Fiscal Quarter FY 66*, pp. 5, 25.

strategic provincial capital of Pleiku was the key to the central high-lands and could not be stripped of protection. No South Vietnamese force would have been spared to help Plei Me without divisional assurance that the city would be safeguarded in its absence. When the relief column was ambushed, division artillery coordination kept the advance moving and insured the breakthrough into Plei Me.

Once the siege was broken, MACV ordered Major General Kinnard's division to locate the NVA forces and render them ineffective. Three brigades were sent in close succession to search out a vast, normally inaccessible territorial wilderness. The North Vietnamese forces withdrawing from Plei Me were unprepared to cope with the division's new style of airmobile warfare. Nothing in NVA training or experience had taught its soldiers how to deal with close helicopter pursuit. The *33d NVA Regiment* was hounded from the area and routed from its normal hiding places. However, the largest enemy units were located through unintended meeting engagements.

The Battles of LZs X-Ray and Albany were both initiated by un-expected North Vietnamese troop concentrations in hostile terrain. The division's campaign losses in large part reflected the severity of such encounters. The ratio of killed to wounded was 334 to 736, or 1:2.2., considerably higher than the 1:4 experienced in World War II and Korea. Most of the battle wounds were caused by small arms fire, with a very large number of head and chest hits, and very few wounds resulted from shell fragments. Most of those killed suffered multiple bullet impacts. The outcome of both actions was decided by massive air and artillery support, as well as by the individual courage and fighting stamina of the division's ground troops.

In the final analysis the Ia Drang Valley campaign was military history's first division-scale air assault victory. The 1st Cavalry Division accomplished all of its assigned objectives. Airmobile rein-forcement insured the survival of a remote but critical outpost; cavalry surveillance followed and found the enemy, and cavalry air assault brought the enemy into battle and pinpointed his strongpoints. Major General Kinnard resorted to strategic B52 bombing to shatter these jungled redoubts once they were identified, as in the Chu Pong after LZ X-Ray. In the process two regular North Vietnamese Army reg-iments were largely annihilated and had to be completely reformed in Cambodia.

The 1st Battalion of the 7th Cavalry returned to LZ X-Ray in April 1966. It wasn't a sentimental visit, as the battalion was providing security for two artillery batteries and preparing to air assault onto the Chu Pong massif. Most of the original battalion members had departed, but there were still quite a few veterans of the original X-Ray battle serving with the unit. Sgt. Steven Hansen had been a forward observer in Captain Nadal's Company A on that fateful day. Now he was a mortar sergeant in Company D.

Sergeant Hansen paced the old perimeter line and gently stepped across the open field. He still remained uneasy standing in the peaceful, grassy clearing where so many troopers had fallen under a hailstorm of bullets. Signs of the battle remained: lots of discarded gear from both sides, a set of American dog tags, and even bone fragments in front of the overgrown foxhole line. In contrast to later engagements, the North Vietnamese had not bothered to bury their dead at LZ X-Ray.

To Sergeant Hansen, the sight of so many howitzers pointing their muzzled tubes at the sky, with their crews lounging nearby, looked out of place on the curled grass of LZ X-Ray, almost as an affront to the sacred soil he stood upon. He remembered the heroism of his comrades, the bone weariness and mental fatigue of the heavy fighting, and how men's speech became halting and hardly audible, if anyone spoke at all. He gazed at the anthill used as Moore's command post; the same mound was being used by his new battalion commander, Lt. Col. Raymond Kampe. When Captain Coleman asked about his feelings, Hansen replied slowly, "It gives me a funny feeling to walk around a place where so many died. In a way I'm glad we came back, but I'd still just rather forget the whole thing."[11]

11. *Army Times*, 11 May 1966, p. 32.

# CHAPTER 4

# Sustained Pursuit

## *Techniques, 1966 Coastal Campaign*

The 1st Cavalry Division's hard-won victory in the Ia Drang Valley was especially important to the allied cause. Before the introduction of the airmobile division to central South Vietnam, MACV was largely powerless to counteract growing Viet Cong influence in this critical region. In harmony with the 1966 allied buildup and burgeoning offensive activity, General Westmoreland ordered Major General Kinnard's division to help clear II Corps Tactical Zone from the border to the coast.

Throughout the new year the airmobile cavalry continued to sweep the rugged central highland interior and strike at North Vietnamese regiments venturing out of Cambodia. However, as the 4th Infantry Division became established in the Pleiku vicinity and took over responsibility for western II CTZ, the 1st Cavalry Division concentrated its major efforts against the Viet Cong–dominated ricelands and adjacent mountain strongholds of Connecticut-size Binh Dinh Province along the South China Sea. MACV's ultimate goal was to break the VC grip over the densely populated and agriculturally important eastern portion of the province and to return this National Priority Area to government control, but this was impossible as long as the region remained unsecure to South Vietnamese authorities.

The geography of the central highlands compressed the fertile, extensively cultivated lowlands into a series of valleys surrounded by jagged ridgelines crowding toward the ocean. Clearing the VC/NVA out of their maze of fortified hamlets and hidden jungle bases throughout the region required the continual application of multidirectional pressure. This style of area warfare differed radically from the linear frontline tactics of conflicts in other wars. Most objectives had to be reswept several times, and troops fought over familiar battlefields. The directionless nature of area warfare often frustrated conventional military solutions, but it offered ideal circumstances for an airmobile division to exercise a basic cavalry task. From late-January Tet-66 through mid-February Tet-67, the 1st Cavalry Division waged a relentless year-long drive against NVA/VC forces throughout eastern Binh Dinh Province. The succession of operations included MASHER/ WHITE WING, JIM BOWIE, DAVY CROCKETT, CRAZY HORSE, THAYER I, IRVING, and THAYER II, and they represented the first airmobile application of sustained cavalry pursuit.

Pursuit is an offensive action against a retreating enemy. Rapid helicopter mobility favored fluid pursuit operations. Throughout the 1966 coastal campaign the 1st Cavalry Division sought to push NVA/ VC units out of their areas of influence, using aerial reconnaissance to disclose enemy locations and then triggering their retreat with helicopter assaults and superior firepower. Ideally, airmobile infantry would envelop the retreating enemy and block escape routes. The division realized that terrain and distance presented serious obstacles, but counted on massive helicopter employment to minimize these problems. Airmobility enabled the attack to be carried into the remote tropical valleys and mist-shrouded canyons which served as the main Viet Cong bases. The division hoped to turn these previously impervious VC redoubts into chokepoints, where the retreating enemy could be finally entrapped and eliminated.

The opening blow of this campaign was Operation MASHER/ WHITE WING, which commenced immediately after the Vietnamese Tet holidays on 25 January 1966. The 3d Brigade, commanded by newly promoted Col. Harold G. Moore, was directed to find and destroy a major enemy regimental recruiting and rice supply center near Bong Son. The cavalrymen became embroiled in heavy combat against a well-defended Viet Cong village at the outset, and this initial confrontation escalated into intense fighting across the brigade front. Airmobile pursuit was initiated, and within three weeks the majority of the 1st Cavalry Division was committed against a full NVA/VC division consisting of the *18th NVA, 22d NVA,* and *2d VC Regiments.*

On the misty foggy morning of 28 January, a phalanx of helicopters combat assaulted Lieutenant Colonel McDade's 2d Battalion, 7th Cavalry, onto the shoreline four miles north of Bong Son. McDade's battalion was having unusually bad luck. His battalion was largely rebuilt after the unfortunate battle at LZ Albany, but a C123 crash outside An Khe caused forty-two deaths in one line company being transported to the Bong Son area before the operation even started. The battalion's first air assault of MASHER was violently opposed as Viet Cong machine gunners hidden in the clusters of beachfront hootches fired into the low-flying aircraft. The helicopters broke formation to avoid the automatic weapons fire and scattered Capt. John Fesmire's Company C in small groups across one thousand yards of open sand in close proximity to Cu Nghi. The village, which surrounded much of the landing zone, was staunchly defended by VC entrenched in earthworks, palm groves, and bamboo thickets. This concealed network of VC mortars, snipers, and machine gun bunkers prevented the separated company from maneuvering.

McDade's other air assault element, understrength Company A commanded by Capt. Joel Sugdinis, landed some distance south of Fesmire. The unit moved overland through numerous hamlets to reach the isolated landing zone, but was stopped just short of its objective. Colonel Moore's brigade was soon mired in combat throughout its axis of advance. Within an hour four CH47 Chinooks were shot down and twelve UH1D Huey troopships badly damaged; by midafternoon twenty-eight helicopters were grounded. One Chinook sling-loading a 105mm howitzer was forced down, and Company B of Lieutenant Colonel Kampe's 1st Battalion, 7th Cavalry, contested the crash site with the Viet Cong. The company finally secured the location by manhandling the artillery piece into firing position, leveling its tube, and firing rounds directly into the charging VC.

At Cu Nghi, Fesmire's men grimly held their positions as the light rain turned into a cold, soaking drizzle. Artillery support was ordered stopped for fear of hitting friendly troops. Captain Sugdinis's advance to reach Fesmire was stalled by VC machine gun nests covering the wet rice paddy between the two companies. The leading troops of Company A could see colored signal smoke from Fesmire's command, but VC automatic weapons fire prevented them from linking up. After an extended firefight in the flat ricefield, both VC weapons positions were destroyed and the drenched American reinforcements reached the main battlefield. Lieutenant Colonel McDade attempted to bring in additional men from Company B late that afternoon, using an artillery barrage to seal off the LZ's eastern perimeter, but all six helicopters were hit by VC fire from positions not masked by the shellfire. He waited until after dark to bring in desperately needed ammunition and medical supplies, but another incoming helicopter was shot down. During the night the exhausted cavalrymen regrouped behind the village's sand burial mounds in the howling wind and rain as enemy grenadiers and snipers intensified their volume of fire.

The air cavalry's mainstay, tactical air support, became available after daybreak. The low overcast lifted enough to permit low-level bombing runs by jet aircraft. Air Force fighter-bombers napalmed village dwellings and trenches, detonating enemy ammunition stocks and causing large fires. Artillery bombarded the front throughout the rest of the morning as Colonel Moore arrived with Lieutenant Colonel Ingram's 2d Battalion, 12th Cavalry, and Kampe's battalion airmobiled into blocking positions north of the village. The cavalrymen overmastered some of the interlocking fortifications and tunnels, but spent another night under close-range fire from the uncleared village. The next day Colonel Moore's combined battalions forced the *7th and 9th Battalions, 22d NVA Regiment*, to retreat from the village. The three-day action in the Cu Nghi vicinity was costly and confused and generally marred by poor coordination between cavalry elements as a result of the weather and unanticipated ferocity of enemy resistance. The battle cost the cavalry 121 killed and another 220 wounded (660 enemy bodies were counted), but division pursuit operations could now be initiated.[1]

On 4 February 1966, as Colonel Moore's 3d Brigade prepared to press pursuit operations to the southwest into the An Lao Valley, the division reinforced the drive with Colonel Lynch's 2d Brigade. On the same day, the cavalry offensive was renamed WHITE WING after President Johnson angrily protested that the original operational title, MASHER, did not reflect "pacification emphasis." The An Lao Valley had been controlled by the Viet Cong since South Vietnam had been created. The valley was one of the most fertile agricultural basins of central South Vietnam, but also one of the most rugged and

---

1. 1st Cav Div, *Seven Month History and Briefing Data, September–March 1966*, dtd 9 June 67; 1st Cav Div, *Operational Report on Lessons Learned*, dtd 5 May 66.

dangerous. Several reconnaissance teams of Special Forces elite Project DELTA (Detachment B-52) were inserted into the valley in conjunction with the division's search pattern, but were quickly overwhelmed and destroyed.

The opening brigade airmobile assault was delayed two days by monsoon storms, marking the first time in division airmobile experience that a major cavalry operation was precluded by adverse weather. The NVA/VC forces used the opportunity to effect an unimpeded retreat as heavy clouds cloaked the densely forested mountainsides and disgorged torrential rains. Pursuing cavalry entered the valley only to find recently abandoned defensive positions.

Opponents of aerial cavalry most often cited its susceptibility to enemy anti-air weapons and weather conditions as valid reasons to discourage the concept. In Vietnam the absence of enemy aircraft and sophisticated antiair defenses meant that weather extremes represented the only real detriment to divisional mobility. However, these opponents considered Vietnam's tropical climate severe enough to undermine airmobile divisional effectiveness. During Operation MASHER/WHITE WING the division deliberately continued to rely on its helicopters and persevered with cavalry pursuit operations despite unfavorable wind and rain conditions. Major General Kinnard proved his division capable of maintaining pressure against an elusive, retreating enemy despite periods of forced inactivity.

Major General Kinnard used Colonel Lynch's newly introduced brigade to search the An Lao Valley mountains. He shifted the division's major pursuit effort farther south by diverting Colonel Moore's brigade into the Kim Son ("Crow's Foot") Valley region. The area was named the Crow's Foot after the shape of the surrounding valley hills on a military contour map. The eight twisting ridgelines around the Crow's Foot compress the bottomland into seven valleys which contain numerous streams and a fast-flowing river. Like the An Lao Valley, this secluded area was an ideal Viet Cong base. It provided concealment and innumerable hiding places for food and weapons caches, controlled entrances and numerous escape routes, excellent water and rice-growing resources, and complete absence of government control over the pro-VC local populace.

Colonel Moore altered his tactics upon entering the Kim Son, deliberately fragmenting his brigade and utilizing terrain in an attempt to outmaneuver any Viet Cong evasion. Helicopters first searched out the many natural valley avenues. Then, using deceptive landings and other flight patterns to confuse enemy scouts, company-size forces with two days' rations were carefully emplaced on the hills and ridges dominating the valley exits. On 11 February the splintered brigade began maneuvering from the hilltops toward the valley floor, while supporting artillery pummeled ravines and trails. Many dead Viet Cong were found downslope where they had been caught by the shower of artillery and rocket fire. The brigade continued its pursuit mode throughout the nights as patrols sortied under flare illumination, attempting to flush out the VC toward prepared ambush positions. The fire missions and ambuscades netted 249 enemy dead at the cost of only 6 cavalrymen killed. One VC battalion headquarters was located through documents found on a fallen enemy soldier, and Captain Diduryk's company of McDade's battalion was airlifted near the Soui Run River to pinpoint the unit before it could escape.

Captain Diduryk's company clashed against prepared VC positions along the densely jungled streambank on the morning of 15 February. Accurate defensive fire stalled two of his platoons, and decisive action was essential to prevent Viet Cong withdrawal before airmobile reinforcements arrived. An airstrike was promptly called for, and just before noon, as the last bombs were falling, the 3d Platoon fixed bayonets and charged the entrenched Viet Cong across the stream. The fury of this frontal assault at bayonet point unnerved the defenders, who fled their lines directly into the pathway of rocket-firing helicopters and company machine guns. The élan and courage of the cavalrymen carried the field, enabling Diduryk's men to thoroughly defeat two VC main force companies before evening. This First Team spirit fused the dash of cavalry enterprise with modern airmobile lethality to power the 1st Cavalry Division war engine throughout the Vietnam conflict.

The persistent pace of pursuit was maintained the next day as Colonel Moore's brigade was switched with Colonel Roberts's fresh 1st Brigade. The new brigade rapidly helicoptered into the virtually inaccessible lower portion of the Kim Son Valley. Lt. Col. Edward C. Meyer's 2d Battalion of the 5th Cavalry helicoptered into the narrow jungle river bottom between densely forested mountain crags, and shortly afterward Company B was engulfed by devastating fire from an upslope heavy weapons battalion of the *18th NVA Regiment*.

The intense recoilless rifle, mortar, and machine gun fire temporarily wiped out artillery liaison and locked the entire battalion into a grueling standoff. The engagement was decided that evening when airmobile reinforcements were flexibly inserted behind the enemy lines, and the NVA were driven from their commanding positions. On the same day, interrogation of a captured NVA battalion commander by Colonel Lynch's brigade staff revealed the location of the *22d NVA Regiment* on the eastern edge of the Kim Son Valley. Lieutenant Colonel Ackerson's battalion (1/5th Cav) led the attack, but became deadlocked in combat against entrenched NVA defending the main camp. Frontal assaults against the formidable earthworks were mired in the thick tropical foliage as hidden machine gun bunkers built flush to the ground suddenly opened fire and cut apart the advancing platoons. Casualties had to be left where they fell, and fighting raged for days around the extensive jungle stronghold. The stalemate was punctuated by attacks and counterattacks on both sides. One of the most serious North Vietnamese sallies was defeated on 20 February after Company A's command post was nearly overrun by three different assault waves. During this period, thirty-three separate battalion attacks, each supported by massive artillery and rocket expenditures, failed to breach the enemy bastion.

North Vietnamese forces trapped in the Kim Son Valley by the sustained cavalry pursuit desperately defended their base, and MACV decided to employ strategic B52 bombers to finish the job. Ackerson's battalion was pulled back on 21 February as the objective area was subjected to high-altitude bombing and then saturated with riot gas. The battalion moved back unopposed into leveled forests and cratered remnants of the NVA position. They found shattered trees tossed through wooden blockhouse ruins, interconnecting tunnels, and even underground stove facilities. The encounter amply demonstrated the futility of defending territory against a determined aerial cavalry onslaught to the North Vietnamese. Contact became increasingly sporadic during the following week. The division terminated its Kim Son (Crow's Foot) Valley sweep at the end of the month. The valley claimed nearly a battalion's worth of American casualties (107 dead and 561 wounded compared to 710 NVA/VC bodies counted), but airmobile pursuit successfully penetrated and led to the elimination of a major enemy redoubt.

The division completed forty-one days of hard campaigning as

Colonel Lynch's brigade scoured the reputed VC stronghold of the seaside Cay Giep Mountains before coming full circle back into the Bong Son Plains. The troops were lowered onto the forested Cay Giep hillmass by CH47-dropped Jacob's ladders suspended through bomb-created clearings, but found few Viet Cong. Operation MASHER/ WHITE WING, the harshest test of airmobile durability to date, ended on 6 March 1966.[2]

Major General Kinnard reaffirmed the airmobile division's staying power in a harsh environment, contrasting sharply with the gently rolling, uninhabited landscape and favorable climatic conditions of the fall 1965 Ia Drang Valley campaign. The 1st Cavalry Division pressed through monsoon rainstorms and fortified NVA/VC defenses to drive the enemy out of villages and mountain hideouts in four main base areas. The effectiveness of modern cavalry pursuit was verified as the division cut a wide circle through a formerly uncontested, densely populated swath of Viet Cong territory. During this time, division aviation flew 77,627 sorties, which included airlifting 120,585 cavalry troops (data includes multiple lifts of the same personnel).[3]

The 1st Cavalry Division's operations were less successful when conducted in response to faulty allied intelligence, a common problem throughout the Vietnam War. For instance, Major General Kinnard retaliated against a Viet Cong raid on the division's An Khe base camp by sending two brigades into the suspected 3,000-strong "Kon Truck" VC staging area during the rest of March (Operation JIM BOWIE). The expedition forced the 1st and 3d Brigades to conduct a fruitless search through very difficult tropical terrain containing few landing zones. Lt. Col. Robert J. Malley's 8th Engineer Battalion airlifted teams with minidozers to carve out fragile clearings on the edge of steep ridgelines and rocky pinnacles. Helicopters swarmed over the sun-baked valleys and deployed a multitude of ambush patrols, which only confirmed that the Viet Cong had executed an orderly withdrawal several days prior to the operation.

The division incurred a large number of losses in spite of the scant opposition. The brigades suffered 380 casualties, mostly from

2. 1st Cav Div, *Combat Operations After Action Report*, dtd 28 Apr 66.
3. 1st Cav Div, *Operational Report on Lessons Learned*, dtd 5 May 66, Appendix 4-3. Aviation Data.

punji-stake wounds and a series of fire-related mishaps. The elephant grass near one landing zone was set ablaze by aerial rocket fire, and the fire was almost extinguished when a hovering Chinook fanned the flames anew. The raging inferno raced two hundred yards through the grass and engulfed an entire mortar platoon. While Operation JIM BOWIE was a marked failure at finding the VC, claiming only 27 confirmed dead, it proved a valuable exercise in refining airmobile doctrine under adverse terrain conditions.[4]

The division was now firmly established in Vietnam, and its record of battlefield success was evident by Viet Cong avoidance of the unit wherever possible. Much of the division's success was directly due to Maj. Gen. Harry W. O. Kinnard, who created the first air assault force in military history and tranformed it into the Army's first airmobile fighting division. He relinquished command of the 1st Cavalry Division to Maj. Gen. John "Jack" Norton on 6 May 1966.

Major General Norton, the son of Col. Augustus Norton, was born 14 April 1918 at Fort Monroe, Virginia. He graduated as first captain of the Corps of Cadets at West Point in 1941 and joined the 505th Parachute Infantry Regiment after paratrooper school a year later. He fought through Europe with the 82d Airborne Division in World War II and served as Secretary of the Army Frank Pace, Jr.'s, military assistant during the Korean conflict. In 1955 Colonel Norton began a series of assignments in the Office of the Chief for Research and Development, which placed him in the forefront of airmobility development. As chief of the Air Mobility Division, Norton became qualified as both fixed-wing and helicopter pilot. He commanded the 2d Battle Group, 4th Cavalry, of the 1st Cavalry Division in Korea before returning to the United States in 1960 as the aviation officer of CONARC. He was on several high-level boards engaged in Army reorganization and airmobile doctrine, including the Howze Board. On 1 April 1963 Norton was promoted to brigadier general and became assistant commandant of the Army infantry school at Fort Benning. He was sent to Vietnam two years later, where General Westmoreland handpicked him to command the 1st Cavalry Division after

---

4. 1st Cav Div, *Combat Operations After Action Report (RCS: MACV J3-32)*, dtd 8 May 66; 1st Cav Div, *Critique of Operation JIM BOWIE*, dtd 15 April 66.

a stint of duty commanding U.S. Army Vietnam support troops. Major General Norton led the 1st Cavalry Division with a firm understanding of both airmobile development and the Army logistical structure in Vietnam, an important resource to the highly technical and equipment-dependent airmobile division.

Major General Norton continued resweeping Binh Dinh Province on 4 May 1966 in Operation DAVY CROCKETT. Colonel Moore's 3d Brigade reentered the Bong Son Plains during the seasonal weather transition, which brought clear weather and high humidity. Flight conditions were enhanced, but troops marched and fought under an unrelenting tropical sun with temperatures of 94 to 110 degrees Fahrenheit. Aerial pursuit was initiated by Lt. Col. James C. Smith's 1st Squadron, 9th Cavalry, which attacked northward, seeking a reported Viet Cong battalion. The chase led to skirmishing the next day at Bing Di, where two battalions of the 7th Cavalry airmobiled to encircle the rapidly moving VC force. A furious artillery barrage inflicted heavy losses, but the VC managed to elude the encirclement during the night. Contact was reestablished when a squadron helicopter was shot down at Than Son village on 6 May, and the division quickly implemented an airmobile response.

The 7th Cavalry's 2d Battalion air assaulted to seal off the village's southern exits while the 1st Battalion moved toward the hamlet from the other direction. Ground reconnaissance troops from the 9th Cavalry, reinforced with mechanized ARVN vehicles, blocked off the east. Twelve F4C Phantom sorties rained high explosives on the VC-occupied hamlet, and both 7th Cavalry battalions advanced toward the fortified VC trenchlines from two sides. At one point, with only three hundred yards separating the advancing cavalrymen, one VC company defensive position was demolished by well-placed 750-pound Air Force bombs, bringing Colonel Moore's accolade that it was "the most accurate display of tactical air precision bombing I have ever seen."[5] The 1st Cavalry Division was most effective when its air-ground teamwork was functioning smoothly throughout the pursuit and final entrapment of the enemy. The battalions made visual contact late in the afternoon, spent the night in vigilant encirclement, and

5. 1st Cav Div, *Seven Month History and Briefing Data: April–October 1966*, dtd 1 May 67, p. 79.

overran the VC battalion and village after a sharp skirmish the next day.

The brigade began searching the Kim Son (Crow's Foot) Valley on 11 May, but few contacts developed, and the mission was being terminated five days later when cavalrymen patrolling the nearby Vinh Thanh Valley clashed violently with the Viet Cong. A cavalry battalion had been dispatched to that area after evidence captured earlier revealed that the Special Forces Vinh Thanh camp might be attacked on 19 May, Ho Chi Minh's birthday. Many major operations in Vietnam were triggered by such small incidents, and the division was "backed into (Operation) CRAZY HORSE by the virtue of the unusual intelligence that was developed." The Viet Cong were discovered in force on the eastern rim of the Kim Son Valley, causing Colonel Moore to remark bluntly at a later operational critique, "How the hell did we finish DAVY CROCKETT without knowing that he [2d VC Regiment] was in the CRAZY HORSE area?"[6]

The clash occurred on the afternoon of 16 May 1966. Capt. John D. Coleman's Company B of the 2d Battalion, 8th Cavalry, landed one helicopter at a time on LZ Hereford near Camp Vinh Thanh, climbed a ridgeline, and encountered the VC in prepared positions. One squad moving forward was annihilated by a sudden Viet Cong counterattack. Attempts to retrieve American dead and wounded only increased casualties and disclosed further VC strongpoints in the dense undergrowth. An afternoon thunderstorm unleashed sheets of rain across the jungle canopy and dimmed the faint sunlight reaching the forest floor. The VC took advantage of the darkened conditions to make repeated attacks, which compressed Coleman's men into a small defensive perimeter under automatic weapons fire from all sides.

The fighting continued into early evening under conditions too close for tube artillery support. The rainstorm seemed to prevent aerial rocket assistance, which was the last-resort weapon available to save an isolated airmobile ground element in trouble. Two armed helicopters of the 2d Battalion, 20th Artillery, led by commander Lt. Col. Morris J. Brady, carefully edged up the ridgeline in the downpour. Guided by radio instructions from the beleaguered company,

6. 1st Cav Div, *Critique Summary—Operation CRAZY HORSE*, dtd 27 June 66, p. 16.

both helicopters loomed over the trees and fired rockets directly into the charging Viet Cong. The massed explosions from their closely delivered salvos shattered the VC assault.

Airmobile reinforcements were dispatched to LZ Hereford, and during the night Capt. John W. Cummings's Company A of the 1st Battalion, 12th Cavalry, reinforced Coleman's lines. The next morning both companies were attacked by a battalion of the *2d VC Regiment*. For two hours throngs of VC surged out of the jungle at intervals and rushed the foxholes, many being brought down and killed just outside the perimeter. Ammunition was so low that many troopers were down to their last rifle magazines and had already fixed bayonets. Another relief force from Lt. Col. William B. Ray's 1st Battalion of the 5th Cavalry airmobiled to the rescue, and these additional reinforcements prompted the Viet Cong to withdraw.

Col. John J. Hennessey's 1st Brigade commenced pursuit with Lieutenant Colonel Ray's battalion and the 2d Battalion of the 12th Cavalry under Lt. Col. Otis C. Lynn. Both units swept east into the mountains in an effort to cut off suspected VC escape routes. The jagged ridges were blanketed by triple-canopy jungle, which sloped into deep heavily vegetated ravines laced with cascading waterfalls and swift streams. Suitable spots for landing zones were so scarce that the Viet Cong were able to keep most under constant surveillance. Adverse skirmishes often erupted in close proximity to them, as Hill 766 (LZ Horse) and when a cavalry mortar platoon was overrun on 21 May (LZ Hereford). On the latter date elements of Lt. Col. Levin B. Broughton's 1st Battalion of the 8th Cavalry also fought a pitched engagement against hillside Viet Cong machine gun bunkers. The knoll's summit was stormed and the VC positions eliminated in an unusual American night assault. In some of these battles the thick jungle caused grenadiers to cease using their weapons, as the M79 projectiles bounded back to explode in friendly lines (later this deficiency was corrected by setting the rounds to arm at a distance from the firer).

By this time Major General Norton had committed the majority of his division to the operation. The bulk of the *2d VC Regiment* remained within the mountains between the Soui Ca and Vinh Thanh valleys, where the difficult terrain effectively masked its movement and location. The division adopted a new tactical methodology on 24 May, when helicopter troop insertions were replaced by massed fire-

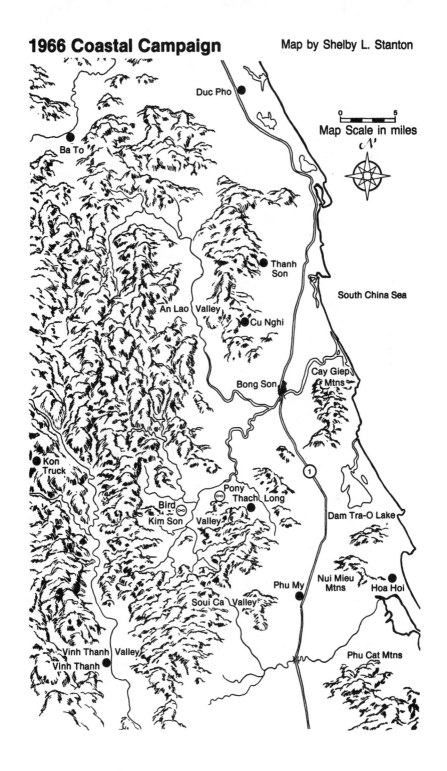

# 1966 Coastal Campaign

Map by Shelby L. Stanton

Duc Pho

Ba To

0          5
Map Scale in miles

Thanh
Son

South China Sea

An Lao Valley

Cu Nghi

Cay Giep
Mtns

Bong Son

1

Kon
Truck

Pony
Thach Long

Bird
Kim Son    Valley

Dam Tra-O Lake

Phu My

Nui Mieu
Mtns

Hoa Hoi

Soui Ca Valley

Vinh Thanh Valley

Phu Cat Mtns

Vinh Thanh

power in an effort to drive the VC out of valley pockets. Ground units were pulled back into a ring of company-size ambush points outside the strike zone, but the area was so large that it could not be patrolled adequately. One large gap had to be covered with a CS gas barrier. Tactical airstrikes, B52 bombing, and artillery concentrations pounded the hillmass interior for three days in an attempt to stampede the Viet Cong out of targeted sectors.

The closest air-ground coordination was required. Flight pattern advisories were constantly radioed in an attempt to prevent aircraft from inadvertently intermixing with artillery shellfire, but the entire sector remained a "rather mad target area," characterized in the best terms as a "nip-and-tuck proposition." Major General Norton himself accompanied Army Secretary Resor on a helicopter from the battlefield to Saigon. During the flight "our chase ship said that artillery out there is awful close—we were lucky not to get hit. When we got back to Tan Son Nhut we found out another Huey had been shot out of the air just five minutes behind us by our own artillery."[7]

Such attempts to dislodge the enemy through firepower neglected the real value of dismounted cavalry (infantry) to the total airmobile cavalry package. The 1st Cavalry Division was a triad of powerful weapons systems—helicoptered infantry, armed aircraft, and mobile artillery. The enemy suffered little sustained damage from artillery and airpower unless infantry followed up to actually seize the ground and completed his destruction. In this case the infantry follow-up really consisted of mere exploratory sweeps to ascertain damage.

Airmobile pursuit efforts in CRAZY HORSE were stymied after the initial fierce firefights. Retreat was triggered, but the rugged terrain, severe heat and humidity, and heightened enemy activity elsewhere precluded a relentless follow-up. The remainder of the operation sputtered into a semisearch through the valley wilderness, which garnered only sporadic contact with the Viet Cong. Although considerable quantities of foodstuffs and supplies were uncovered, results were rapidly diminishing. Renewed NVA activity in the western portion of II CTZ required division presence elsewhere. Major General Norton was forced to decide how long such a large and logistically expensive effort in a rough area like the Vinh Thanh Valley was

7. Ibid., p. 11.

worthwhile. The division kept its aerial reconnaissance squadron and four rotating battalions in the area until 5 June 1966, when he ordered the operation terminated. Operation CRAZY HORSE, with its toll of 79 KIA, 1 MIA, and 356 WIA (compared to 350 enemy killed by body count and another 330 estimated), was a costly lesson in the limits of sustained pursuit.[8]

The 1st Cavalry Division turned its attention to enemy threats elsewhere for the next several months. Two operations were conducted around Tuy Hoa in Phu Yen Province, followed by engagements in the central highlands and a return to old division haunts in the western Ia Drang–Chu Pong region. In the meantime Binh Dinh Province remained only partially subdued by the Korean Capital Division, which occupied its southeastern portion. Reliable intelligence indicated that the *3d NVA Division* (also known as the *610th*) was still using the An Lao, Soui Ca, and Kim Son (Crow's Foot) valleys as important assembly and supply base areas. In mid-September 1966 the division returned to the coast from the Cambodian border to begin an extended seventeen-month campaign to pacify northeastern Binh Dinh Province. Major General Norton reinitiated cavalry pursuit by launching Operation THAYER I, the first stage of this renewed campaign.

For three days prior to the operation, numerous B52 bombing runs were made to separate the NVA/VC from their various havens and neutralize or drive them toward the Kim Son region. Colonel Smith's 1st Squadron of the 9th Cavalry provided aerial surveillance on all strikes, but was unable to render the necessary ground observation because of the lack of landing zones in six of the targeted areas. The exact dispositions of the North Vietnamese remained largely unknown.

On 13 September 1966 the division conducted its largest air assault to date as more than 120 Hueys and Chinooks lifted five battalions of Col. Archie K. Hyle's 1st Brigade and Col. Marvin J. Berenzweig's 2d Brigade into a circular configuration on the ridges around

---

8. 1st Cav Div, *Combat Operations After Action Report (RCS: MACV J3-32)*, dtd 10 Sep 66; 1st Cav Div, *Critique Summary—Operation CRAZY HORSE*, dtd 27 Jun 66; various 14 MH Det opns chronologies and summary fact sheets.

the Crow's Foot. The *18th NVA Regiment* quickly split up, side-stepped the advance, and slipped away. For the next two weeks the brigades made only scant contact as troop-laden helicopters leap-frogged battalions in airmobile pursuit of the fleeing enemy columns. Several food and clothing caches, a major hospital, and even a grenade and mine factory were uncovered, but the only significant personnel claim was one song-and-dance troupe specializing in musical propaganda, captured while traveling between villages.

Although progress seemed disheartening, an NVA regiment had been displaced from the Kim Son Valley base area and forced to retreat an even greater distance from its supply sources. The relentless cavalry drive apparently caused considerable consternation among the *7th* and *8th Battalions* of the *18th NVA Regiment*, which decided they had to fight their way out of the situation. The NVA force exposed its location by making an unsuccessful nighttime attack against an ARVN regimental command post on 23 September and then moved farther east onto the coastal plain. The division maintained its momentum of pursuit and entrapped both battalions there four days later.

The two identified NVA battalions were pocketed into an area bounded by the South China Sea, the Phu Cat Mountains to the south, and the Nui Mieu hillmass to the north. Aggressive airmobile cavalry maneuvering blocked all routes of egress back west into the valley regions. Major General Norton tightened his cavalry screen to make enemy exfiltration more difficult and exchanged the Berenzweig brigade for Col. Charles D. Daniel's fresh 3d Brigade. Additional South Vietnamese and Korean forces were brought in to complete the encirclement, and THAYER I was declared terminated as preparations for Operation IRVING began.[9]

Operation IRVING, actually an extension of THAYER I, commenced on 1 October 1966 as five battalions air assaulted into the seacoast pocket. Colonel Hyle's 1st Brigade fought an opening two-day battle at Hoa Hoi, which became a classic demonstration of combined airmobile tactics. In true cavalry fashion, aerial reconnaissance started the battle as 9th Cavalry "White" scoutships spotted several

---

9. Hq 1st Bde 1st Cav Div, *Combat Operations After Action Report*, dtd 29 Oct 66; Hq 2d Bde 1st Cav Div, *Combat Operations After Action Report*, dtd 28 Oct 66.

enemy soldiers on the sandy northern tip of the Hung Lac peninsula. Lt. Col. George W. McIlwain's Troop A of the 1st Squadron, 9th Cavalry, aggressively exploited the initial contact with "Red" gunships and its "Blue" rifle platoon to determine the size of the opposing forces. A sizable North Vietnamese contingent was confirmed occupying the hedgerows, dikes, and natural defensive bulwarks of beachside Hoa Hoi village.

Colonel Hyle's brigade responded with optimum airmobile flexibility. The situation was relayed to Lt. Col. James T. Root, commanding 1st Battalion, 12th Cavalry, who dispatched Company B under Capt. Frederick Mayer, already in flight to another mission, to the scene of action. Captain Mayer's men air assaulted onto the open beach and were mortared as they maneuvered into line formation. Two exploding rounds wounded Mayer, who, despite profuse bleeding, remained in charge and directed the company through the well-prepared enemy bunker and trench system crisscrossing in front of Hoa Hoi. The rest of the battalion was rapidly airmobiled into nearby blocking positions. The line companies then fought closer toward the village's main defenses in carefully phased and coordinated attacks.

One advancing platoon was momentarily stopped by intense fire, but the men quickly recovered, stood up with rifles blazing, and charged the first trench. The gallantry of two privates, one (Pfc. Roy Salazar) killed leading a squad to breach a strongpoint and the other (Pfc. Francis Royal) mortally wounded carrying a wounded comrade to safety, established the pace of action for the duration of the battle. Throughout the action the cavalrymen adhered to the Rules of Engagement, when the easier and safer course would have been to ignore them. Lt. Donald Grigg of 3d Platoon, Company A, was leading his men across an open field when he saw several civilians suddenly walk aimlessly onto the field in the direct line of fire between the two forces. Immediately Lieutenant Grigg threw down his weapon, web gear, and helmet and raced more than fifty yards through enemy automatic weapons fire to carry two small children back to his own lines, followed by the rest of the old men and women.

The fighting in the village outworks raged throughout the day. At dusk the battalion pulled back from the village to form a tight cordon, preventing enemy exfiltration during the night. A continuous naval and field artillery bombardment was conducted under flarelight. Several bands of NVA soldiers tried to probe and shoot their way out of the encirclement, but each attempt was repulsed. The battalion made its final assault against the village the next morning. Fighting was heaviest in the final trenches, but continued unabated through the bunker-studded hootches themselves. Several times the cavalrymen were temporarily halted by the desperate resistance of heavy weapons strongpoints, but each time the soldiers rallied and carried the attack forward, sometimes in hand-to-hand combat. Elements of the *7th* and *8th Battalions, 18th NVA Regiment*, lost 233 killed by body count and 35 captured at Hoa Hoi, compared to the relatively slight cavalry casualties of 6 killed and 32 wounded.[10]

While the coastal pursuit continued, the division also realized that continual military presence was required to discourage enemy return to long-held base areas. By 13 October the division reconcentrated in the Soui Ca and Kim Son region, where fast reconnaissance sweeps were interspersed with artillery raids. These tactics yielded more significant cache discoveries and denied the NVA/VC any unimpeded opportunity to reconsolidate. When Operation IRVING was terminated at midnight on 24 October, the division's aviation had again rendered remarkable mobile service, airlifting the equivalent of forty-six infantry battalions and thirty-six artillery batteries during Operations THAYER I/IRVING.[11]

Operation THAYER II, which commenced 25 October 1966 with the return of the northeast monsoon season and continued into 1967, was a two-brigade sustained pursuit effort to exploit the success of the previous five weeks of almost continuous contact with the NVA/VC in the rich coastal plain and the Kim Son and Soui Ca valleys to the west. Strong surges of monsoon weather dominated the operation with turbulent, wind-driven rainstorms and excessive humidity. Division aviation struggled though the dense morning fogs and after-

10. 1st Cav Div Unit Historical Rpt #6, *The Battle of Hoa Hoi*; 1st Cav Div, *Report of Action 2–3 October 1966*. As a sidenote, the first platoon, under Lt. Joe Anderson, had a French film team attached under producer Pierre Schoendoerffer. The film later produced, *The Anderson Platoon*, devotes a significant portion to the Hoa Hoi battle.
11. 1st Cav Div, *Combat Operations After Action Report*, dtd 13 Jan 67; and *Operational Report on Lessons Learned*, dtd 22 Nov 66, Appendix 5-3.

noon thunderstorms to lift the equivalent of 142 infantry battalions and 70 artillery batteries during the operation.

The *18th NVA Regiment* was critically short of food because of the incessant cavalry offensive, since many rice-gathering details were destroyed, captured, or surrendered. Several firefights erupted in the flooded valleys as the fractured enemy battalions desperately sought to replenish their caches with the recently harvested lowland rice. While most encounters were cavalry victories, two large battles were fought under confusing and tactically unsound circumstances, partially reflecting the unfavorable impact on the division of personnel turbulence and the long strain of campaigning.

On 16 December 1966 Colonel Daniel's brigade was replaced by Col. James C. Smith's 1st Brigade, while Col. George W. Casey's 2d Brigade continued operating. The next day seven cavalry companies from the newly inserted brigade responded to a 9th Cavalry clash with two NVA companies in the Crow's Foot near Thach Long, but control difficulties between elements nullified the vital coordination required in all fast-moving airmobile operations. Poor scheduling led to helicoptered units arriving at the same time as airstrikes, so that reinforcements were kept circling while the battle was raging below. Some platoons sat idle for hours on pickup zones, and entire companies were fed piecemeal into the battle. Time and time again arriving forces walked straight into the killing fields of well-camouflaged enemy hedgerow bunker positions, some of which were previously detected, and were decimated in lethal cross fires. Only the courage of individual cavalrymen allowed units to push forward, but ironically this further locked depleted cavalry forces in adverse situations from which extrication was very difficult. The Viet Cong ended the battle by withdrawing virtually unhindered after dark. Lt. Col. George D. Eggers's 1st Battalion, 12th Cavalry, suffered heavy casualties, and its Company D ended the day with only thirty-five troops left.[12]

The division's supporting howitzers were concentrated on two large landing zones in the Crow's Foot, LZs Pony and Bird, which could fire supporting artillery anywhere in the Kim Son Valley. They were obviously prime targets for enemy action, and Division Artillery warned

12. 1st Cav Div, *The Battle in the 506 Valley, 17 Dec 66*, Unit Historical Rpt #15.

them to expect an attack immediately following the Christmas Truce on 26 December. Almost unbelievably, the *22d NVA Regiment* was able to emplace supporting fire weapons and stage a massive surprise close assault which nearly overran LZ Bird in the early morning darkness of 27 December 1966. Approximately 700 North Vietnamese regulars crawled to within fifteen feet of the landing zone perimeter without being discovered. Covered by well-placed machine guns and recoilless rifles, they surged forward with bayonets fixed, screaming, "GI, you die!" as a sudden mortar barrage swept through the American lines.

The perimeter cavalrymen of Company C, 1st Battalion, 12th Cavalry, were quickly overwhelmed, and the NVA charged through all five 155mm howitzer positions of Battery C, 6th Battalion, 16th Artillery, as well as half of the 105mm howitzers of Battery B, 2d Battalion, 19th Artillery. The waves of NVA soldiers became intermixed with retreating cavalrymen. Burning ammunition bunkers were exploding, communications were knocked out, and all cohesion disappeared under the weight of attack. Some of the most violent hand-to-hand fighting transpired as gun crews were killed making last stands around their howitzers.

The executive officer of the light howitzers, 1Lt. John D. Piper, frantically loaded a Bee Hive round into the lowered tube of one of his last remaining weapons and aimed it at hundreds of NVA swarming around an overrun 155mm howitzer. The Bee Hive round, composed of more than 8,500 steel flechettes, had been specifically designed to stop mass infantry assaults. Lieutenant Piper was unable to find the flare to alert possible friendly troops in its pathway and yelled, "Bee Hive!" repeatedly. Sergeant Graham, who had been forced out of the targeted position and was now in a drainage ditch out front, screamed back, "Shoot it!" He recalled that it sounded like "a million whips being whirled over my head." Piper could see the resulting carnage in the flarelight, yelled, "Tube left," quickly chambered another Bee Hive round, and pulled the lanyard. The North Vietnamese attack was stopped.[13]

The combination of Bee Hive rounds and overhead aerial artillery

13. 1st Cav Div, *The Attack on LZ Bird*, Unit Historical Rpt #2, p. 13.

rocket fire caused the North Vietnamese attack to falter, and the enemy withdrew before daylight. Landing Zone Bird was left in shambles, and the 266 dead North Vietnamese were interspersed with 58 dead and 77 wounded Americans. While the defending units were later awarded the Presidential Unit Citation in recognition of their valiant defense of LZ Bird and the individual valor exhibited there, disturbing questions over proper security were left unresolved. The 1st Cavalry Division immediately launched pursuit operations, which continued for the next several days as the *22d Regiment* attempted to withdraw north to the An Lao Valley, but meaningful contact was never regained. Even so, the division could justifiably point to the severe losses inflicted on the regiment, which temporarily knocked it out of action.

On 3 January 1967 the 3d Brigade of the 25th Infantry Division was placed under the operational control of the 1st Cavalry Division to support its own engaged six battalions oriented against the National Priority Area of eastern Binh Dinh Province. The continuous battering rendered the *18th NVA Regiment* mostly combat-ineffective. The unit suffered heavy losses, which included all original company commanders, and an intercepted message of 10 January revealed that the enemy division commander considered the unit unreliable because of its low morale. Scattered by several large engagements and uncounted bush contacts, the regiment fragmented into small groups which attempted to escape northwest into the An Lao Valley to reequip. Cavalry patrols continually brushed with these exfiltrating elements.[14]

Operation THAYER II, which ended after the Tet truce of 8 to 12 February 1967, was typified by long periods of relatively unopposed search operations punctuated by sharp contacts, and marked the final stage in the 1st Cavalry Division's year of sustained pursuit. There were negative aspects in the total campaign. It was uneven and often hampered by insufficient intelligence and competing requirements to reinforce other fronts, especially battles in the western highlands. In certain areas the high cost of continued search ruled out continued expenditure of effort for large blocks of time. Some battles

14. 1st Cav Div, *Operation THAYER II Combat After Action Report*, dtd 25 Jun 67.

were tactically mishandled, and a critical division artillery firebase was even surprised and almost destroyed. The highly proficient and elusive NVA/VC units were often able to take advantage of adverse weather and the rugged jungle to evade many airmobile thrusts and to avoid absolute annihilation. Above all, the division's human cost was staggering. From 31 January 1966 to the end of January 1967, the division suffered 19,512 casualties in all operations: 720 killed in action; 3,039 wounded; 2,304 nonbattle deaths and injuries; and 13,449 as a result of disease.[15]

Yet the positive military gains were most impressive. The cumulative effect of sustained cavalry pursuit greatly reduced NVA/VC control in most provincial sectors by wearing down effective resistance. The campaign disorganized the Viet Cong control structure, creating havoc among VC tax gathering, recruiting, medical services, and administration. Viet Cong government members evading death or capture were forced to work less openly and with much less effectiveness.

In summation the cavalry pursuit of the 1966 coastal campaign established the basis for the cavalry clearing operations of 1967. In many ways this campaign also marked the final evolution of Major General Kinnard's airmobile doctrine into a battlefield staple of the Vietnam War. The 1st Cavalry Division exerted persistent airmobile pressure, found and engaged strong enemy forces, maintained a steady pace of extended helicopter operations, and triumphed over weather and enemy adversity.

15. 1st Cav Div, *Operational Report on Lessons Learned*, dtd 5 May 66, p. 40; dtd 15 Aug 66, p. 8; dtd 22 Nov 66, pp. 8–9; dtd 15 Feb 67, p. 8.

# CHAPTER 5

# Clearing Operations

*Techniques, 1967 Coastal Campaign*

The 1st Cavalry Division began the campaign for military control of Binh Dinh Province's coastal plains, narrow valleys, and rugged mountains in 1966. During 1967 the division still had the job of finding and destroying the NVA/VC military and support network, but it emphasized pacification as a part of clearing operations as MACV expanded Major General Norton's priority list.

Great political emphasis was being placed on doing more than just killing Viet Cong. Ellsworth Bunker replaced Henry Cabot Lodge as ambassador and insisted that the military get more forcefully involved in pacification efforts. In May President Johnson's special ambassador for pacification, Robert Komer, created CORDS (Civil Operations and Revolutionary Development Support) directly under Westmoreland's chain of command to consolidate the previously disjointed Allied efforts. Komer was anxious to eliminate the VC infrastructure and tax-collection system, and recognized that divisions might serve as excellent vehicles for security duty.

The 1st Cavalry Division, designed as a swift and powerful formation able to influence battles by dint of its airmobility, was hardly formulated for occupation tasks. Its cannons, aircraft, and automatic weapons were in the hands of skilled personnel trained to seek out and annihilate NVA/VC main force units. Nevertheless, with a minimum of guidance, but a great deal of confusing high command directives, the 1st Cavalry Division found itself intimately involved in trying to help the South Vietnamese government assert administrative control over the rich agricultural eastern area of Vietnam's most populous province.

The 1st Cavalry Division's clearing offensive in the 1,600 square miles of Binh Dinh Province was labeled Operation PERSHING, and it would last from 11 February 1967 until 21 January 1968. It might have continued indefinitely, except that the regular North Vietnamese Army divisions, which the politicians consistently underrated or ignored (and which would actually blitzkrieg South Vietnam into destruction during 1975), forced the cavalry's redeployment to I CTZ. In the meantime, with his troops committed to endure another annual cycle of heavy northeast monsoon rains and dry southwest monsoon heat along the central coast, Major General Norton set up his command post at LZ English outside Bong Son.

The burden of implementing a pacification program that supplemented combat operations with meaningful civic action fell on the shoulders of the cavalry provost marshal, Lt. Col. James P. Oliver. As a military policeman, he simply combined the divisional 545th Military Police Company with the 816th South Vietnamese National Police Field Force (NPFF) to form an ad hoc cavalry-advised NPFF battalion which became operational the same day CORDS became official: 26 May 1967. The police battalion would seal off selected hamlets and search them for tunnels and caches while interrogating the residents. Colonel Oliver strictly enforced the Rules of Engagement, since everyone at least agreed that proper troop conduct was basic to winning the respect and cooperation of the local population.

Operation PERSHING was essentially a clearing operation emphasizing population control and area security. Most of it consisted of slow and tedious searches aimed at breaking VC village-level power. To the soldier's eye this part of the operation was deceptively unglamorous—consisting of searches day after day through homes and compost piles, often in pouring rain or searing heat—and tedious, since he was keenly aware that he was under constant observation by an enemy quick to capitalize on his slightest mistake. The innumerable, monotonous cordon-and-search missions could be marred by sudden and violent hamlet firefights, and the NVA/VC defended enough fortified villages and valley passes to kill and maim cavalrymen in numbers surpassing all division operational losses of 1966.

Regardless of allied pacification intentions, the fact was that the 1st Cavalry Division still faced a viable enemy main force threat in Binh Dinh Province and adjacent areas. Therefore, Operation PERSHING contained numerous platoon actions, brigade emergency displacements, long-range airmobile raids, and some of the hardest-fought engagements of the division's Vietnam service. The 1st Cavalry Division's massed helicopter airlift, vertical air assault muscle, and swift aerial and artillery firepower were all significant in subduing the province's pro–Viet Cong population and its armed units. To this air-oriented dimension, the 1st Cavalry Division added armor and mechanization for the first time. Tanks provided essential fortifications suppression and gave the psychological edge in ground attacks. The 1st Battalion of the 50th Infantry (Mechanized), attached to the division in September, was used either way. The armored personnel carriers were employed either as fighting vehicles in a mounted role or as mobile gun platforms with minimum crews as the companies were helicoptered into combat as airmobile infantry.

The division's 1st Squadron of the 9th Cavalry remained in the forefront of all coastal campaign action. The aerial recon squadron was the sole Army unit of this type at the time, but already its unique scout and gunship composition was proving a deadly effective combination over the battlefield. The squadron's mission was direct and simple: find the enemy. To avail the widely separated brigades of its valuable service, the squadron parceled out one air cav troop to each. The ground troop (Troop D) was composed of fast-riding gunjeeps backed up by attached M42 Duster self-propelled flak guns and was used as a mobile light infantry reserve that protected the engineers who were sweeping mines and replacing blown bridges along Highway 1.

The 9th Cavalry thrived on speed in the hunt and quick reaction to any contact. Typical of its utilization was the June action at An Quang near Dam Tra-O Lake, a tidewater basin connected to the South China Sea. Troop C of the squadron was scouting for Col. Fred E. Karhohs's 2d Brigade, and a pair of light H13 observation "White team" helicopter pilots buzzing An Quang at treetop level spotted suspiciously fresh diggings and field work but no farmers. The sector was normally quiet, but had seen action in the past, and the troop commander decided to investigate with his "Blue" rifle platoon. The ground cavalrymen landed, found a large boulder whitewashed with "Welcome to the VC and NVA" in Vietnamese, and were fired upon when approaching the village. They called for several aerial rocketing runs by armed "Red team" helicopters and withdrew to block the southern exit from the village.

Colonel Karhohs arrived overhead in his command helicopter and immediately ordered the 2d Brigade quick reaction force platoon, 1st Platoon of Company B from Lt. Col. Joseph C. McDonough's 2d Battalion, 5th Cavalry, to land in support. The company was air assaulted beyond the village to block the northern direction, and its helicopters were fired upon while descending. The 9th Cavalry squadron commander, Lt. Col. R. H. Nevins, Jr., kept a swarm of armed and scout helicopters circling over the lake to the west. Judging from the amount of enemy return fire, Colonel Karhohs estimated that elements of two NVA companies were in the village complex and radioed for reinforcements. Even the "Blue" platoon was bolstered by a platoon of riflemen from Troop D that was airlifted to its assistance. What had started as a scouting report by the Troop C leader was now an opportunity for decisive brigade action. When Lieutenant Colonel McDonough arrived to take charge on the ground less than two hours after the initial contact, he had four and a half cavalry battalions surrounding An Quang.

Preparatory to his ground attack, McDonough massed a liberal diversity of fire support to soften the village defenses. Working with several controllers and observers, he coordinated the firepower of artillery, aerial rocket helicopters, regular gunships, Navy and Air Force tactical airstrikes, naval gunfire, medium battle tanks, M42 Duster 40mm self-propelled guns, and even CH47 "Guns A-Go-Go" mini-gun-armed Chinooks. Despite the destruction wrought by this heavy explosive ordnance, both Companies B and D were hit midway through the smoldering village. Two Viet Cong suddenly dashed out from spider holes and heaved grenades into the cavalry ranks, and machine guns and snipers swept the companies with accurate close-in fire. Dead and wounded Americans littered the open ground where they had been cut down next to weapons in tunnel entrances. A pair of tanks moved forward to blast the treetops with canister Bee Hive discharges, allowing the cavalrymen to pull back their wounded and get out of the village. They left behind one burning M42 Duster which had been knocked out in the fighting.

With evening approaching and regular brigade troops in position, the aerial squadron would have normally extracted its elements to continue reconnoitering or block other possible exfiltration routes. In this case, however, it was necessary for the two squadron ground platoons to stay situated and help seal off the village complex. The

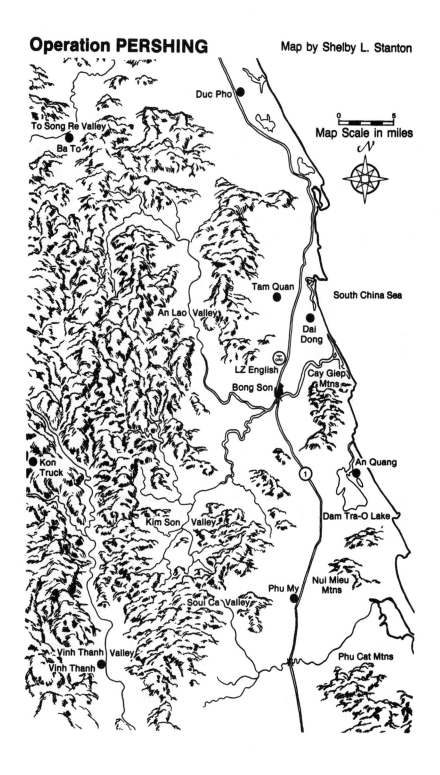

# Operation PERSHING

Map by Shelby L. Stanton

Duc Pho

To Song Re Valley

Ba To

Tam Quan

South China Sea

An Lao Valley

Dai Dong

LZ English

Cay Giep Mtns

Bong Son

Kon Truck

An Quang

Kim Son Valley

Dam Tra-O Lake

Phu My

Nui Mieu Mtns

Soui Ca Valley

Vinh Thanh Valley

Phu Cat Mtns

Vinh Thanh

0   Map Scale in miles   5

N

North Vietnamese decided to evade during the night despite the bright moon and continuous illumination flares. They left a rear guard in An Quang which still had to be destroyed. The following day thirty-three airstrikes and several artillery barrages were directed against the village complex. Lieutenant Colonel McDonough's battalion assaulted through the interlocking fire of the remaining bunkers and secured the hamlet. A total of 89 NVA bodies were found, and more were believed to be buried in the collapsed bunker ruins. Later a prisoner claimed that his *18th NVA Regiment's 9th Battalion* lost 150 of its 250-man complement in the action and that the survivors reached the Cay Giep Mountains only by slipping through the water and reeds around the northern edge of the lake.[1]

Throughout the 1967 coastal campaign, the aerial reconnaissance squadron sparked the majority of division contacts in the same fashion. "White" scout team helicopter sightings of NVA/VC activity were followed up by rocketing and strafing from the "Red" aero weapons teams and exploited by "Blue" aero rifle platoons. The contacts produced a variety of brigade-size battles, platoon firefights, and firings recorded only in flight logs, but the work was always extremely dangerous. All contacts, regardless of their length or significance, were likely to be challenged by some type of enemy antiaircraft fire with weapons up to 12.7mm AA machine guns in size.

Over the course of the squadron's 343 days in the PERSHING campaign, its forward reconnaissance role exacted such a heavy toll that its aircraft were replaced twice over. The 1st Squadron, 9th Cavalry, which operated with 88 helicopters and 770 personnel, was taken under fire 931 times, resulting in 250 helicopters being hit. Of these, 102 helicopters were so badly damaged that they had to be stricken from inventory, and 14 were shot down and fully destroyed. During this same time, the squadron lost 55 killed, 1 missing, and 264 wounded members in aerial and ground combat.[2]

Behind this advance umbrella of 9th Cavalry aerial scoutships, Major General Norton's three cavalry brigades and one attached infantry brigade from the 25th Infantry Division fanned out through

1. 1st Cav Div, *The Battle of Dam Tra-O*, Unit Historical Rpt #16.
2. Hq 1st Sqdn, 9th Cav, *Memorandum for Record, Operation PERSHING*, dtd Feb 68, pp. 6–7, 24.

Binh Dinh Province. Operation PERSHING began as Colonel Smith's 1st Brigade and Colonel Casey's 2d Brigade slashed into the Bong Son Plains in a wave of air assaults that took several hamlets by storm and flushed large numbers of hiding enemy soldiers from tunnels, wells, and concealed underground bunkers. Col. Jonathan R. Burton's 3d Brigade reconnoitered the forbidding An Lao Valley, and the attached 3d Brigade of the 25th Infantry Division covered area development chores of the ARVN 22d Division and Korean Capital Division as far south as the Soui Ca Valley and Phu My Plains.

Learning from its bitter lessons at Ia Drang and other early encounters, the division reserved one full battalion as a ready reaction force (RRF). The RRF conducted normal operations, but was prepared for swift consolidation and pickup by division helicopters specially earmarked for emergency utilization. The division RRF stood ready to land a company quick reaction force anywhere in the PERSHING area within just thirty minutes. This lead strike unit could be followed by the rest of the battalion RRF in three to four hours. Each brigade maintained a miniature company-size RRF, with one platoon designated as its quick reaction force. Throughout the upcoming campaign the airmobile reaction reserves offered the 1st Cavalry Division an unprecedented flexibility in dominating the battlefield.

The sister 1st and 2d Battalions of the 5th Cavalry battled across the village-studded Bong Son Plains through February as they wrestled more villages from the *22d NVA Regiment*. Two large engagements overshadowed a rash of platoon skirmishes and countless boobytrap and mechanical ambush device incidents. Engineer dozers were used to level any structures potentially useful as fortified strongpoints, but contact dwindled as search operations intensified. The division adopted a new stratagem to keep NVA/VC activity low in its old haunts of the mountains west of the coastal plains.

The 1st Cavalry Division instituted drastic clearing measures against the most troublesome VC base areas. The Kim Son (Crow's Foot), Soui Ca, and An Lao valleys were all written off as too remote and too hazardous to be effectively occupied. Classified as "denial areas," the division made final sweeps of them and forcibly removed the remaining inhabitants. Once depopulated, the valleys were smothered with Agent Orange by the Vietnamese Air Force, which flew repeated crop-destruction missions. The division hoped that liberal application of this toxic chemical would poison all future rice production in the valleys, ruining their usefulness as enemy havens. The mass roundups also denuded the land of VC labor and military recruits, but produced more than 93,000 refugees. The displacement problem became so acute that plans for other denial areas had to be dropped.[3]

The small sweeps and patrols became routine, but they always required a mastery of basic soldiering and leadership. Contact was normally light, but numerous mines, booby traps, snipers, and sudden firefights continued to decide the cavalrymen's survival. The fragmented division was waging a platoon-level war in its clearing campaign, which demanded the highest degree of judgment, discipline, and tactical expertise. Action on the Bong Son front simmered in March, but Colonel Casey's brigade engaged the *18th NVA Regiment* in several skirmishes around the Cay Giep Mountains and Dam Tra-O Lake. One encounter resulted in a brigade-size battle against well-defended NVA village defenses from 19 to 22 March near Tam Quan.

With Operation PERSHING well underway, and in keeping with MACV's annual rotation of division commands during the Vietnam War, Major General Norton relinquished command of the 1st Cavalry Division to Maj. Gen. John J. Tolson III on 1 April 1967. General Tolson, the Commandant of the U.S. Army Aviation School since 1965, fulfilled all the prerequisites shaping the airmobile division command ticket. He was a paratrooper veteran and a seasoned aviator, and he had long been in the forefront of airmobility development. Born 22 October 1915 in North Carolina, he graduated from West Point in 1937 and participated in the first tactical air movement of Army ground forces two years later. During World War II, Colonel Tolson served with the paratroopers in the Pacific, making combat jumps into New Guinea, Corregidor Island, and the Philippines with the 503d Parachute Infantry. In 1957 he became an aviator and later served as Director of Army Aviation.

Major General Tolson continued divisional searches in the coastal region and mountain valleys, but was also directed immediately to assist Marine Operation LEJEUNE in the Duc Pho region, just north of the Bong Son Plains. Major General Norton had been urging cav-

---

3. 1st Cav Div, *Combat After Action Report*, dtd 29 Jun 68, Tab 30; Ltr dtd 14 Jul 68, Incl. 7, Significant Contacts.

alry pursuit north of the Bong Son Plains for some time before his departure, and the division was anxious to explore the area. MACV commander General Westmoreland also deliberately slated this "fire brigade" reaction as a model exercise to test changes of operational direction with minimal advance warning. Assistant division commander Brig. Gen. George S. Blanchard was placed in charge of the sudden flurry of activity accompanying Colonel Karhohs's 2d Brigade airmobile expedition. Fortunately, April was a transition month of fair weather between the northeast and southwest monsoons, and the brigade enjoyed optimum atmospheric and sea conditions.

The entire brigade was airlifted into Duc Pho in a day and a half to permit rapid Marine redeployment. The rushed timetable and hectic helicopter shuffling caused some loss of air traffic control, mostly because of the lack of coordination between Marine and Army aircraft channels. Helicopters continually roared across unit boundaries in the confined beach area, dropped off gear and personnel in unsatisfactory locations, and then moved them around again. Rotor blades kicked up sand, knocked down tentage, and scattered equipment. The radio waves were cluttered with irate transmission outbursts typified by, "If you blow my tent down one more time, I'm going to shoot you out of the air!" but everything was soon in place without serious mishap.

The most impressive display of division capability during Operation LEJEUNE was the 8th Engineer Battalion's incredible airfield construction feat. More than two hundred tons of heavy equipment were airlifted by CH54 Flying Crane and CH47 Chinook helicopters to build a forward combat airfield in just twenty-four hours. The "Skybeaver" engineers worked around the clock for two more days making the field acceptable for C123 cargo transport aircraft. The Marines were awestruck by the lavish amounts of cavalry equipment and helicopter support, but expressed open concern about snipers as the airmobile engineers toiled nightly under floodlamps and vehicle headlights. Working with great skill in record time, Lt. Col. Charles G. Olentine's engineer battalion proved that the airmobile division could promptly build the airfield facilities necessary for its own support.

The 2d Brigade helped to build another airfield, secured the beach landing site as the Marines departed, conducted numerous search-and-destroy sweeps, and policed the Vietnamese as they harvested VC-planted rice.

The 1st Cavalry Division also touted a geographical first, since the move placed the division outside II CTZ for the first time since its arrival in Vietnam nineteen months before: Duc Pho was in Quang Ngai Province of I CTZ. On 19 April, with his mission accomplished, Colonel Karhohs turned over the Duc Pho sector and its recently constructed airfields to the 3d Brigade of the 25th Infantry Division, which was released from division control three days later. The excursion demonstrated the airmobile division's ability to transplant quickly a major task force into an unfamiliar area on short notice. This was one of the most valuable advantages of the aerial cavalry division to the MACV command.[4]

The 1st Cavalry Division's clearing operations began driving the NVA/VC main force units out of northeastern Binh Dinh Province and into the mountain ranges beyond the coastal valleys. To reach them, Major General Tolson mounted cavalry raids, which were time-honored cavalry tactics in a new airmobile mode. Fast and light, the cavalry battalions struck northwest of the An Lao Valley and stabbed into distant NVA/VC base areas. In early May, airmobile cavalry staged out of the remote Ba To Special Forces camp and searched for the suspected headquarters of the *3d NVA Division*. In August the 3d Brigade leapfrogged northward from the An Lao Valley in a series of airmobile thrusts which carried it into the long-suspected VC haven of the Quang Ngai Province's Song Re Valley. The twisting valley floor was suspiciously free of visible inhabitants, but filled with fertile ricefields between the jungle hillocks.

The 2d Battalion of the 8th Cavalry, under Lt. Col. John E. Stannard, had just completed a month's tour of duty guarding the division main base at Camp Radcliff. His battalion was attached to 3d Brigade and became part of a cavalry raid into the Song Re Valley. Once in the valley, Lieutenant Colonel Stannard planned to sweep his battalion toward blocking positions set up by one company airmobiled ahead onto a small ridge near the abandoned airstrip of Ta Ma, which would then move downslope and establish its positions.

On the morning of 9 August 1967, following five minutes of preparatory light artillery fire on the grassy ridgeline, Capt. Raymond K. Bluhm, Jr.'s, Company A was air assaulted into LZ Pat. The last helicopters were descending with the weapons platoon when heavy

4. 1st Cav Div, *Operation LEJEUNE*, Unit Historical Rpt #10.

North Vietnamese antiaircraft guns suddenly opened fire from two higher hills dominating the ridgeline on either side. Two 9th Cavalry helicopter gunships orbiting overhead were immediately shot down. An H13 observation helicopter and the brigade command and control ship were also quickly put out of action. The enemy flak guns turned to sweep the exposed ridge with intensely accurate fire, pinning Captain Bluhm's 120-man company close to the ground.

The company was unable to maneuver, and Viet Cong troops hidden in spiderholes and log bunkers on the ridgeline itself began firing into the cavalry lines. Several cavalrymen were killed in quick succession. One trooper was mortally wounded by a 12.7mm AA round that tossed him back five feet. Medical Sp5 Andrew Conrad became the first aidman killed when he was struck in the forehead by a bullet while trying to assist a wounded comrade. The increasing number of wounded could not be evacuated because the heavy antiaircraft fire blanketed the landing zone.

SSgt. John Stipes, the weapons platoon leader, quickly emplaced his 81mm mortar to fire against the muzzle flashes on the neighboring hillsides, but the tube stuck up like a stovepipe at such close range. The enemy returned a volley of mortar rounds against the obvious target, forcing Stipes to cease firing. Extra mortar ammunition was scattered in discarded packs, lying all over the LZ. Ammunition bearer Pfc. Prentice D. Leclair was shot through the head while trying to collect them.

With all recoilless rifle and mortar ammunition either expended or unreachable, the company's few M60 machine guns rattling defiantly at the adjacent jungled slopes constituted its main firepower. One by one they were knocked out. Gunner Sp4 Michael Hotchkiss had already lost several crew members when a mortar shell landed on his back and disintegrated the entire position. Platoon Sgt. Frank M. Theberge, who suffered a broken ankle after leaping eight feet from a helicopter when the firing started, crawled to a small knoll and took charge of the machine gun crew there. While trying to direct the gun, he was struck in the back of his head by a bullet and knocked unconscious.

A1E Skyraiders dived along the enemy-held ridges and spilled clusters of bombs directly against the enemy flak positions. Three medical evacuation helicopters braved concentrated fire to lift out the most seriously wounded. Close bombing passes by F4C Phantoms and F100 Supersabres blasted the surrounding hills. After forty-two sorties and an expenditure of 82,500 pounds of bombs, 28,500 pounds of napalm, and 22,600 pounds of 20mm cannon fire, enemy AA fire slackened enough to allow helicopter extraction of Bluhm's battered company before nightfall. The Battle of LZ Pat was a dour lesson in raiding a formidable enemy strongpoint with only light artillery and limited helicopter support. The Song Re Valley expedition served as a valuable dress rehearsal for stronger, division-size cavalry raids in the coming year.[5]

The 1st Cavalry Division continued to battle the NVA/VC across the Bong Son Plains and into the An Lao Valley during September. In early October the 3d Brigade was transferred to southern I CTZ to permit further Marine redeployments northward, and the division posted more emergency task forces to other fronts. By November, when Col. Donald V. Rattan's 1st Brigade was airlifted into the western highlands because of the raging Dak To campaign, Operation PERSHING had become essentially a holding action. I Field Force Vietnam commander Lt. Gen. Stanley R. Larsen expressed open concern over the worsening situation in the PERSHING area on 16 December 1967. While recognizing the fact that the 1st Cavalry Division had been assigned, for the time being, an economy of force role, he indicated that any further draw-down of his forces could have an adverse effect on the clearing operations in Binh Dinh Province. Whenever containing pressure weakened, the North Vietnamese slipped out of the hills and attempted to reestablish themselves in the coastal plains and ricelands. The NVA/VC resurfaced whenever the cavalry division dispatched fire brigades to Kontum Province or other locations.

The 1st Cavalry Division did not complete its clearing operations in Binh Dinh Province until 21 January 1968, but the coastal campaign culminated in the mid-December victory over a fortified seacoast village complex near Tam Quan. The action began on 6 December as a routine sighting in the midst of a dozen squad and platoon-size incidents throughout the PERSHING area. Aerial scoutships of the 9th Cavalry observed a communications antenna being pulled in near the village of Dai Dong, and shortly afterward enemy machine guns opened fire on an H13 observation helicopter.

5. 1st Cav Div, *The Battle of LZ Pat*, 14 MHD.

Troop A's rifle platoon was air assaulted into the vicinity late that afternoon, but became embroiled in combat and unable to disengage. A platoon of the squadron's Troop D inserted to assist became stranded as well. The North Vietnamese occupied an extensive network of spider holes and fortified strongpoints built into trenchlines around the terraced rice paddies and hamlets. The enemy positions were embedded in thick hedgerows formed by cacti and dense underbrush, and also interwoven into the numerous dwellings, bamboo thickets, and palm groves on a sandy barrier island.

Colonel Rattan dispatched several units to reinforce and rescue the isolated recon troops before dark from their untenable positions. One of the first in was his quick reaction force, Company B of Lt. Col. Christian Dubia's 1st Battalion, 8th Cavalry, which was air assaulted into the engagement. Shortly after landing, the reaction force was struck by extremely close-range automatic weapons and grenade fire erupting from positions concealed in the nearby hedgerows and shrubbery. The fighting was at such close range that the North Vietnamese surged out of their trenches to loot American wounded. The 2d Platoon clubbed its way out to prevent their mortally wounded lieutenant from being choked to death by NVA soldiers. In another area four armored personnel carriers sent from Company A, 1st Battalion of the 50th Infantry, were stopped by a dike at the edge of the barrier island. One of the mechanized vehicles became mired in paddy mud just short of the enemy trenchline and received a direct hit from a B40 rocket.

The battered reaction company pulled back and reorganized with the remaining three armored personnel carriers. After nightfall, as artillery and helicopter gunships pounded and rocketed the enemy defenses, one of the vehicles sped over to extract the trapped reconnaissance troops. The artillery bombardment was maintained throughout the night under aircraft searchlights and flare illumination. Colonel Rattan used the time to move the 40th ARVN Regiment into blocking positions around the general area and ordered in more mechanized support to include flamethrowing carriers. The rest of Lieutenant Colonel Dubia's battalion moved onto the battlefield.

Although the weather was cool and overcast, with intermittent rain showers and early morning ground haze, it never interfered with aerial support. In the morning helicopter gunships rocketed the village then doused it with riot gas. Four Duster self-propelled flak guns clanked into position to fire through the dense foliage covering the enemy lines. Dozers from the 8th Engineer Battalion pushed up a causeway across the muddy paddy water so that additional armored personnel carriers could fully support the renewed attack.

At 9:00 A.M. the cavalrymen started across the marshy ricefields, supported by several armored personnel carriers. They were met by a hail of machine gun, rifle, and grenade fire. Company A's advance was stopped in a heavily overgrown area, and on the left flank a platoon of Company B was pinned down by a heavy machine gun nest. Snipers were registering extremely accurate fire on the mechanized carriers, and many vehicle commanders and drivers were killed. This first assault was called off shortly after one of the mechanized vehicles was destroyed by a mine while carrying wounded to the rear. The units pulled back, allowing more artillery and airstrikes to be placed on the enemy fortifications.

The two companies assaulted the NVA lines later that morning with seven armored personnel carriers in front. The advancing cavalrymen had gained only one hundred yards when they were hit with a fusillade of devastating sniper, automatic weapons, and grenade fire. Almost instantly, one vehicle driver was killed and three armored vehicle commanders were severely wounded. Company A lost twenty men trying to cross over one low hedgerow, and the open field was covered with dead and wounded. The battalion was forced to retreat and reorganize under the cover of artillery fire, while twelve helicopter loads of wounded were medically evacuated.

That afternoon another attack was launched. As the cavalrymen moved forward, the armored personnel carriers slowly proceeded in front of them with shielded machine guns blazing. One armored flamethrowing carrier accompanied the advance. Although there were two mechanized flamethrowing carriers during the battle, only one could be used at a time. The other mechanized flamethrower was to the rear taking on a fresh mixture of napalm, and they rotated in this fashion throughout the action. As recoilless rifle fire and rocket-propelled grenades slammed into the advancing troops, one carrier exploded and stopped Company B's drive. The gush of smoke rising from the antitank weapon backblast revealed the enemy position, and it was scorched by the flamethrower.

Company A was also having difficulty, as one of the tracked vehicles in front of the unit threw a track and became immobilized. The enemy fire intensified, but the remaining three carriers suddenly put on a burst of speed fifty yards from the main trenchline. The engines sputtered from a walking rate to fifteen miles per hour, enabling the machines to smash into the trench. The unexpected violence of this maneuver completely disorganized the North Vietnamese, who tried to flee the onrushing vehicles. Several groups tried to climb the armored carriers only to be crushed under their steel tracks or shot down by the machine guns and rifles of the crew members. The infantry quickly caught up, and by evening the first trench was in cavalry hands. The limit of advance had been reached for the day.

Lieutenant Colonel Dubia airlifted Company C of his battalion into the line on the morning of 8 December to relieve Company B. The attack was continued, but opposition was already considerably weaker. The armored personnel carriers were followed by engineer dozers and demolition teams destroying emplacements and clearing lanes as the infantry pushed ahead. Hard fighting transpired in other nearby hamlets, and the entire engagement lasted several days. Every night the Americans pulled back to night laagers ringed with armored vehicles. The 1st Battalion of the 12th Cavalry was brought in as reinforcement from Dak To, and more NVA pockets of resistance were eradicated throughout the area. On 19 December 1967 the final action was fought by a company of Lieutenant Colonel Stannard's battalion against a Viet Cong force dug into the northern bank of the Bong Son River.

The Battle of Tam Quan was fought over a relatively large area on the Bong Son Plains between the towns of Tam Quan and Song Son from 6 to 20 December 1967. Colonel Rattan's brigade used its attached mechanized forces to optimum advantage in mauling both the *7th* and *8th Battalions, 22d NVA Regiment*. With the battle's conclusion, organized enemy regular forces were largely finished in northeastern Binh Dinh Province. The Battle of Tam Quan was costly to both sides. The 1st Cavalry Division lost 58 soldiers killed and 250 wounded, while more than 600 North Vietnamese bodies were found in the smashed trenches and charred strongpoints. The engagement was considered one of the most significant encounters fought during Operation PERSHING, and it represented the successful air cavalry utilization of mechanized support on a well-defended battlefield.

Operations in Vietnam placed the 1st Cavalry Division in the security business for the first time since its initial inception as a border patrol division in the southwestern United States. Clearing operations in Operation PERSHING brought a new dimension to airmobility as well. Traditionally favored air assaults, aerial surveillance, and rapid reaction capabilities were tailored to meet new division needs. The airmobile techniques most commonly used in PERSHING were either specifically innovated or refined for the clearing campaign: cordon and search, swooper, snatch and selective snatch, bushmaster, lightning bug, hunter-killer, minicav, artillery ambush, trail running, and artillery raids.

Cordon-and-search missions applied to temporary village occupation. Under the cover of early morning darkness, a cavalry rifle company marched to a selected hamlet and surrounded it before dawn. Just after first light a South Vietnamese field police platoon was airlifted in to thoroughly search the village. One police team set up a screening and collection point for the villagers while the rest of the platoon searched each home and questioned its inhabitants. Persons detained during the search were whisked out by helicopter to a separate collection center at brigade level. The other villagers were assembled and listened to a propaganda team explain the U.S. presence and South Vietnamese government aims, and were encouraged to give information about the Viet Cong. At the same time, division medical personnel established a MEDCAP medical clinic in the hamlet.

At division and brigade level the provost marshal established police operations centers jointly staffed by the division military police, NPFF, special branch police, and officers from the ARVN 22d Division G2 and G5 sections. Here village detainees were subjected to closer scrutiny, and division military intelligence experts produced the feared counterintelligence "Black Lists" in the division police operations center. The magnitude of this effort was reflected by the 10,407 detainees processed by the 545th Military Police Company's "dragnet" screening points at division and brigade level. They ranged from individual farmers scooped up while tilling rice in selective snatch missions to whole regional populations forcibly evacuated from zones such as the An Lao Valley. From 26 May 1967, when the joint cavalry-NPFF force conducted its first cordon and search, the division conducted 946 such missions, which checked 319,313 undetained "innocent" civilians.

Speed and surprise were essential in cordon-and-search missions because the Viet Cong quickly fled villages being approached by al-

*Skytroopers of the 1st Cavalry Division prepare to disembark from a UH-series Huey helicopter during the Ia Drang Valley Campaign in November 1965* (Army News Features).

*1st Cavalry Division pathfinder guides a gaggle of UH-1D Huey helicopter troop transports into a Vietnam landing zone* (U.S. Army).

*The CH-47 Chinook helicopter was used for a variety of cargo missions and could deliver troops using Jacob's ladders into difficult jungle terrain, as demonstrated here* (Army News Features).

*A heavy Hunter-Killer team consisting of one OH-6A "white" observation helicopter and two AH-1G "red" Cobra gunships on a reconnaissance mission over III CTZ, 21 February 1969 (U.S. Army).*

*The giant CH-54 Flying Crane allowed the 1st Cavalry Division to airlift medium 155mm howitzers onto remote mountaintop landing zones in Vietnam (U.S. Army).*

*Air Force C-130 aircraft, here preparing to fly 1st Cavalry Division advance troops from Nha Trang to An Khe on 25 August 1965, were used to transport division elements throughout the war* (593d Signal Company Audio Visual Detachment).

*The division aviation resources included six OV-1 Mohawk reconnaissance aircraft, but their Vietnam performance was disappointing* (U.S. Army).

*Dismounted cavalrymen cautiously advance through a coastal village near Bong Son during Operation PERSHING on 15 March 1967* (U.S. Army).

*Suppressing NVA bunkers was one of the many dangerous tasks conducted by crack "Blue" cavalry reconnaissance troops of the 1st Squadron, 9th Cavalry, in Vietnam* (U.S. Army).

*The 7.62mm machine gun was one of the most valuable infantry weapons of the airmobile cavalry and each line company was authorized six of them (Author's Collection).*

*Heavy jungle slowed cavalry movement on the ground in Vietnam, and demanded constant teamwork in crossing innumerable water obstacles (U.S. Army).*

*A 155mm howitzer of the divisional 1st Battalion, 30th Artillery, renders medium fire support from a forward position in War Zone C (U.S. Army).*

*The 8th Engineer Battalion contained a variety of heavy construction equipment used for building airfields, such as this one at Duc Pho prepared during Operation LEJEUNE in April 1967 (1st Cavalry Division PIO).*

*Helicopter losses in Vietnam were less than expected, but still took a heavy toll. This AH-1G Cobra of Battery A, 2d Battalion, 20th Artillery, crashed near Tay Ninh on 13 January 1970* (Author's Collection).

*Combat infantrymen of the 1st Battalion, 8th Cavalry, at a forward aid station with female medical personnel attached to the division* (Author's Collection).

lied military units. The timing and methods of surrounding villages were constantly changed to avoid setting patterns. Companies were often airmobiled around villages on swooper missions. Considerable surprise could be achieved by sudden swooper airmobile insertions if the time of day was varied sufficiently to throw VC guards off balance. Sometimes the cavalry even amphibiously landed near seaside hamlets from naval craft covered by swift boats.

Snatch missions tried to capture Viet Cong among the people working in the fields outside the villages. Developed in late July, a typical snatch mission used a pair of scout helicopters and a third helicopter, which carried the battalion operations officer. He randomly surveyed the ricefields for large groups of people and called for a snatch mission by radioing the standby airmobile rifle platoon and Vietnamese police team. Escorted by two gunships, the troop helicopters corralled any selected group of people by landing around them. The platoon riflemen got out of the helicopters and compressed the surrounded farmers, who were usually men, women, and children of all ages, toward one spot for screening and inspection by the police. Since snatch missions could be conducted in one hour and netted many VC suspects, they were considered very successful.

Within a few weeks, however, people no longer gathered in groups large enough to make a snatch mission worthwhile. The division responded by developing the selective snatch. These missions normally involved two Huey troopships with three riflemen from battalion headquarters on each, escorted by two gunships and a pair of scout helicopters. The battalion operations officer flew above the ricefields looking for anybody who appeared suspicious and directed the two Hueys to descend swiftly on both sides of suspects to allow apprehension by the six cavalrymen. The selective snatch mission generally terminated when the lift ships were full of suspects.

Division bushmaster missions were night infantry ambushes along suspected NVA/VC infiltration routes, employed by platoon-size elements. Multiple ambush forces were usually fielded within reinforcing distance of their company forward base and were mutually supporting. During Operation RICE GRAIN, a suboperation guarding the October rice harvest, bushmaster missions were conducted to prevent night harvesting for possible VC consumption.

Lightning bug missions were another nighttime activity to detect and inhibit enemy travel, using special searchlight-fitted helicopters at division level. Since helicopter-mounted spotlights were almost useless if dense foliage existed, these "firefly" aircraft usually probed the darkened coastal region. A lightning bug team consisted of one searchlight helicopter, a team of two helicopter gunships, and a flare-dropping helicopter. The gunships fired on targets revealed by the powerful spotlight beams of the searchlight helicopter. Alternatively, the lights could be turned off and targets spotted with starlight scopes, in which case the flare-dropping helicopter provided target illumination for the gunships. Often a SLAR-equipped aircraft flew ahead of the lightning bug team to scan for likely searchlight targets such as sampans.

The hunter-killer missions were battalion-level night helicopter searches. One Huey helicopter carried a starlight scope operator, who was chosen by battalion headquarters, and he marked targets with tracer rounds for the two helicopter gunships which made up the rest of the hunter-killer team. All nightly surveillance was kept deliberately on an irregular basis.

Minicav missions were small airmobile search operations which normally air assaulted a rifle platoon onto an objective, with other airmobile reinforcements on standby in case of contact. The minicav mission differed somewhat from ordinary platoon sweep operations because the platoon was under the control of a flight leader overhead in an observation helicopter. He moved the platoon to check out his visual sightings and could rapidly extract and reinsert the platoon with great flexibility to search wide areas.

Artillery ambushes and trail-running missions were division artillery night firings. Artillery shelling was used in Vietnam for harassing and interdiction purposes on a nightly basis. To find targets automatically, artillery ambushes were triggered by seismic intrusion devices or field-expedient trip flares along trails and suspected pathways. An artillery section or battery was prepared to fire a barrage on signal and could switch to firing illumination rounds for helicopter surveillance or additional aerial rocketing if desired. Artillery ambush effectiveness was enhanced during 1967 by electronic Sandia Devices, miniature seismograph sensors capable of detecting footsteps, which transmitted the signals to receiver sets. Trail running was simply the placement of artillery fire along the length of trails or ridgelines.

Artillery raids were conducted if worthwhile NVA/VC targets were reported beyond the range of normally positioned division artillery. Airmobile infantry secured a forward location, and CH47 Chinooks brought in an artillery battery to the new landing zone. Observers in scout helicopters spotted targets for the artillery raiding battery. Lucrative sightings could be engaged also by the infantry as the howitzers switched to a fire support role. The artillery raid was brief, usually being completed within six hours, and offered Division Artillery an ability to react rapidly to targets of opportunity.

Searching, swooping, and raiding across half a province for an entire year demanded large amounts of manpower. The 1st Cavalry Division was always up to strength, but there were critical shortages of infantry, aviation, artillery, and medical personnel during certain periods. These occurred because of Army-wide shortages, peak rotational times, and other personnel management problems. From October through December, for example, serious shortages of artillerymen and medical personnel developed. Since replacements in those fields were not forthcoming from the United States, the divisional artillery firepower was significantly diminished, while medical support was only hindered (medical service could be increased by cutting out hamlet MEDCAP clinics).[6]

The 1st Cavalry Division casualties in Operation PERSHING totalled 852 troopers killed in action, 22 missing in action, 286 killed in noncombat circumstances, and 4,119 wounded, which exceeded all division operational losses during 1966. With actual division strength averaging 19,571 personnel throughout Operation PERSHING, these casualties amounted to 27 percent of available manpower, not counting injuries or disease. Most losses were taken by the infantrymen, and USARV responded quickly to send infantry replacements, but loss rates were still too high to permit smooth transition in training and experience among division personnel.[7]

The success of the division's clearing campaign in Operation PERSHING was difficult to measure. There was no precise way to gauge whether the Viet Cong were being ferreted out of the hamlets

---

6. 1st Cav Div, *Combat After Action Report,* dtd 29 Jun 68, Tab 13: MOS Shortages.
7. Ibid., Tab 12, and Incl. 4 to cover ltr dtd 14 Jul 68, Subj: Recommendation for PUC.

or were simply lying low. The pacification effort's success in winning over the people in Binh Dinh Province to the South Vietnamese government was impossible to ascertain. The division offered considerable tangible evidence to show that its airmobility enhanced the security process. Highway 1 was opened for commercial traffic through Binh Dinh Province for the first time in years, and government-sponsored elections were held for the first time on 3 September. The division claimed 2,029 NVA killed and 3,367 VC killed in Operation PERSHING, with another 236 NVA and 2,123 Viet Cong captured. However, perhaps the most telling evidence supporting the 1st Cavalry Division's claim to victory was one inescapable military reality. During the major NVA/VC Tet-68 offensive, which engulfed the entire country only a week after PERSHING ended, the former communist stronghold of Binh Dinh Province was one of the least-affected regions in Vietnam.

# CHAPTER 6

# Flexible Response
## *Techniques, Tet-68*

At the beginning of 1968, allied concerns about clearing Binh Dinh Province were cast aside as events worsened in the northernmost part of South Vietnam. While the 1st Cavalry Division was waging a slow-paced double war of search and pacification in the sandy hamlets and jungle valleys along the central coast, the Marines were combating entire North Vietnamese divisions driving across the DMZ. The major Marine border bastion at Khe Sanh was being challenged by freshly infiltrated NVA forces, and there were disturbing signs of increased NVA activity throughout northernmost Quang Tri and Thua Thien provinces. On 15 January 1968 MACV deputy commander Gen. Creighton W. Abrams ordered Major General Tolson to move his airmobile division northward to reinforce I Corps Tactical Zone at once.

When Tolson received notice to transplant his flag to Gia Le in upper I CTZ immediately, his division was still embroiled in Operation PERSHING. Although the bulk of the airmobile cavalry was concentrated in the central highlands on this major clearing operation, a number of secondary MACV missions had elements scattered from Phan Thiet, northeast of Saigon, to the Que Son Valley below Da Nang. The division had not been together under a single commander for nearly two years. As an airmobile formation, the 1st Cavalry Division was designed for flexible battlefield mobility, but it was sent to Vietnam before concept tests on such a vast scale could be conducted at Fort Benning.

The emergency movement north, coded Operation JEB STUART,

was the first actual test of rapid airmobile division displacement between combat theaters. This was also the first MACV undertaking of such magnitude, and the transfer would have been extremely difficult even in fair weather and the best of circumstances. Each zone had to be independently supplied in the absence of secure north-south communications lines. The overtaxed Navy supply system which governed I CTZ was woefully unprepared to cope with the arriving airmobile division's high rates of supply consumption. The incomplete logistical arrangements were further aggravated because the unprecedented relocation was made in direct response to a major battle zone crisis and had to be executed with great rapidity. Uprooting the 1st Cavalry Division and moving it two hundred miles to an entirely new military zone demanded optimum flexibility, quick reaction, and mastery of adverse weather conditions.

The 1st Cavalry Division, like all American formations in Vietnam, was an extremely large organization. It was tied to a huge, sophisticated main base complex which provided the vast amounts of necessary support and sustenance. Once emplaced, allied divisions rarely moved from their assigned geographical sector because of the expense and time required to shift the support base. This need to keep divisions within the logistical operating radius of their base camps inevitably transformed them into static security formations. Returning the 1st Cavalry Division to a flexible response posture meant cutting the An Khe umbilical cord. Such action would unfortunately reduce divisional combat power during the transition period.

Operation PERSHING was immediately curtailed as the division scaled down offensive activity in Binh Dinh Province to local patrolling. The widely separated units packed up their gear and streamed back to either the main An Khe garrison or Landing Zone English. Fleets of transport aircraft shuttled troops from An Khe in the central highlands and LZ English on the Bong Son Plains to Quang Tri and Hue–Phu Bai along the northern coast. Long truck convoys crowded the winding road from An Khe to the Qui Nhon docksides where the division cargo was transferred to Navy ships streaming toward Da Nang. Overhead, flights of division helicopters droned through overcast skies to their new helipads.

General Tolson moved his command post into a graveyard north of Phu Bai called LZ El Paso, but the barren landing zone was unsatisfactory for division headquarters. On 23 January General Abrams agreed that the 1st Cavalry Division should be relocated to Camp Evans, a former Marine regimental base. This move also fortuitously displaced Colonel Rattan's 1st Brigade to LZ Betty, just outside the key communications hub of Quang Tri, as the Marines withdrew on 25 January. The 3d Brigade under Col. Hubert S. Campbell was already in I CTZ, having spent four months fighting the *2d NVA Division* in the Que Son Valley, twenty-five miles south of Da Nang. Campbell's brigade was recalled to Quang Tri the same day, and the 2d Brigade was left in Binh Dinh Province to guard the old PERSHING area.

General Westmoreland wanted Tolson to have a full division of three working brigades in his new operational area. MACV attached Col. John H. Cushman's 2d Brigade of the 101st Airborne Division, which had just arrived in Vietnam, to the cavalry and transferred the new brigade from Cu Chi, west of Saigon, to Gia Le. General Tolson sent this brigade to LZ El Paso on 27 January, and it began transforming the innocuous site into Camp Eagle. The camp was destined to become one of the largest military field posts in the world after it became the main base of the 101st Airborne Division (Airmobile).

Operation JEB STUART I officially began on 21 January 1968. Unaware of the impending NVA/VC storm of Tet-68, which would sweep through Vietnam within a week, the division's original purpose was to help III Marine Amphibious Force (MAF) safeguard the stretch of territory between Quang Tri and Hue–Phu Bai. Colonel Rattan began helicoptering search parties west of the cities into the mountainous enemy base areas. These longstanding strongholds were known to be honeycombed with fortifications, supply bunkers, hospitals, training sites, and even recreation facilities. While the 1st Cavalry Division was preparing to thrust into the enemy-held jungles, the NVA/VC were making their own preparations for attack.

The NVA/VC targeted the city of Quang Tri, the capital of South Vietnam's northernmost province, as part of a country-wide wave of attacks aimed at capturing important population centers and provoking a general uprising against the Saigon regime. The enemy offensive was timed for the *Tet Nguyen Dan*, lunar new year, holiday celebrations to achieve as much surprise as possible. MACV's military forces were observing the Tet-68 truce period, and many ARVN soldiers were absent from their units. Allied intelligence was generally unaware of any unusual enemy plans or dispositions.

The original plans to capture Quang Tri were made long before the 1st Cavalry Division moved into I CTZ but never altered. Enemy planners knew that the division was present, but watched as its brigades engaged in mountain search efforts some distance to the west. The NVA/VC apparently discounted the airmobile cavalry's ability to reorient one of these brigades in time to affect the battle for Quang Tri.

The assumed inability of the 1st Cavalry Division quickly to shift internal resources was not unreasonable. The airmobile division's poor logistical posture was further impaired by the unexpected onslaught of Tet-68, engulfing the formation's new operational area just days after its arrival. Although many supplies for the division were pre-positioned in the new zone, they were placed in anticipation of allied directives prior to Tet and not where the division was actually sent. When the enemy offensive suddenly sliced the road networks, many essential logistical items—especially aviation fuel and artillery munitions—were reduced to fractional amounts delivered by C130 aircraft parachute drops.

The 1st Cavalry Division's logistical nightmare compounded itself in a vicious cycle. The troops were still building fuel storage revetments at Camp Evans when the Tet offensive started, and the limited containers on hand required daily refilling. The absence of a written requisition (an administrative error) prevented this resupply the day before Tet started, leaving the division with only ten thousand gallons of JP4 aviation fuel. A lack of helicopter fuel and the foul weather conditions limited available airlift to emergencies, so that stock levels remained dangerously low. This critical situation was aggravated by the marginal condition of overworked division aircraft trying to build up supplies and respond to tactical field missions, since insufficient maintenance elements accompanied them to I CTZ.

The cold northwest monsoon period of drizzling "crachin" rain presented the worst possible weather for airmobile operations. The low, misting clouds and dense ground fogs lasted for twenty-seven days straight, limiting aircraft-controlled airstrikes to five hours daily and forcing much artillery fire to be adjusted by sound alone. The bad flying weather frequently canceled helicopter gunship support and interrupted critical aerial replenishment, medical evacuation, and troop airlift.

The North Vietnamese and Viet Cong intended to take joint control of Quang Tri by infiltrating a sapper (engineer demolition) platoon of the *10th NVA Sapper Battalion* into the city before the main attack. The sappers would create as much confusion as possible with explosives and sabotage, weakening the town defenses for the primary assault by the *812th NVA Regiment* and two VC main force battalions from the outside. The battle began at 2:00 A.M. on 31 January 1968 as the sappers destroyed communications lines and attacked other critical points precisely on schedule. Fortunately for the allies, the North Vietnamese regimental advance was delayed more than two hours by rain-swollen streams and lack of terrain familiarity. This gap in timing later proved fatal, for the 1st ARVN Regiment in and around the city was quickly alerted once the sappers revealed themselves. The South Vietnamese battalion posted within Quang Tri eliminated most of the infiltrators before the main attack struck in the predawn darkness at 4:20 A.M.

The *814th VC Battalion* stormed through the outlying hamlet of Tri Buu, where the 9th ARVN Airborne Battalion was monitoring a revolutionary development program. The South Vietnamese paratroopers were pushed back into Quang Tri and desperately tried to shore up the inner defenses. The Viet Cong and North Vietnamese infantrymen rushed the city walls from several directions. The ARVN soldiers slowed the combined attack, but heavy fighting continued unabated throughout the morning. The *812th NVA Regiment* penetrated the city defenses at several points and advanced toward the sector headquarters. By noon on 31 January the outcome of the battle was still uncertain.

Shortly after noon the Quang Tri senior province advisor, Mr. Robert Brewer, urgently conferred with Colonel Rattan to assist the thin ARVN lines. Mr. Brewer briefed him that the situation at Quang Tri was "highly tenuous," with at least one enemy battalion already inside the city, and that the defenders might not be able to hold out. Since the NVA/VC firing positions were located on the eastern and southern fringes of the city, it appeared that he was reinforcing for the final blow from the east. Colonel Rattan hastily called division headquarters for authority to counterattack at once from the air, even though it was already late afternoon. General Tolson granted him the authority to use the limited division helicopters on hand.

The lead elements of Rattan's brigade had been in the Quang Tri area for only two weeks, and much of his command for only six days. Since then, he had tackled the southwestern approaches to Quang Tri by sending his brigade to a suspected enemy mountain base area nine miles away, with one firebase as far as twelve miles out. LZ Betty and the other fire support bases had been under rocket and mortar attack since dawn, as the North Vietnamese attempted to lock the cavalry in place. Despite the problems imposed by lack of advance reconnaissance, unfamiliar terrain, distance, and harassing fire, Rattan felt he could quickly airmobile two battalions to the aid of the city. The battle plans were drawn in one hour with the help of Mr. Brewer, who pointed out the most probable enemy infiltration and support routes. Selected assault areas were planned with the idea of blocking the enemy from reinforcing troops already engaged in the city, eliminating enemy fire support by landing on top of his supporting guns, and trapping whatever enemy forces were already in Quang Tri.

Additional helicopters were requested from Division Aviation, the aerial reconnaissance squadron and the aerial rocket artillery battalion were alerted, and the 1st Brigade issued its attack order at 1:45 P.M. Lt. Col. Daniel W. French's 1st Battalion of the 12th Cavalry, which was given priority on airlift, executed its lightning air assault into the middle of the North Vietnamese heavy weapons sites. The helicopters carrying Company C skimmed low underneath the clouds and banked sharply to land the Skytroopers among the mortars, recoilless rifles, and AA machine guns of the NVA fire support center for the *K-4 Battalion, 812th NVA Regiment*.

The North Vietnamese machine gunners frantically shifted their guns to fire directly into the descending helicopters, but were unable to stop the aerial assault from overwhelming the position. The cavalrymen leaped off the skids of the lowering helicopters as bullets peppered the doorframes and jumped into action with their M16s blazing. The cavalry squads quickly maneuvered forward as the enemy gunners turned more weapons against the surprise air assault. Company B also became engaged in heavy fighting as it landed on the other side of the enemy positions. After hours of bitter fighting, resistance tapered off after twilight as the North Vietnamese began abandoning the field. By landing two companies against the *K-4 Battalion's* heavy weapons support and destroying it, one-third of the

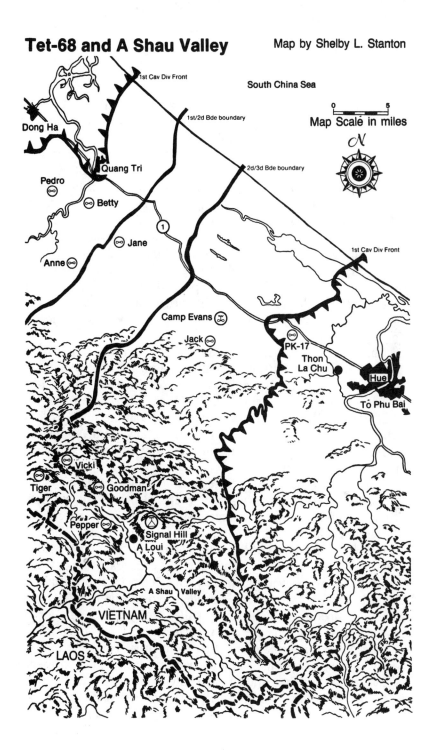

# Tet-68 and A Shau Valley

Map by Shelby L. Stanton

1st Cav Div Front

South China Sea

1st/2d Bde boundary

Map Scale in miles
0       5

Dong Ha

2d/3d Bde boundary

N

Quang Tri

Pedro ⊗

Betty ⊗

1st Cav Div Front

1

Jane ⊗

Anne ⊗

Camp Evans ⊕

Jack ⊗

PK-17 ⊗

Thon
La Chu

Hue

To Phu Bai

Vicki ⊗

Tiger

Goodman ⊗

Pepper ⊗

Signal Hill
A Loui ▲

A Shau Valley

VIETNAM

LAOS

NVA regiment was pinned and rendered combat-ineffective between Colonel Rattan's airmobile troops in their rear to the east and the Quang Tri defenders in front to the west.

Shortly after Lieutenant Colonel French's battalion launched its attack, Lt. Col. Robert L. Runkle's 1st Battalion of the 5th Cavalry air assaulted southeast of Quang Tri into the rear of another one of the NVA regiment's battalions. Company C was airmobiled onto one side of Highway 1 as Company A landed just south of the road to set up blocking positions. Runkle's troopers scrambled toward the raging battle and smashed into the rear guard of the *K-6 Battalion, 812th NVA Regiment*. Supporting helicopter gunships rocketed and strafed the enemy lines as the Skytroopers pressed forward. Like its sister battalion, the *K-6 Battalion* found itself wedged between ARVN forces and advancing cavalrymen and was quickly destroyed as an effective fighting unit.

The cavalry thrust was so demoralizing to the NVA regiment that its attack on Quang Tri was discontinued after nightfall. All enemy efforts turned to using the darkness to get off the battlefield. Unable to conduct an orderly withdrawal, the North Vietnamese broke into small groups. Sporadic combat flared throughout the night as these elements sought to avoid the allied forces. Many North Vietnamese and Viet Cong escaped by mixing in with crowds of refugees streaming away from the town.

The next day the 1st ARVN Regiment completed clearing Quang Tri as Colonel Rattan's cavalrymen swept into close pursuit of the fleeing enemy. The cavalry forces helicoptered in ever-increasing concentric circles around the city, seeking to engage any NVA regimental remnants. The attached 1st Battalion of the 502d Infantry found a North Vietnamese contingent holed up in a cathedral south of Quang Tri. Aerial gunships were summoned, and Company D of Lieutenant Colonel French's battalion air assaulted into the firefight to insure numerical superiority. Similar but smaller firefights flared up for the next ten days, long after the city was cleared.

The North Vietnamese and Viet Cong were confident and superbly equipped when the battle opened, but their battle experience against the Marines had offered them only limited opportunity to witness airmobile tactics. Marine helicopters were comparatively rare and used as transports rather than as an integrated armada of aerial war machines. The NVA/VC were completely unprepared to cope with the dazzling pace and devastating firepower of air cavalry tactics. Not realizing their vulnerability if caught in the open, the North Vietnamese often "played dead" and seldom returned fire as helicopters approached. This primitive response cost them dearly as division helicopters swarmed over the fields and cut loose with rockets, cannons, machine guns, and grenade launchers into the prone enemy ranks.

The Battle for Quang Tri was a resounding allied victory which not only denied the NVA/VC an important Tet-68 objective, but also cost the enemy 914 killed along with 86 men and 331 weapons captured. The 1st Brigade, situated in the western highland foothills when the battle commenced, had wheeled its battalions around and helicoptered them to the rescue in the finest traditions of historic American cavalry.

For the first time in airmobile division history, vertical air assault was used to decide a major battle by conducting a classic surprise pincer counterattack. It was a "textbook" maneuver previously only dreamed of in military tactical planning sessions. The sudden airmobile blitz straddled the North Vietnamese heavy weapons positions and eradicated the fire support needed by the Quang Tri attackers. Trapped between the newly airlanded cavalrymen and the defending garrison of Quang Tri City, five enemy battalions were forced to quit the battlefield in complete disarray. The flexible response of modern aerial cavalry at Quang Tri gave MACV one of its most decisive successes during the long, discouraging weeks of Tet-68.

As Colonel Rattan's 1st Brigade was mopping up the last enemy resistance around Quang Tri, a much larger battle was shaping up in Hue. The enemy had over seven thousand troops in control of large portions of the ancient imperial capital when the Tet offensive started. The available airmobile cavalry in the area consisted of Colonel Campbell's 3d Brigade, which had just deployed around Camp Evans. Like Colonel Rattan's brigade, it was constructing firebases to the west, preparing to search out remote enemy base areas. Again a major city was attacked while the cavalrymen were carrying out assignments orienting them in the opposite direction. This failure of allied intelligence to appraise properly enemy intentions forced the cavalry brigade to make a complete turnabout with very limited helicopter resources in extremely poor weather conditions.

As the Marines and South Vietnamese struggled to recapture the city itself, Colonel Campbell's brigade attacked toward Hue from the northwest on 2 February. The brigade was assigned the mission of interdicting the northern and western approaches into Hue. If the brigade could cut off NVA/VC supply lines, further enemy access to the city would be denied, and his reinforcements would be prevented from reaching the raging battle. Estimates of the enemy situation were mostly guesswork, but it was suspected that five battalions were engaged in Hue, an unknown force probably occupied the hamlet of Thon La Chu just outside Hue, and other regiments or battalions were deployed to the west or southwest to protect enemy supply channels. Ambushes along Route 1 indicated that the enemy intended to block the main highway.

The 2d Battalion of the 12th Cavalry, commanded by Lt. Col. Richard S. Sweet, was given the mission of moving toward Hue, contacting the enemy, fixing his location, and destroying him. The battalion was helicoptered from Camp Evans, where it was providing base security, to a landing zone just outside PK-17, a South Vietnamese army camp six miles from Hue City. Early the next morning Sweet formed a diamond-shaped battalion formation with his line companies and began the advance parallel to and south of Highway 1 toward Hue. The low rural area consisted of continuous rice paddies, with slightly rolling hills and sparse scrub brush, interrupted only by scattered stone tombs and peasant houses composed of mud and straw.

At 10:30 A.M. Colonel Sweet halted his battalion after lead elements passed through a patch of woodland and spotted enemy soldiers milling about on the other side of a broad rice paddy in front of Thon La Chu. The hamlet had been captured at the outset of Tet-68 and was being used as the support and staging base of the *7th* and *9th Battalions, 29th Regiment, 325C NVA Division,* which had just marched into the area from the Khe Sanh front. Thon La Chu was an elongated settlement surrounded by thick vegetation and, as a model Revolutionary Development project, contained sophisticated defenses designed by U.S. Army advisors.

During the next several hours, the battalion assaulted across the ricefield toward the far woodline. Capt. Robert L. Helvey's Company A led the attack, but the rolling ground fog and rainy haze prevented the usual helicopter support. Most division gunships were grounded. Two aerial rocket helicopters from the 2d Battalion, 20th Artillery, braved the dense fog to spew 2.75-inch rockets in front of the cavalrymen. This extra measure of support allowed some of Captain Helvey's men to reach the woodline and clear an area along the northern edge of the settlement. The formidable North Vietnamese machine gun, recoilless rifle, and mortar positions prevented any further advance. Helvey recalled, "In the Que Son [Valley] we fought the *2d NVA Division* in several knock-down, drag-out fights, so we knew what we were getting into. We reacted the way we should have reacted, but we were outnumbered and outgunned."[1]

Lieutenant Colonel Sweet pleaded for artillery support throughout the day, but the dismal weather prevented howitzers from being airlifted into range of the battle. Finally, two CH47 Chinook helicopters flew under the low overcast during the afternoon and brought two 105mm howitzers of the 1st Battalion, 77th Artillery, into PK-17. The cannoneers wrestled their artillery pieces into action despite enemy mortar fire, but the cavalrymen needed more than one section of two tubes in support.

As darkness fell, the 2d Battalion, 12th Cavalry, established a tight perimeter to better maintain control in close proximity to the enemy village because of the extremely low visibility. During the cold night of 3 February, the cavalrymen received only a few mortar rounds in their positions, but they were forced to sit miserably awake in fighting positions without packs, ponchos, or poncho liners to ward off the damp chill.

At dawn the North Vietnamese regiment launched a mass counterattack. Hundreds of mortar shells smothered the shrunken American perimeter, which measured only 150 yards across. It quickly became apparent that the enemy was making an all-out effort to eliminate the American force and regain his lost positions. The cavalry grenadiers and riflemen hurled back waves of NVA soldiers who were running at them firing AK47 automatic rifles from the hip as machine gunners laid down grazing cross fires in the fog. Enemy mortar rounds exploded through the compact battalion and scored several direct hits against crowded weapons pits and foxholes. By noon the 12th Cavalry lines were surrounded. Losses were heavy, and only a few medical evacuation helicopters were able to penetrate the intense, close-range fire to retrieve the seriously wounded.

---

1. 14th MHD Report on Tet-68, dtd 15 Apr 68, p. 17.

With an entire battalion isolated outside Hue, Colonel Campbell air assaulted Lt. Col. James B. Vaught's 5th Battalion, 7th Cavalry, into a landing zone south of PK-17 and astride Highway 1. The battalion prepared to move toward the stranded cavalrymen the following day, and more artillery was brought forward. However, Colonel Sweet realized that his men couldn't stay where they were another night. They had had less than six hours of sleep in the past forty-eight hours and were double fatigued by two days of desperate fighting for their survival. Ammunition, food, and canteen water were almost exhausted, and the troops were already skimming muddy rainwater from the wet clay to drink.

Late in the afternoon Sweet huddled with his battle-hardened officers and senior sergeants to devise a plan to extricate the battalion before it was annihilated. They decided to slip past the enemy after dark by going three miles deeper behind his lines to a hill overlooking the surrounding lowland, rather than pulling back as expected. It was a bold gamble and would require the entire night, but the poor visibility and misty cold conditions would assist the deception.

The troopers began gathering their equipment together singly at different times so that nothing unusual could be observed by the enemy. Loose gear was tied down and padded. Stretchers were improvised to carry wounded if action occurred during the march. Excess equipment belonging to the dead and injured was centrally collected in each company area and buried in a pit for timed detonation. Many of the troops rigged dummies in their foxholes, using sticks, spare clothing, and broken weapons.

The daring night march commenced at 8:00 P.M. Only six light howitzers were available to support the battalion, but their concentrated fire provided enough diversion to allow the battalion to assemble discreetly and start moving out. Smoke grenades were popped to create a smoke screen as the most reliable point man, Pfc. Hector L. Comacho, carefully led the battalion through the ankle-deep water of the rice paddies. "It was dark," Private Comacho said, "but I trust myself. The hardest part was finding some place where everyone could go, and making sure that everyone could keep up."[2]

The troopers were instructed not to fire under any circumstances,

2. 14th MHD, *The Battle for Hue*, undtd, 1st Cav Div files, p. 4.

and if fired upon to just drop to the ground and remain silent. Only company commanders could give the orders to return fire, and if this was necessary, only machine guns would be used. The battalion proceeded in a column of files with two companies abreast. The night was so dark that individuals moved within an arm's length of each other. The men trudged slowly west across the muddied ricefields. The enemy remained quiet and unaware of the escape. At one point the five-hundred-yard-long column froze when someone forward thought he heard an enemy rifle bolt slam forward, but when nothing happened, the cavalrymen began moving again. The battalion silently snaked through the quiet landscape.

As the battalion approached the river, the ground became boggy, and soon both files were sloshing noisily through the wet mud. The river was twenty feet wide and four to five feet deep, with a bottom of spongy mud. The troopers crossed individually, helping each other up the slippery far bank. As they were crossing the river, the equipment left behind and set for detonation exploded in a huge ball of fire. The cavalrymen at the rear of the column saw trip flares around the perimeter go off, and rifle fire started barking in the distance. An artillery barrage was used to discourage any North Vietnamese probing.

It was raining, and the bone-penetrating cold pierced the rolling ground fog. Everyone was extremely tired, and several wounded soldiers were trying to keep up. The battalion became noisier as the troops waded through the flooded ground, and sergeants occasionally lost contact with elements in front as they worked their squads around various obstacles. Whenever the lead element halted to let the column close, some of the exhausted men fell asleep on their feet, while others fell to the ground with a muddy splash. The sleeping soldiers were jostled awake as the column began moving again.

As soon as everyone was across the stream, the battalion swung south and traveled across the remaining two and a half miles of terraced paddies and rough pastureland. Along their route many noticed numerous combinations of signal lights flashing at them from woods and hamlets as they progressed southward. Later they surmised that these lights were part of some enemy regular route-marking system used on all passing NVA/VC units. The drowsiest soldiers were jarred awake stumbling across submerged dikes and looked up to see ghostly flares illuminating the skyline over Hue itself.

Finally, as full daylight flooded the landscape shortly after 7:00 A.M. the next morning, the ordeal ended. The weary, shivering cavalrymen climbed the hill which offered them defensible terrain and temporary respite from close-by NVA forces. Lieutenant Colonel Sweet stated, "We had men who had refused to be medevaced that afternoon. They hid their wounds so they could stay with the battalion. . . . And we found guys who were moving along; you'd see them limping; there was no talk. No noise at all. I've never seen such discipline in a unit. Little by little these guys started popping up—you'd find that the man up ahead of you who was dragging a foot had a bullet in his leg, and had it there for almost 24 hours. That's why the night march worked."[3]

By daybreak on 5 February, as Sweet's men safely reached their objective, Colonel Campbell realized that there was a multibattalion enemy force and perhaps a regimental headquarters at Thon La Chu. Radar-controlled bombs and naval gunfire pounded the North Vietnamese positions every day. The fresh troops of Lieutenant Colonel Vaught's reinforcing battalion moved against the northern edge of the village. In the meantime Sweet's men were rested and resupplied and then moved northwest through the sniper-filled hamlet of Thon Bon Tri to reach the enemy's southern flank. After attacking successive treelines on 9 February, the battalion was forced to halt in front of Thon La Chu's inner defenses that night. The actual extent of the enemy preparations in the fortified village was still unknown.

Captain Helvey led a fourteen-man volunteer patrol to scout the enemy positions that night. They crossed the darkened field between the enemy and cavalry lines until Helvey reached a graveyard with a deserted cement house. The patrol occupied the structure in the middle of no-man's-land, allowing him to scan the area with a starlight scope while the other patrol members fired M79 grenade launchers into the far treeline. There was no return fire, as the North Vietnamese refused to disclose their positions. The cavalry patrollers made two trips to the other side of the field past enemy lines.

On the second trip the patrol was spotted by a North Vietnamese soldier who unwittingly thought that Sp4 Michael Oberg, a short

3. 1st Cav Div Rpt on Tet-68, dtd 15 Apr 68, p. 19.

American, was a fellow Oriental. When the NVA soldier tried to engage him in conversation, Oberg shot him. About the same time, Sp4 David Dentinger stepped on something which started moving. He glanced down in horror to see the muzzle of an AK47 rifle and the firer frantically trying to pull it from underneath his foot. Dentinger emptied his M16 magazine into the soldier at point-blank range, and the patrollers scrambled back toward their own lines. A recoilless rifle shell slammed into the cement building as they moved past it, hastening their departure, but Captain Helvey's patrol arrived in friendly lines unscathed.

Lieutenant Colonel Sweet postponed a planned dawn attack based on the patrol's findings. Helvey's men discovered entrenched positions complete with 57mm recoilless rifles, B40 rocket launchers, and heavy machine guns in a double treeline, which meant that any attacking force reaching the first treeline would still have another to penetrate. The Company A executive officer, Tony Kalbli, remarked, "To attack would have been suicide. In that sense alone, the fourteen volunteers saved the battalion from almost complete destruction."[4]

Early that morning Lieutenant Colonel Vaught's battalion assaulted the northern side of the fortified hamlet. Company C poured flanking fire into one NVA company shifting positions to reinforce the main defensive line, dropping numerous bodies into the river. However, the battalion was forced to pull back as more mutually supporting bunkers opened up. Airstrikes throughout the rest of the day hit the village with sixteen tons of bombs and five tons of napalm.

Major General Tolson moved Col. Joseph C. McDonough's 2d Brigade north from Bong Son in II CTZ to rejoin the division. This additional reinforcement freed Colonel Campbell's brigade from all security duty and allowed him to concentrate it against Thon La Chu. Four battalions made the final attack on 21 February 1968. Lieutenant Colonel Vaught's battalion hit Thon La Chu from the north, with Lt. Col. Joseph E. Wasiak's 1st Battalion of the 7th Cavalry on the right flank, while the attached 2d Battalion, 501st Infantry, swung in from the west, and Lieutenant Colonel Sweet's battalion attacked northeast from their southern positions.

4. 1st Cav Div Rpt on the Battle for Hue, dtd 15 Apr 68, p. 6.

Lieutenant Colonel Vaught's men pushed into a fiercely defended treeline near the northwest corner of the hamlet. To destroy the NVA fortifications, the cavalrymen maneuvered troops with M72 antitank rocket launchers onto the berms. They fired just ahead of the advancing platoon point men, keeping the bunker occupants pinned down. Light H13 observation helicopters darted overhead, raking the backsides of the bunkers with machine gun fire to prevent enemy use of blind spots and to isolate entrances or adjacent earthworks. The ground point men coordinated with smoke grenades and radios and, on signal to cease supporting fire, rushed forward to push pole charges and satchel charges into bunker openings to explode and cave them in.

Two platoons were pinned down in a shallow ditch under mortar fire in front of one sniper-filled concrete bunker. Point man Pfc. Albert Rocha slowly crawled forward along the ditch toward the bunker as bullets clipped the dirt around him. One bullet smashed the handguard of his rifle. He reached the bunker and slithered on top of it, where he was joined by 1Lt. Frederick Krupa of Company D. While Rocha lowered his rifle to fire into the bunker aperture, Krupa jammed a ten-pound shaped pole charge into the bunker slit. The snipers inside frantically tried to push the charge back out, but the lieutenant kept it there until it exploded. One North Vietnamese soldier suddenly raced out the back exit, spotted Rocha, and broke into a broad grin as he aimed his rifle. Rocha quickly shot him.

Once the outer strongpoints were destroyed, the battalion swiftly continued its advance through the hamlet to the east and linked up with Lieutenant Colonel Wasiak's battalion as it drove south and Lieutenant Colonel Sweet's battalion advancing north. When the brigade consolidated, the fight for Thon La Chu was over. That night a soldier spotted a bypassed enemy tunnel position, grabbed a .38-caliber pistol and flashlight and went into the hole and returned with an NVA captive. The prisoner stated that throughout the battle the thousand North Vietnamese defenders rarely left their fighting positions. They were replenished with food, water, and ammunition in their bunkers by the Viet Cong, who suffered the bulk of the constant artillery and aerial pounding.

The action at Thon La Chu was the turning point in the division's battle at Hue. Colonel Campbell's brigade fanned out to scour the western approaches and sever NVA logistical lifelines into the city. At the same time, the 1st Cavalry Division's own supply difficulties were eased as supply convoys began rolling down Highway 1 from Quang Tri to Camp Evans. More Chinooks and Huey helicopters brought supplies to the field battalions. The Skytroopers were able to secure adequate rest and eat hot meals flown in each day at breakfast and supper. Morale peaked as the drive toward Hue resumed.

The cavalry brigade's determination was reinforced by a grim discovery made by an attacked battalion from Colonel Cushman's brigade. The soldiers found the bodies of fifteen women and children who had been savagely executed in a tiny hamlet only two miles west of Hue. The civilians had been herded into a trench by the North Vietnamese occupiers and shot at close range. Later a significantly larger NVA massacre inside Hue, involving thousands of slain civilians, would be uncovered.

On the night of 22–23 February, Sweet's battalion made another night march closer to Hue. This time they got within two miles of the city before the North Vietnamese opened up with automatic weapons, rockets, recoilless rifles, and mortars from solidly constructed ARVN positions captured at the beginning of the Tet offensive. The extensive fortifications and trench networks were over a mile long and nearly as deep and emplaced in thick jungle. The battalion spent three days clearing the well-defended obstruction.

Hue was attacked from the north by Lieutenant Colonel Vaught's battalion, which was stopped just a half-mile short of the city walls. A cleverly concealed NVA roadblock shattered the lead squad and engaged Capt. Michael S. Davison, Jr.'s, Company C in locked combat. When the firing started, Sp4 William Phifer edged his way through a cemetery on the right flank of the stranded company and tossed two grenades into a bunker. Both detonated, but had little effect. Phifer fired point-blank into the firing port with his pistol and pitched in another grenade. His grenade struck a Chicom grenade being thrown out at him, and they both exploded, lifting him about two feet off the ground. Miraculously, he was only shaken, but the four-man NVA heavy weapons crew was wiped out. The battalion fought past the roadblock and reached Hue's outer wall the next day.

On 23 February Lieutenant Colonel Wasiak's battalion, also advancing upon Hue from the north, ran into a mortar barrage just outside the city. NVA grenades and machine guns lashed the cavalrymen struggling forward through the waterlogged rice paddies. Sensing a slackening of enemy fire to the right, the lead company attacked in that direction. The North Vietnamese promptly shifted their troops and frantically began digging new positions. Rocket-firing helicopters darted through the low overhanging clouds to discharge volleys of rockets directly into the North Vietnamese soldiers. The intensive return automatic weapons fire still kept the cavalrymen flat on their stomachs in the freezing paddy water. Wounded were extracted by inflating air mattresses, rolling bloodied comrades over onto them, and then pulling the floating mattresses out behind crawling volunteers.

During the night the battalion spotted large numbers of North Vietnamese soldiers trying to exit Hue. They called in artillery bombardment on top of the enemy files and shelled the trails all night, producing terrific carnage. During the morning, Wasiak's men joined Vaught's battalion along the city walls. The North Vietnamese conducted one last-ditch counterattack against the 3d ARVN Regiment within the city, which was destroyed by concentrated artillery fire. At 5:00 A.M. on 24 February, the Viet Cong banner, which had flown over the Hue citadel since the beginning of the month, was torn down and the red-and-yellow flag of the Republic of Vietnam was hoisted.

On the morning of 25 February, Lieutenant Colonel Sweet's battered battalion reached the west wall and assaulted the final enemy trenchline. He chose his strongest companies to clear the last opposition in front of them, but each of the depleted companies sallying forward had been reduced since the drive started to a mere forty-eight men. The bloody battle for Hue was declared over, although mopping up continued for the next several days. Although the major brunt of the city combat was taken by U.S. Marines and South Vietnamese fighting block by block inside Hue, the 1st Cavalry Division brought tremendous pressure to bear against the NVA staging and reinforcement areas, stifling the enemy's capacity to hold out.[5]

After the Battles of Quang Tri and Hue, the NVA/VC forces sought to avoid contact and gain time to regroup their shattered forces by withdrawing far into mountain base areas. The 1st Cavalry Divi-

5. 1st Cav Div Rpt on the Battle for Hue, dtd 15 Apr 68; 2d Bn 12th Cav, *Battle for Hue: 2–5 Feb 68;* 3d Bde 1st Cav Div, *Operational Report—Lessons Learned,* dtd 11 Mar 68; 14th MHD, *Combat After Action Interview No. 5-68,* dtd 4 May 68; and Maj. Miles D. Waldron and Sp5 Richard W. Beavers, 14th MHD Study No. 2-68, *Operation Hue City,* dtd Aug 68.

sion maintained its flexible response through airmobility and pursued the enemy into their most remote strongholds. Actually, this penetration of enemy base areas was the original concept of Operation JEB STUART. Colonel Campbell's brigade redeployed back through Camp Evans, reopened LZ Jack in the mountains, and began helicopter sweeps of the rugged jungle. During the month of March, the brigade conducted forty-eight reconnaissance missions and fourteen search-and-destroy operations in the region. Colonel Campbell's main clearing effort, however, was directed against the bunker-studded lowlands and rice cache areas of the northern coastal plains.

Colonel Rattan's brigade established LZ Pedro and swept into the mountains west of Quang Tri. The brigade used search-and-clear, cordon-and-search, and swooper operations to pursue the NVA/VC during the day and hunter-killer teams and night ambushes after dark. Like the 3d Brigade, the 1st Brigade also devoted considerable attention to the sandy coastal plains and cleaned out the remnants of the enemy units which attacked Quang Tri.

The last elements of Colonel McDonough's brigade arrived in I CTZ as the Battle of Hue was ending. The command post was set up at LZ Jane between the other two brigades, and on 1 March the fresh unit relieved the attached 2d Brigade of the 101st Airborne Division in the same sector. The two 2d Brigades had carried out ninety-nine reconnaissance missions and seventy-seven search-and-clear operations in the JEB STUART area by the time the operation was over at the end of the month.

Operation JEB STUART, which encompassed the division's hard-fought Tet-68 response, had lasted only forty-two days when it was cut short to enable the 1st Cavalry Division to relieve the beleaguered Marines at Khe Sanh. During this short time, the division lost 276 killed in action, 18 missing, and 1,498 wounded in I Corps Tactical Zone. The high casualty rates easily surpassed 1967 levels, and the personnel situation was worsened by great turnover in the ranks. Also, 2,484 division members were rotated routinely to the United States within this period; the division received 5,345 replacements from 22 January until the end of March alone.[6]

6. 1st Cav Div, *Combat Operations After Action Report*, dtd 2 Jul 68, Tab L (Adjutant General Services) and Tab T (Casualty and Medevac).

The tremendous toll on aviation resources was reflected in the fact that twenty-four helicopters were totally destroyed after being shot down and seventy-six aircraft were dropped from accountability, most of them as a result of battle damage, during Operation JEB STUART. The strain of combat, marginal weather, and lack of ready helicopter maintenance reduced aircraft availability to all-time lows.[7]

In exchange the 1st Cavalry Division's flexible response was instrumental in crushing several NVA/VC units, recapturing key cities and towns, and clearing critical territory during the large-scale enemy Tet-68 offensive. The airmobile division's success probably killed more than 3,200 NVA/VC troops (the actual body count was 313). The division secured a vital stretch of Vietnam's most valuable overland supply route, Highway 1. More important, the division assisted Marine and South Vietnamese forces engaged in battles of great political significance to the United States. For the first time in airmobile history, aerial cavalry proved its true worth as a national investment on a foreign battleground.

The 1st Brigade, miles from Quang Tri City when it was attacked on 31 January–1 February and moving in the opposite direction toward another objective, executed a complete turnabout and air assaulted troops into the battle within hours of notification. The Skytroopers landed between the enemy forces fighting inside Quang Tri and the enemy reserve, trapping considerable numbers of NVA and VC between the airmobile infantry and the South Vietnamese town garrison. The shock of this sudden countermove completely disrupted the enemy bid to overrun Quang Tri, enabling the city to be resecured within twenty-four hours. In the ensuing pursuit, cavalry artillery and helicopter gunships decimated the demoralized enemy and drove them into the mountains.

The 3d Brigade, advancing south along Highway 1 in February, fought a determined month-long battle for the critical northern and western approaches to Hue. Since the foggy, rainy weather impeded airmobile operations, the cavalrymen often switched to a conventional infantry foot advance. They defeated large enemy forces composed of elements of nineteen battalions, severed enemy reinforcement and supply lines, and insured the encirclement of the greater battlefield.

7. Ibid., Tab AE (Logistics).

The courage, adaptability, endurance, and fighting skill of this brigade underlined the highest expectations which MACV accorded the airmobile cavalry. Some of the most bitter Army fighting in Vietnam, under the most stressful conditions, was waged by the veteran battalions on this one prolonged drive. Having seized the initiative, the 1st Cavalry Division relentlessly consolidated its gains and kept the enemy retreating from the population centers. The division pushed into the NVA/VC staging areas in the rugged mountains west of Hue and Quang Tri. Throughout March the airmobile battalions carved out firebases and prowled the dense jungles, uncovering vast quantities of weapons, ammunition, and food in formerly secret enemy sanctuaries. These operations were supplemented by division activity in the northern coastal plain, specifically designed to deny the enemy rice or recruits and to weed out the Viet Cong infrastructure. The division was called upon to deploy rapidly to another combat sector as the month ended and to undertake yet another highly critical mission: to reach the besieged Marine fortress of Khe Sanh in Operation PEGASUS.

# Cavalry Raids

*Techniques, Khe Sanh and A Shau*

The cavalry raid has been one of the most valuable functions of mounted horsemen throughout history, and the 1st Cavalry Division brought this ability to Vietnam with helicopter-riding cavalrymen. Raids can be defined as rapid attacks into enemy territory to carry out specific missions. Without the intention of holding terrain, the raiding force promptly withdraws when its mission is accomplished. Like screening and scouting, fast raiding is a natural attribute of the airmobile cavalry.

Although most raids are carried out by small forces with very limited objectives, the 1st Cavalry Division executed two classic division-scale cavalry raids just after Tet-68. The first was the airmobile drive to raise the siege of Khe Sanh, and the second was the airmobile strike into the remote A Shau Valley enemy base area. Both cavalry raids were expedient attacks with precise objectives, completely divorced from terrain occupation, and involved expeditious withdrawals.

After reaching Khe Sanh, the division was immediately withdrawn to air assault into the A Shau Valley because long-range weather forecasts predicted April as the last month of favorable weather before monsoon rains would prevent helicopter flight in the valley. The division scheduled withdrawal accordingly. However, the most important cavalry raid in Vietnam was the division's attack to reach the isolated Marine fortress at Khe Sanh.

The Marine combat base at Khe Sanh was established in the far northwest corner of South Vietnam close to Laos as the most westerly strongpoint of the main Marine defensive lines facing North Vietnam.

Formerly a small Army Special Forces camp, the Marines built up the Khe Sanh bastion on the strategically located plateau and hills just north of Route 9 and garrisoned it with the reinforced 26th Marines. During January 1968, a series of violent hill fights around Khe Sanh disclosed that at least two NVA divisions had moved into the area and surrounded it. The battle for Khe Sanh mushroomed into a major confrontation between the United States and North Vietnam. Control of the citadel acquired overriding political importance as a test of national willpower under President Johnson.

Throughout the weeks that the 1st Cavalry Division was battling the NVA/VC Tet-68 offensive at Quang Tri and Hue, the besieged 26th Marines fought for Khe Sanh's survival under heavy bombardment and periodic ground attack. Enemy approach trenches extended to within a few yards of the outer wire, which was already breached in places by the bangalore torpedoes of NVA sappers. The few patrols sent out by the defenders were ambushed and destroyed. NVA heavy cannon, artillery, mortars, and recoilless rifles pounded Khe Sanh daily, and often more than a thousand rounds impacted within the perimeter every twenty-four hours. The airstrip was in shambles, and the Marines were soon cut off from both overland and airlanded supplies.

The North Vietnamese ringed the Marine lines with entrenched infantry and a multitude of antiaircraft weapons. Dense fogs and rain-swollen overcasts shrouded the jungled mountains. During February, 679 parachute drops were flown to keep the garrison alive. On the night of 7–8 February 1968, North Vietnamese tanks overran the outlying Special Forces fort at Lang Vei. On 23 February the beleaguered Marines endured their heaviest barrage of the siege and six days later hurled back a major North Vietnamese assault. Khe Sanh achieved paramount importance in American wartime direction because of President Johnson's fixation over its possible loss. He considered the situation completely desperate and demanded immediate MACV response. The Marines hung on through March as General Westmoreland mustered the powerful forces needed to achieve a breakthrough.

The MACV call for help went to Major General Tolson's 1st Cavalry Division as early as 25 January 1968, when the airmobile division was flown into I CTZ and prepared contingency plans for either the relief or reinforcement of Khe Sanh. The unexpected blows of Tet-68 interrupted the allied scheme as divisions and brigades were shifted to recapture and safeguard lowland cities and towns. The brunt of this enemy offensive in the northern zone was shattered by 2 March. At the same time, Hue was officially declared back in South Vietnamese hands. However, the Marines at Khe Sanh were still in danger, and Deputy MACV Commander General Abrams was anxious to send a relief expedition to their rescue at once.

On the second day in March, he summoned Tolson to Da Nang to brief III Marine Amphibious Force commander General Cushman on division concepts to break the siege. General Tolson suggested a lightning airmobile assault which would slash through enemy lines, over terrain and defensive obstacles, much like a division-size cavalry raid. The momentum of this aerial offensive would greatly assist the two Marine and ARVN divisions expected to advance on Khe Sanh up Route 9. After listening to Tolson's presentation, Generals Abrams and Cushman told him to commence final preparations for the attack. The operation would be labeled PEGASUS, named for the flying horse of mythology.

The 1st Cavalry Division began detailed planning on 11 March. Although the mission to strike into Khe Sanh, reopen Route 9, and destroy all enemy forces along the way was simple, the amount of coordination and meticulous planning involved was staggering. As division chief of staff, Col. George W. Putnam supervised the staff sections producing the tactical and logistical arrangements; Tolson helicoptered several times into surrounded Khe Sanh to confer directly with Marine defense commander Col. David E. Lownds.

Within three days of the division being alerted to orient toward Khe Sanh, the 8th Engineer Battalion was near Ca Lu, alongside Navy Seabees and Marine engineers, building the massive airfield and storage facilities required for the upcoming attack. Under the personal direction of Assistant Division Commander-B, Brig. Gen. Oscar E. Davis, Landing Zone Stud was transformed into a major airfield staging complex and supply depot. In only eleven days the construction included a 1,500-foot runway, ammunition storage bunkers, aircraft and vehicle refueling facilities, a communications center, and a sophisticated air terminal. Still retaining its landing zone designation, although larger than many bases, the compound became the advance operations center for PEGASUS.

On 25 March (D-Day minus six) the countdown to attack began.

For the next six days Lt. Col. Richard W. Diller's 1st Squadron of the 9th Cavalry was unleashed over the planned offensive axis of advance, along and on both sides of Route 9, toward Khe Sanh. Allied intelligence of enemy dispositions was vague and often unreliable, forcing the division to rely almost exclusively on its own 9th Cavalry scoutships to develop accurate data about actual ground conditions, find suitable landing zones, chart enemy defenses, and destroy potentially devastating AA positions.

The reconnaissance helicopters and gunships found the targets, destroyed what they could, and reported the rest. The division moved 8-inch and 105mm artillery batteries to Ca Lu and LZ Stud to supplement the 175mm-gun and howitzer units already pounding the newly located enemy. Tactical airstrikes by fighter-bombers, rocket and strafing runs by armed helicopters, and Arc Light heavy bombing by B52s blasted known and suspected enemy concentrations and fieldworks. Landing zones were selected and hit with tactical airstrikes using specially fused "Daisy-Cutter" bombs and other explosive ordnance to clear potential resistance.

As D-Day approached, division reconnaissance and construction efforts were stepped up. On D minus one, the day prior to the attack, Tolson moved his command post to LZ Stud, and Colonel Campbell's 3rd Brigade initial assault elements helicoptered to their final marshaling areas. On the morning of the attack, thick ground fog and low-hanging clouds merged to blanket the landscape in total overcast. The rows of helicopters lined up along the landing zone runway were shrouded in haze, but still the hub of activity as trooploads were sorted, instruments checked, and fuel topped off. However, they appeared idle to the Marines, whose reservations about airmobility seemed confirmed as their infantrymen stepped off the line of departure in full battle gear and began advancing toward Khe Sanh.

At noon the tropical sun began baking away the mists, the veteran cavalrymen clambered aboard their Hueys, and the shrill whine of starting helicopter engines surged into a deafening roar as hundreds of rotor blades whirled into life. At 1:00 P.M. sharp the first waves of dozens of troopships soared into the air as the largest cavalry raid in American history commenced. The Marines silently trudging along the road under the strain of their heavy packs heard an increasing drone in the distance over the clatter of their equipment. They lifted

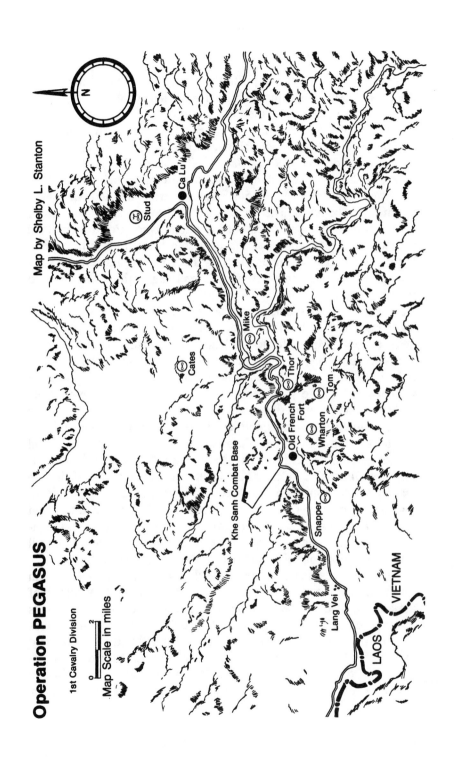

# Operation PEGASUS

1st Cavalry Division

Map Scale in miles
0          2

Map by Shelby L. Stanton

Stud

Ca Lu

Cates

Mike

Thor

Old French Fort

Wharton

Tom

Khe Sanh Combat Base

Snapper

Lang Vei

LAOS

VIETNAM

their heads as the throbbing pitch of helicopters resonated overhead. The overcast sky was filled with swarms of helicopters racing ahead with all three battalions of the 7th Cavalry. Lieutenant Colonel Wasiak's 1st Battalion roared over the Marines marching on the road below and continued flying toward LZ Mike, alongside Route 9 halfway to Khe Sanh. The 2d Battalion, under Lt. Col. Roscoe Robinson, Jr., came directly behind it, while Lieutenant Colonel Vaught's 5th Battalion airmobiled into LZ Cates two miles to the north. The spectacular 7th Cavalry air assaults were breathtaking to the aerial observation pilots, who circled their little scoutships out of the way as the troopship formations approached. The pilots reported seeing as many as thirty Hueys and Chinooks simultaneously descending onto an LZ, seemingly filling the air with machines and men.

The division's initial reconnaissance confirmed North Vietnamese Army intentions of blocking or delaying any allied attempt to reach the beleaguered Marine fortress at Khe Sanh. Elaborate enemy strongpoints occupied key hilltops and terrain features both north and south of Route 9. However, the NVA defenders were completely stunned and outwitted by the swift aerial intrusion of cavalry troops in front of, behind, and around the flanks of their positions.

The combined power, speed, and surprise of an airmobile division also became obvious to the Marines as a startling demonstration of combat accomplishment: in one afternoon a full infantry brigade was projected within five miles of Khe Sanh. The thoroughness of the 9th Cavalry's reconnaissance and target work became instantly evident. Not one round was received by any incoming helicopter, and this was in an area that had been bristling with AA positions just seven days earlier. The flak guns which greeted the first division scout helicopters had been put out of action during the ensuing week.

Operations escalated as more cavalrymen were airlanded at LZ Stud in Chinook and Caribou transports, shifted to Huey troopships, and air assaulted to open new landing zones. Operation PEGASUS was proceeding so successfully that schedules were accelerated, and Colonel McDonough's 2d Brigade was sent into the drive a day early on 3 April. Two days later Colonel Stannard's 1st Brigade was airlifted onto the battlefield. A South Vietnamese task force of three battalions was also air assaulted by the division south and west of

Khe Sanh. In one week Major General Tolson had deployed fifteen thousand combat soldiers into action.

The 1st Cavalry Division blasted open seven new landing zones in five days, each bringing the allies closer to Khe Sanh and driving more enemy soldiers from their defenses. Each air assault was prefaced with withering artillery fire, fighter-bomber passes, and final aerial rocketing against the field below, ending just seconds before the Skytroopers leaped from the open cabins and skids of their Hueys. The cavalrymen dashed out to form a quick perimeter. Within minutes Chinooks lumbered overhead with howitzers and slingloads of ammunition. The artillery was quickly unlimbered, ammunition crates were smashed open, and minutes later the sharp boom of howitzer fire echoed through the vegetation. The artillery tubes either shelled enemy defenses closer to Khe Sanh or sent final barrages into other fields chosen as LZs for the bounding infantry.

For the first time the cavalry artillery was answered by North Vietnamese artillery. As the fire support bases were set up on landing zones, artillery duels began. LZ Wharton was hit by twenty rounds from long-range 130mm cannon after it was established on 3 April. The division's quick-draw batteries lashed back by pumping out hundreds of rounds in counterbattery fire. The Chinooks of the 228th Aviation Battalion were soon hauling five hundred tons of ammunition a day to the forward tubes. LZ Stud was bombarded once by enemy artillery, but the forward observers were spotted on a nearby ridgeline and killed, and the base was not threatened again.

Typical of the fire support that paved the way for the cavalry advance were the exploits of 1st Battalion, 30th Artillery, forward observer 1Lt. Stephen Esh on 7 April. Lieutenant Esh flew in an OH6 Cayuse light observation helicopter. On the first mission of that day, he spotted four NVA soldiers and called in artillery, which resulted in two confirmed kills and two probables. His second mission took him over gently rolling hills two miles south of Khe Sanh and less than a mile from Laos. He spotted twenty NVA soldiers trekking through the elephant grass. The light helicopter made two passes over the enemy, coming in low and fast as the lieutenant hurriedly plotted the positions on his folded map and radioed for artillery. On the third pass he pinned down the enemy with M16 rifle bursts, lifting away just as the artillery shells began to hit the area.

While the artillery barrage swept the NVA, Esh scanned the vicinity further and spotted an NVA convoy of five trucks and one Russian-built tank on a nearby road. He immediately called for rocket-firing helicopters, and Cobra gunships swiftly arrived to demolish all six vehicles. Lieutenant Esh directed his helicopter low over the burning wreckage to count the clusters of dead North Vietnamese and noticed stenciled markings on some of the backpacks. Suspecting that they contained valuable intelligence, he ordered the pilot to land. The crew chief leaped out to get the packs as the lieutenant stood guard and shot down two North Vietnamese soldiers charging from the brush.

After stopping at LZ Stud and grabbing a quick meal, Lieutenant Esh picked up a fresh helicopter and crew and flew farther south. He directed the helicopter to circle an area only four hundred yards from the Laotian border and soon spotted another NVA truck convoy parked beside a road in a nearby valley. He directed artillery fire which destroyed seven trucks and killed large numbers of enemy troops. Secondary explosions rocked the jungle as a petroleum dump and two ammunition dumps suddenly detonated as well. The explosions and fires raged for hours, and Esh departed the burning target area as the helicopter fuel ran low. Such remarkably effective use of artillery observers in helicopters allowed the airmobile division to extend its artillery capability well beyond advancing ground troops.

As the advance continued and the enemy showed increasing signs of disorganization, General Tolson took advantage of the airmobile division's inherent flexibility to rapidly shift his battalions onto LZs and in directions not part of the original attack plan. On 2 April Lieutenant Colonel Robinson's battalion air assaulted into LZ Thor, a key position along Route 9 closer to Khe Sanh, and began moving west. Everywhere the cavalrymen went they were astonished to find huge piles of weapons and equipment littering the battlefield. This was unusual behavior for an enemy which just weeks earlier during JEB STUART had taken great risks to pick up any fallen man's weapon (where one weapon was retrieved for every five NVA killed). Around Khe Sanh the cavalry and Marines captured 763 individual and crew-served weapons that had been left on the ground, and it was apparent the North Vietnamese were in full retreat.

The next day Lieutenant Colonel Sweet's 2d Battalion, 12th Cavalry, seized LZ Wharton on a critical hilltop only four miles southwest of the Marine fortress. Between LZ Wharton and Khe Sanh was an old French fort, and its defenses were upgraded and held by what was estimated to be an NVA battalion. Lieutenant Colonel Runkle's 1st Battalion, 5th Cavalry, was stopped below the fort by heavy mortar shelling which caused many casualties and mortally wounded the battalion commander. The battalion was extracted and replaced by the 2d Battalion of the 5th Cavalry under Lt. Col. Arthur J. Leary, which flanked the fort from the west. The North Vietnamese fled, and the fort was taken without resistance.

In the meantime Lieutenant Colonel Robinson's battalion was steadily pressing forward along Route 9, but was stopped 7 April by a final NVA defensive line. The enemy bunkers were on a ridge overlooking the road, only two miles short of the beleaguered Marine base. After bombarding the ridge with artillery and helicopter rockets, Robinson at once air assaulted four of his companies onto the enemy positions. Three companies touched down around the enemy position, while the fourth landed behind the blocking force like a hammer against an anvil. The North Vietnamese were routed from their positions in a sharp battle, and the road to Khe Sanh was finally opened.

At 8:00 A.M. on 8 April 1968, the cavalrymen linked up with the Marine garrison after walking the final two miles up the twisting narrow road into the Khe Sanh fortress. Pfc. Juan Fordoni, from Puerto Rico, was the first trooper to make contact as he clasped hands over the barbed wire with a Marine lance corporal, one of the defenders who had weathered the heaviest siege of the war. The simple handshake was sealed as Lt. Joe Abodeely blew a triumphant blast on a tarnished North Vietnamese bugle found during the final march along the roadside with other discarded NVA equipment. The siege of Khe Sanh was ended, exactly one week after the cavalry raid commenced.

Mopping up continued, and two days later the 1st Cavalry Division recaptured the overrun Lang Vei Special Forces camp against light rearguard resistance on 10 April. That same morning, General Tolson was suddenly ordered, without previous notification, to extract the entire division and prepare to air assault into the A Shau Valley. Operation PEGASUS formally terminated on 14 April 1968.

Tolson's swift and powerful cavalry raid had smashed through the enemy lines and broken the siege of Khe Sanh in the first division-scale air assault in history. Every line battalion was helicoptered directly onto the battlefield in the first airmobile division attack to use all three brigades. The raid's success can be attributed to many factors: the excellence of its aerial reconnaissance, the coordination of its elements, and the logistical improvement in division operations. The cavalry raid was spearheaded throughout by the 1st Squadron of the 9th Cavalry. For a week prior to the upcoming division assault toward Khe Sanh, the dauntless squadron closely integrated its reconnaissance skills with the firepower of tactical airstrikes, artillery, and B52 strategic bombing to locate and destroy targets in the intervening enemy-held territory. The cavalry reconnaissance squadron brilliantly demonstrated its ability to prepare a divisional axis of advance despite the absence of higher command information about the enemy. The intelligence gathered by the division's aerial reconnaissance arm not only added immeasurably to the success of PEGASUS, but raised air cavalry to a new level of military acceptance.

The 1st Cavalry Division effectively coordinated an airmobile drive of eight cavalry battalions with a ground advance by seven Marine and four South Vietnamese infantry battalions. The pace of the division's aerial onslaught was set by waves of helicopters catapulting battalions of Skytroopers over successive enemy barriers. The multiple airmobile infantry prongs were both preceded and screened by rocket-firing Cobras and helicopter gunships directed by the reconnaissance squadron's observation craft. The combination of air assaulting infantry, aerial rocket attack, and scoutship harassment forced the NVA to abandon carefully prepared defenses and to retreat without regard to his planned directions of withdrawal. The hasty enemy departure was evidenced by the staggering amounts of munitions, emplaced weapons, and equipment left in defensive positions.

The division renewed emphasis on its supporting foundation, including the proper pre-positioning of supplies, as a result of lessons learned in the divisional transfer to I CTZ and Tet-68 battles during Operation JEB STUART. This favorable logistical posture enabled the division to increase the tempo of the drive despite continually unfavorable weather. Eleven complete battalions were helicoptered onto the battlefield by the seventh day of the raid (D plus six).

During Operation PEGASUS, the 1st Cavalry Division scored a decisive airmobile victory by quickly reaching the besieged Marine Khe Sanh bastion without setback or heavy losses, all within fifteen days. The careful planning and preparation preceding the raid was backed up by aggressive and innovative tactics during its execution.

At a cost of 315 casualties (including 59 KIA and 5 MIA), the division chased the North Vietnamese forces off the battlefield into Laos, forcing them to leave behind at least 638 dead soldiers and much valuable equipment.[1] Rarely has the potential of airmobile cavalry been more brilliantly applied.

Operation PEGASUS was summarily concluded in order to start Operation DELAWARE, the code name for General Tolson's next cavalry raid into the heart of the remote North Vietnamese–held A Shau Valley. The tropical valley was a mile-wide slash of flat bottomland covered by rain forest and elephant grass, wedged between mist-covered mountain ranges on the Laotian border. The North Vietnamese wrested control of the forbidding region from the allies by overrunning the A Shau Special Forces camp in 1966 and then turned the valley into their primary staging area for the assault on Hue during Tet-68. Because of its location and jagged topography, both Vietnam's northeast and southwest monsoons brought heavy rains, hail, and unpredictable storms raging through the valley's primeval jungle. This combination of terrain and weather made it inaccessible by road and difficult to navigate by air, but General Westmoreland was determined to strike deep after Tet-68 and eliminate the NVA bases located there.

General Westmoreland believed the 1st Cavalry Division was ideally suited to penetrate the A Shau for two simple reasons. First, the division was the only formation in the allied inventory that could airlift large numbers of troops into relatively inaccessible areas on short notice. Time was essential if the allies were to search the valley in 1968, because the brief transition period of mid-April to mid-May (between monsoons) offered the only respite in valley weather. (Unfortunately, this proved erroneous: as events were to prove, the premonsoon interval of fog and low clouds in the valley produced worse flying weather.) Secondly, no one knew what reception the NVA had prepared for allied intrusion. The 1st Cavalry Division was considered to be one of the toughest MACV divisions, able to triumph over whatever might be encountered.

Allied knowledge of enemy dispositions in the A Shau Valley was

---

1. 1st Cav Div, *Combat Operations After Action Report*, dtd 11 Jul 68, Tabs D and K.

even scantier than the intelligence provided prior to PEGASUS. Allied ground forces stayed out of the A Shau Valley, and aerial reconnaissance was nearly impossible. MACV could only guess at NVA dispositions inside the valley by judging the enemy forces which came out the south end. This estimate was very discouraging; whenever North Vietnamese units emerged from the valley, they were well organized, well equipped, and ready to fight. Although the extent of enemy fortifications inside the valley was unknown, aircraft overflights were challenged by extensive antiaircraft positions.

Lieutenant Colonel Diller's 9th Cavalry scouting squadron was sent into the valley to report all they could see or find, but almost immediately bad weather curtailed their activity. The raid was postponed two days to allow the reconnaissance craft more time to gather information. The light observation helicopters swept along the steep mountain slopes and rocky outcrops, using their nimble craft as bait to locate and chart the positions of dug-in batteries of heavy and light antiaircraft guns. The squadron paid a price—50 aircraft hit, of which 5 were destroyed and 18 damaged beyond repair, but fighter-bombers and strategic bombers responded by hitting the pinpointed targets with 209 tactical airstrikes and 21 B52 bombing runs preparatory to the raid.[2]

The cavalry raid into the A Shau Valley was much bolder than the PEGASUS expedition. The division would not only be raiding under marginal weather conditions, but also its forces would initially air assault beyond the supporting artillery fires of division howitzers. General Tolson wanted to achieve surprise and believed that this would more than offset the advantages of close artillery at the start of the raid. He gambled that aerial rocket artillery and other air support would suffice until the Chinooks airlifted howitzers in right behind the assaulting infantry.[3]

To conduct the raid, Tolson utilized seven of his nine line battalions (the 1st and 2d Battalions of the 5th Cavalry under 2d Brigade were temporarily attached to the Marines), but reinforced his division with a South Vietnamese brigade-size task force. All other division

2. 1st Sqdn 9th Cav, *Combat After Action Report*, dtd 4 Jun 68, p. 4.
3. 14th MHD Interview with MG John J Tolson by Cpt JWA Whitehorne, dtd 27 May 68, p. 4.

components were committed. The original plan envisioned Colonel Stannard's 1st Brigade making the initial assaults in the central A Shau Valley to secure the overgrown airfield of the lost Special Forces A Loui camp, which had been destroyed three years earlier. However, unsuppressed antiaircraft fire in this region led Tolson to open the raid instead by air assaulting Colonel Campbell's 3d Brigade into the extreme northern part of the valley. This switch destined Colonel Campbell's lead brigade of PEGASUS to be in the forefront of the second air cavalry division raid in history as well.

The cavalry raid commenced on 19 April 1968 as swarms of troopships and their gunship escorts lifted high into the clouds from Camp Evans. The helicopters crossed west over the highlands, bathed in a cloudy froth exposing only the highest peaks, and, once past the near mountain chain of the A Shau Valley, descended into the gloomy mists of the overcast valley. Capt. John Taylor, who commanded Company A of the 5th Battalion, 7th Cavalry, described the opening air assault: "The feeling the majority of the men had upon first coming into the valley was a sort of fear, distinctly different from that felt at Hue or Khe Sanh. We had heard so many stories about A Shau, like the possibilities of running into large concentrations [of flak]. We had a fear of the unknown. We thought that just around any corner we would run into a battalion of North Vietnamese."[4]

A wall of red antiaircraft tracers suddenly ripped through the lowering helicopter formation. Well-camouflaged mobile 37mm antiaircraft guns blazed continuously at thirty rounds every ten seconds. The shower of steel tore through twenty-three helicopters of two battalions and sent ten spiraling in flames to crash on the valley floor. The first two battalions air assaulted through the flak to establish landing zones on twin peaks overlooking the northern end of the valley. Lieutenant Colonel Vaught's battalion landed on LZ Tiger, but the unit suffered numerous casualties, including the battalion commander. Chinook helicopters managed to place a battery of light howitzers on LZ Tiger immediately following the assault. Lieutenant Colonel Wasiak's battalion landed on LZ Vicki, but deteriorating weather, the late hour of the assault, and intensified AA fire prevented artillery from being set down to reinforce them.

---

4. 1st Cav Div Ltr, Subj: Recommendation for PUC, dtd 15 Apr 69, p. 30.

In one of the most daring opening episodes of the attack, the division's Company E, 52d Infantry (Long Range Patrol), accompanied by combat engineers of the 8th Engineer Battalion and volunteers from the 13th Signal Battalion, rappelled from helicopters to establish a vital radio relay site on a five thousand-foot mountain peak which they dubbed Signal Hill. They worked frantically to complete the communications facility, which was needed to link the division communications at Camp Evans with its units on the valley floor. Bad weather set in, supplies stopped, and the North Vietnamese quickly used the opportunity to probe the defenses on the night of 20 April, killing four cavalrymen and wounding three others. The next day the clouds began to part, dozers and howitzers were lifted in by Flying Cranes, and Signal Hill was soon in full operation.

The thundering storm which masked Signal Hill swept through the entire valley for several days. The flashing lightning, severe wind gusts, and torrential rains confirmed the worst division apprehensions about A Shau weather. Visibility dropped to near zero and threatened logistical support of LZ Tiger. Despite the low cloud ceiling and almost blind flying conditions, division aviators were able to transport one company of Lieutenant Colonel Robinson's battalion farther south along the same ridgeline to LZ Pepper, to give the cavalrymen a better chance at resupply. Unfortunately, the lead Huey was shot down on the landing zone, and the wrecked helicopter blocked further lifts until engineers were able to cut out a larger clearing.

Wasiak's cavalrymen on LZ Vicki were in the worst predicament, as the battalion could not be lifted out, and attempts to sustain them on Vicki had to be abandoned. Their position was untenable, and Colonel Campbell was left with no choice but to direct Wasiak to march his men overland to LZ Goodman, a more favorable spot four miles south on the valley's eastern edge. Colonel Wasiak personally led the difficult trek for three days as the troopers struggled through the broken triple- and double-canopy jungle, following the ridge's tortuous terrain as it twisted and doubled back on itself. The drenched marchers became chilled and sick. They subsisted on ration tins and went without sufficient sleep. Late in the afternoon of 22 April they finally reached and secured the map location marked Goodman. Along the way they were amazed to find two Soviet-built dozers driven up into the hillside and carefully concealed. The equipment was the first significant find of the operation.

In spite of the marginal weather, the 5th Battalion, 7th Cavalry, began pushing downhill and crossed a major branch of the Ho Chi Minh Trail emptying into South Vietnam—Route 548 running through the middle of the A Shau Valley out of Laos. They found the NVA highway to be a hardened dirt road, reinforced by sections of corduroy logs and mud as well as steel planking, with trees along each side tied together at the top to form a concealing canopy overhead. Colonel Campbell's entire brigade was soon ranging throughout the northern valley, but the unsatisfactory weather continued.

Helicopter pilots were forced to leave Camp Evans by climbing individually through ceilings of nine thousand feet on instruments, reforming over the cloud layer broken only by the highest peaks, and fly into the valley through holes in the overcast. Switching back over to instruments, the young aviators probed through the murky gloom at near-zero visibility to find the cavalry positions. The normal ten-minute flight from Camp Evans in clear weather took at least an hour, and only the sheer flying heroics of the division's 11th Aviation Group made the raid possible.

On 24 April Colonel Stannard's brigade began air assaulting into the central valley around the abandoned A Loui airstrip, the original insertion area of the raid's planning. Despite intensive gunship preparation over LZ Stallion, the landings were opposed by considerable antiaircraft fire and a number of machine guns on the field itself. Lt. Col. John V. Gibney's 1st Battalion, 8th Cavalry—the first brigade battalion in—lost two CH47 Chinooks and a Huey, and only three howitzers could be landed the first day. The commander of the 8th Cavalry's 2d Battalion, Lt. Col. Christian Dubia, was medically evacuated during his unit's air assault the next day.

The seizure of A Loui permitted the 8th Engineer Battalion to begin airfield rehabilitation on 29 April. Flying Cranes lifted in the heavy construction equipment, and by 2 May the first C7 Caribou transport aircraft were landing. Logistical problems were greatly eased by the establishment of this division airhead. In the meantime the cavalry companies reconnoitering the valley found large quantities of abandoned trucks, wheeled 37mm AA guns, and other weapons. Contact remained light as Company D of Lieutenant Colonel Stockton's battalion brushed with an NVA platoon trying to evade the area on the night of 27 April.

The next day Company D of Lt. Col. George C. Horton's 1st

Battalion, 8th Cavalry, discovered a mile-long depressed corduroy road containing huge storage bunkers and defended by an entrenched NVA company with one tank in support. The cavalrymen pressed forward, wearing gas masks to ward off North Vietnamese chemical grenades, and Sgt. Hillery Craig wriggled forward to destroy the tank with two well-aimed M72 antitank rocket rounds. The North Vietnamese retaliated by trying to outflank the company, forcing it to withdraw. The cavalry reinforced, and the "Punchbowl" area was taken on 3 May after several days of fighting.

The Punchbowl turned out to be a large logistical center complete with hospitals and a headquarters site of a regiment-sized component of the *559th NVA Transportation Group*. During the first few days of May, the two cavalry brigades crisscrossed the valley and uncovered numerous well-stocked caches of tools and equipment. On 5 May the North Vietnamese began to strike back with increasing amounts of 122mm rocket, artillery, mortar, and recoilless rifle fire. The nearby border with Laos enabled the enemy to strike cavalry positions in the A Shau Valley by accurate indirect fire attacks with complete immunity from cavalry pursuit.

The cavalry raid was planned for termination in accordance with the northward advance of the monsoon. On 7 May, with the weather front fast approaching, Tolson decided to begin withdrawing his cavalry raiding force three days later. On 11 May the valley was deluged with torrential rains which quickly washed out the improved dirt A Loui airstrip. The division was forced to withdraw its raiding force by helicopters alone. As the last battalions were extracted under heavy rainstorms, Operation DELAWARE terminated on 17 May 1968.

Operation DELAWARE was conducted under far more arduous circumstances than PEGASUS; yet it was successfully confirmed that the large cavalry raid was a viable tactical role for employment of an airmobile division. The raid into the A Shau Valley achieved its objectives admirably. The raid determined enemy dispositions and area utilization, disrupted a principal supply area and infiltration route, and harassed NVA forces. The tangible success of this division cavalry raid was evidenced by the incredible amounts of enemy equipment captured, including 1 tank, 73 vehicles, 2 dozers, more than a dozen 37mm antiaircraft guns, 2,319 rifles and submachine guns, 31 flamethrowers, and 1,680 hand grenades. The cavalry raid was conducted under adverse weather and in the face of sophisticated antiaircraft defenses, and its casualties reflected these conditions: 86 killed, 47 missing, and 530 wounded troopers.[5]

Like the PEGASUS drive to relieve Khe Sanh, the division-scale cavalry raid to scour the A Shau Valley was a classic manifestation of the airmobile division's ability to conduct a traditional cavalry mission of great value to modern warfare. Both division-scale cavalry raids were further milestones in developing airmobile doctrine and further testaments to the proper wedding of airmobility and cavalry in the marriage of the cavalry division (airmobile) during the Vietnam War.

5. 1st Cav Div, *Combat Operations After Action Report*, dtd 11 Jul 68, Tab I.

# CHAPTER 8

# Cavalry Screen

## *Safeguarding a Capital*

The 1st Cavalry Division had completed three and a half months of unremitting combat by the time its helicopter-conveyed raiding forces departed the A Shau Valley on 17 May 1968. Fighting from Hue to Quang Tri into Khe Sanh and the A Shau, Major General Tolson's spectacular division had served as the backbone of the Army's versatile striking power in Vietnam. Airmobility was largely responsible for the allied spring victory in I Corps Tactical Zone.

The division regrouped and performed clearing operations through the rice-growing coastal lowlands and NVA/VC mountain strongholds in eastern Quang Tri Province until the last month of the year. The brigades opened new firebases, invaded the enemy jungle havens of Base Areas 101 and 114, and found large supply and food caches in Operations JEB STUART III and COMANCHE FALLS. Although sharp firefights and sudden clashes sparked throughout the summer and fall campaigns, the pace of these "rice and salt hunts" was slower, and the division needed the rest. The 1st Cavalry Division, deployed to I CTZ as an emergency mobile reaction force, was withdrawn from the northern region of the country after the situation stabilized and other Army formations were well emplaced in the area.

During its stay in I CTZ, the division's flexible response, raiding, and clearing operations cost combat casualties of 745 killed, 4,063 wounded, and 138 missing troopers in slightly more than eleven months. The incessant problem of personnel turbulence within division ranks was underlined by the loss of 18,681 veterans through rotation (in addition to combat casualties, injuries, disease, or nonbattle deaths) and the absorption of 23,202 new replacements. With an average assigned strength of 19,717 personnel during its service in I CTZ, the 1st Cavalry Division was completely refilled at least once within the span of less than a year.[1]

The Army temporarily retitled airmobile divisions as air cavalry divisions when the 101st Airborne Division was taken off paratrooper status and began conversion into an airmobile configuration. The air cavalry division was a term that the 1st Cavalry Division unofficially bestowed upon itself in Vietnam, especially by widespread use of the common abbreviation 1 ACD. On 27 June 1968 DA directed that the 1st Cavalry Division (Airmobile) and the 101st Airborne Division be redesignated as the 1st and 101st Air Cavalry Divisions (Airmobile). The directive provoked a great amount of dissatisfaction among the traditionalists, since both were proud divisions with independent heritage. As a result of extensive complaint, the Army officially revoked the terminology on 26 August 1968. The 1st Cavalry and 101st Airborne Divisions reverted to their original titles, using (Airmobile) as a mere cognomen.[2]

The leadership of the 1st Cavalry Division changed as well, as Major General Tolson departed on 15 July 1968, temporarily turning over the formation to his Assistant Division Commander-A, Brig. Gen. Richard "Dick" L. Irby. The new commander, Maj. Gen. George I. Forsythe, was already selected, but undergoing aviator training prior to assuming command. In fact, Forsythe actually expected to lead an infantry division because he lacked aviator wings. When Westmoreland told him that he was taking over a division, Forsythe was surprised because all the infantry divisions were filled. He replied, "Well, that's great news, sir. Which one?" Westmoreland smiled, "The First Cav."

1. Divisional averages assigned strengths determined by following total assigned strengths of the division: Opns JEB STUART I, 18,943; PEGASUS, 19,877; DELAWARE, 20,294; JEB STUART III, 19,757; Source: 1st Cav Div Recom for PUC, dtd 15 Apr 69, Incl 4; Casualties determined from figures in the following documents: 1st Cav Div COAAR dtd 15 Apr 69, Tab G; COAAR dtd 11 Jul 68 DELAWARE, Tab I; COAAR dtd 11 Jul 68 PEGASUS, Tab K; COAAR dtd 2 Jul 68, Tab L; ORLL dtd 26 Aug 68, Tab L.
2. MACV, *Command History*, 1968, Volume I, p. 245.

Forsythe was momentarily unable to respond because he knew that command of the elite airmobile division was considered one of the plum assignments within the Army and that the traditional ticket to the position included pilot qualification. He replied, "Well, that's great news, but I guess you know, sir, that I'm not an aviator." Westmoreland responded easily, "Oh, that's easy. We'll make you an aviator." With that authority, Maj. Gen. Forsythe dashed back stateside to complete a rush aviation course at Fort Rucker, Alabama, and returned to Vietnam to assume command of the 1st Cavalry Division on 19 August 1968 at Camp Evans.[3]

George I. Forsythe was born in Butte, Montana, on 21 July 1918 and graduated from the University of Montana with a degree in business administration in 1939. A reserve officer ordered to active duty with the 30th Infantry Regiment at the Presidio of San Francisco in 1940, he became a Regular Army officer in February 1942 and participated in the invasions of Aleutian Kiska Island and Kwajalein Atoll in 1943 and 1944. Promoted to lieutenant colonel in March 1944, Forsythe spent the rest of the war as the operations officer with XIX Corps in Europe. In 1954 he was promoted to colonel, later became paratrooper-qualified, and took over the reactivated 502d Airborne Infantry. After graduation from the Air War College in 1958, Colonel Forsythe was posted to Vietnam as the first senior advisor to the South Vietnamese Army's Field Command. Returning to Vietnam as a major general in June 1967, he served as General Westmoreland's deputy for CORDS until chosen to lead the 1st Cavalry Division.

While the NVA/VC menace decreased in I CTZ, substantial enemy force developments inside Cambodia threatened the South Vietnamese capital of Saigon in late 1968. Earlier that year Saigon was penetrated by sizable Viet Cong units in both February (Tet) and May (mini-Tet), resulting in great political embarrassment to the American government. The new MACV commander, General Abrams, was determined to block future enemy stabs into the capital. Allied intelligence reported at least four North Vietnamese divisions building up strength along the Cambodian border of northern III CTZ during October and estimated that a major attack against Saigon was imminent.

3. USAMHI, *Senior Officers Oral History Program*, Lt. Gen. George I. Forsythe Interview, Carlisle Barracks, Pennsylvania, p. 435. Hereafter cited as USAMHI, Forsythe Interview.

The 1st and 25th Infantry Divisions normally covered the enemy approaches between Cambodia and Saigon by guarding War Zones D and C, respectively. However, as part of General Abrams's emphasis on increased pacification efforts, both divisions were being pulled back from the frontier wilderness to support South Vietnamese military units and to assist pacification in more heavily populated regions. Since Abrams did not want to upset the progressive stability that this arrangement brought to his "One War Plan," he decided to shift the 1st Cavalry Division south and to use it as a corps covering force for II Field Force Vietnam which would screen and safeguard the capital.

On the afternoon of 26 October 1968, General Abrams ordered the cavalry moved into northern III CTZ immediately. General Abrams was keenly aware of the division's past record of air assault, sustained pursuit, clearing operations, flexible response, and cavalry raids. He now wanted the airmobile division in a screening role to meet the North Vietnamese on the border if they came across. Military screening missions are assigned to provide timely warning of enemy approach, maintain visual contact and report on enemy movement, destroy or repel small enemy forces, and impede the advance of larger enemy forces.

General Abrams did not expect that one division spread over such a vast area could stop a determined multidivisional NVA attack, but he knew that the cavalry's airmobile infantry and firepower could chew it up. He ordered Forsythe to get his cavalry into position on the Cambodian front at once and if the North Vietnamese came across, to "ride them with your spurs all the way down, down to the point where, if and when they do get to the populated areas, they will be a relatively ineffective fighting force!"[4]

Ninety minutes after notification that the move would start within twenty-four hours, Forsythe and selected staff members flew south to Long Binh. The U.S. Army Southeast Asia Signal Training Facility was placed at their disposal and became the advance command post. Continuous communication would have to be maintained between all units, as the division would be participating in three major operations on two fronts simultaneously.

When Forsythe inquired about special precautions to keep the move

---

4. USAMHI, Forsythe Interview, p. 443.

secret, such as taking off cloth insignia, reinforcing NVA/VC uncertainty about the extent of division redeployment, Abrams would have none of that. He told Forsythe that he specifically wanted to show the North Vietnamese that "you could move a division 600 miles overnight," and to "leave the cav patch painted on their [helicopter] noses to show them" the tremendous flexibility the airmobile division afforded the MACV command.

The task of moving the 1st Cavalry Division, coded Operation LIBERTY CANYON, represented the largest allied intratheater combat deployment of the Second Indochina War. The division withdrew its scattered battalions from the jungled mountains at one end of the country and moved them more than 570 miles by air, land, and sea for commitment into flat territory against an unfamiliar enemy at the other end. Operation LIBERTY CANYON commenced 27 October 1968 as Brigadier General Irby began sending the cavalry battalions south at the rate of one per day.

Lt. Col. Frank L. Henry's 2d Battalion of the 8th Cavalry "Mountain Boys" began packing on 27 October. After stashing all their equipment into CONEX containers, which were trucked to the docksides in Hue for shipment by sea, the troops camped on the Quang Tri airstrip with only their combat gear. Two days later C130 transport aircraft ferried them into Quan Loi, where they spent two days preparing to air assault into LZ Joe on Halloween, the last day of the month. Rocket-firing gunships and artillery pounded the woodlines as the battalion conducted the first cavalry division air assault in III CTZ. Waves of supply helicopters followed with materials as a new fire support base was hastily constructed.

Lt. Col. Addison Davis's 2d Battalion of the 7th Cavalry was flown to Quan Loi, paused for breath, and airmobiled onto LZ Billy in the forested borderland on 1 November. The order of the day was simply "Dig down or build up, but hurry." Reinforced by a battery from the 2d Battalion, 19th Artillery, and two squads of engineers, the troops felled trees with chain saws, cleared fields of fire with explosives, dug foxholes in the swampy soil, set up observation posts, and started building bunkers with steel planking, sandbags, logs, and sod. The bunker walls were stacked with hundreds of dirt-filled ammunition crates, quickly rendered excess as the light howitzers pumped shells into the nearby forest. In two days 181 helicopter sorties lifted in food, ammunition, fortification materials, light vehicles, radios, tents, and other equipment to establish the new fire support base. Rockets slammed nightly into the perimeter, and local patrols were already clashing with the Viet Cong. Company D's probe of a nearby woodline embroiled the battalion on its first southern firefight against a VC battalion just days later, on 6–7 November 1968.

On 27 October Lt. Col. James W. Dingeman learned that he would be moving his 2d Battalion of the 12th Cavalry south in approximately a day and a half and began planning to pull his companies in from the mountains. By noon on 29 October, his troops were assembled. Whipped by dust and pebbles from the twin rotors of descending Chinooks, they clambered aboard and were whisked to the Quang Tri airport for transport by C130 cargo planes into their new territory.

With three battalions locked into III CTZ, the 3d Brigade relocation was complete, and Col. Robert J. Baer's 1st Brigade began arriving to take over the southeastern portion of the former brigade's area. The inherent airmobile division flexibility allowed the screen to be adjusted wherever needed. For instance, Lt. Col. John F. McGraw, Jr.'s, 5th Battalion, 7th Cavalry, was originally ordered to Phuoc Vinh, but was shifted to "The Fishhook" area, a sharp bend in the border, where Lieutenant Colonel Henry's battalion encountered the enemy. The 2d Brigade lingered in I CTZ on COMANCHE FALLS until the operation was terminated 7 November and moved south the next day, where it was taken over by Col. Conrad L. Stansberry before the end of the month.

The 11th Aviation Group flew its own four hundred aircraft and 2,164 men down the coast from Da Nang to Bear Cat. From there the helicopters were flown to helipads and fire support bases being built near Army Special Forces campsites along the border. This arrangement provided some mutual security, allowed aircraft to operate out of prepared airstrips, and enabled battalions to be briefed on their individual areas by Special Forces teams. The 1st Cavalry Division headquarters deployed to its new main camp at Phuoc Vinh, a former 1st Infantry Division brigade base, on 7 November. Operation LIBERTY CANYON was concluded as the last essential combat equipment of the division arrived in III CTZ on 15 November 1968.

The amount of personnel and material moved during the transfer was staggering. During sixteen days of frantic Air Force aircraft shuttling, the 834th Air Division's 437 C130 transport sorties carried 11,550 troops and 3,399 tons of cargo from Quang Tri, Camp Evans, and

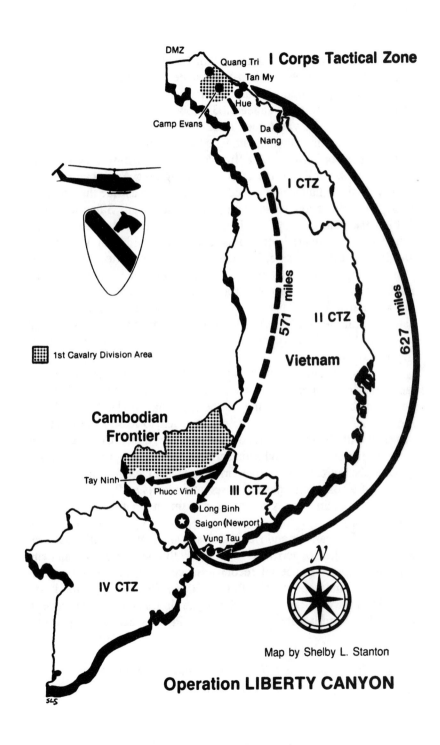

**I Corps Tactical Zone**

DMZ

Quang Tri

Tan My

Hue

Camp Evans

Da Nang

I CTZ

571 miles

627 miles

II CTZ

**Vietnam**

1st Cavalry Division Area

**Cambodian Frontier**

Tay Ninh

Phuoc Vinh

III CTZ

Long Binh

Saigon (Newport)

Vung Tau

IV CTZ

*N*

Map by Shelby L. Stanton

**Operation LIBERTY CANYON**

Phu Bai and landed them at Tay Ninh, Quan Loi, Phuoc Vinh, Bien Hoa, and Long Thanh North. At the same time, the Navy mustered a flotilla of ships ranging from the carrier *Princeton* (LPH-5) to auxiliary landing vessels and sailed 4,037 troops and 16,593 tons of cargo from Hue to the Newport dock at Saigon.[5]

The 1st Cavalry Division stretched its screen across 4,800 square miles of the northern III CTZ frontier by establishing a belt of fire support bases, similar to the forts used in fighting American Indians, to provide surveillance and armed reconnaissance astride the principal NVA/VC infiltration lanes from Cambodia toward Saigon. In this fashion the nine cavalry battalions on one side of the international boundary were squared off against several secure North Vietnamese divisions on the other side. The cavalry picket line extended from the rolling, jungled plains of the "Sheridan Sabre" area, covering The Fishhook and northern approach routes, to the flat ricefields and marshy Plain of Reeds in the "Navajo Warhorse" area, covering the western Saigon corridor facing The Angel's Wing and Parrot's Beak. The screen was patrolled by infantry and buttressed by helicopter reconnaissance flights day and night.

As division helicopters began skimming over the grassy woodlands, they encountered far greater NVA/VC antiaircraft fire than that encountered previously in the northern coastal lowlands of I CTZ. Aerial operations were immediately adjusted to lessen the threat of this frequently heavy flak. Whenever possible, attack Cobra gunships flying "high bird" escorted scoutships to provide suppressive fire and to guide them around dangerous firing sites and clearings in their flight paths. Rifle companies pushed observation posts and patrols well beyond their landing zones to insure maximum security for resupply helicopters.

In the flat marshes and rice paddies of the Navajo Warhorse area, a dangerous slice of territory saturated with enemy booby traps and trip-wire explosives, aerial reconnaissance over the sparsely vegetated, open landscape usually limited NVA/VC activity to the hours of darkness. Roving cavalry ambush patrols maintained vigilance at night. The plentiful waterways around the Parrot's Beak, jutting within

5. 14th MHD, *Operation Liberty Canyon*, dtd 30 Jan 69.

thirty miles of Saigon, were screened with cavalrymen on Navy river patrol boats in joint "Nav-Cav" operations. The Nav-Cav search patrols swept through the Plain of Reeds and often crossed into the adjacent IV Corps Tactical Zone of South Vietnam's delta region. The 1st Cavalry Division became the only Army division to serve in all four Vietnam corps tactical zones.

Search operations in War Zone C's tropical rain forests pitted the cavalry against well-fortified, superbly camouflaged bunkers built for mutually interlocking fire and always designed in unique arrangements. Fields-of-fire, invisible to the advancing cavalrymen, were cut in the thick overgrowth only a few feet off the ground. Caught in such killing zones, entire platoons could be wiped out in a matter of seconds. The lethal bunker complexes could be mastered only by using carefully coordinated, overwhelming fire support and airpower. Even in the absence of such fieldworks, maneuvering cavalry was targeted by increased use of close-range enemy B40 rocket launchers. The companies reduced this danger by changing locations daily, aggressively sweeping the flanks of moving units, staking out night ambush sites, and establishing listening posts around perimeters at night.

The cavalrymen, accustomed to combating NVA entrenched into the monsoon-laden mountains who concealed their signal lines, found enemy communications wire simply strung along the trails. In one instance the wire was tapped as the enemy was relaying traffic. However, the troops quickly learned that following the wire often led to disaster for the point unit. Safe wire tracking required that units move in arcs every fifty yards, relocating the wire farther down the trail, then repeating the procedure until the wire's source was discovered.

The joint aerial cavalry reconnaissance and fire support base patrolling screen inhibited the flow of enemy supplies. At midnight on 14 November 1968, the enemy made its first determined bid to smash the cavalry screen in the corner of War Zone C. The *95C Regiment* struck Fire Support Base Dot, held by the ARVN 36th Ranger Battalion under the division's operational control and backed up by 2d Brigade gunships, artillery, and scout helicopters. Preceded by a heavy mortar and rocket barrage, thousands of NVA infantrymen surged forward, trying to overrun the base. The South Vietnamese rangers lowered their artillery tubes to fire point-blank into the massed charges, which were also mauled by defensive artillery, helicopters, and F100 fighter-bombers. The attackers retreated with heavy losses, and division gunships rocketed and strafed the defeated remnants for four miles as they streamed back to Cambodia.

During the month of December, the allies gained evidence that the North Vietnamese were planning a multidivision repeat attack against Saigon during the Tet-69 period. The *5th VC Division* was assigned the task of moving down Adams Road (the Song Be corridor) to eliminate the allied command's strategic Bien Hoa–Long Binh complex outside Saigon. This division's movement was the linchpin of the enemy's battle plan. The closer *1st, 7th,* and *9th Divisions* would continue to reconnoiter and stash forward caches, but would not move toward Saigon until the *5th VC Division* was in position on the eastern flank. The *1st NVA Division* was given the diversionary mission of marching out of War Zone C to draw the allied reserves from their positions. The two other divisions would then advance on the capital itself, the *7th NVA Division* from the north down the Saigon corridor and the *9th VC Division* from the west directly out of The Angel's Wing.

All NVA/VC offensives required high levels of supplies prestocked in advance depots. In anticipation of the upcoming offensive against Saigon, the enemy increased his flow of materials into Vietnam. Supply lines such as the X-Cache Route, Saigon corridor, Serge's Jungle Highway, Adams Road, and Jolley Trail were shifted or strengthened to pierce the airmobile screen. Although December was generally a period of light, sporadic contact, the 1st Cavalry Division's battalions opened and closed fire support bases in rapid succession as they tried to remain ahead of the NVA forces infiltrating into attack positions.

Col. Karl R. Morton took over the 3d Brigade on 15 November and shifted brigade efforts to cover Serge's Jungle Highway, a critical enemy midzone infiltration lane, on 1 December 1968. That same day, Lt. Col. George D. Hardesty, Jr., assumed command of the 2d Battalion, 7th Cavalry. Captain Fitzsimmons's Company D had been moving northwest of Quan Loi for several days, engaging only small pockets of resistance and occasional sniper fire. The field first sergeant, Sfc. John Allison, a veteran of the same company during his previous Vietnam tour in 1966–67, noticed that the scant contact was making the troops restless and that they were becoming lax. On the night of 2 December, Captain Fitzsimmons announced that the company would be air assaulted into a new area. He turned to Sergeant Allison and said, "Six Mike (Allison's call sign), we are going in without a prep or chopper gunships working over the LZ prior to the troops coming in on helicopters." Sergeant Allison was aghast. Fitzsimmons quickly replied that he was only joking, and everyone sighed with relief.

On the following morning the 116-men company airmobiled by increments into LZ Eleanor. Artillery and armed helicopters ceased pounding the horseshoe-shaped woodline around the landing zone as the first troopships glided toward the LZ. Helicopter door gunners raking the trees and dense undergrowth were not challenged during the final descent, and the signal "LZ Green!" (meaning safe or secured) was given. The first troopers nonchalantly moved through the waist-high grass and around small anthills on the two-hundred-yard-wide field. An hour before noon the helicopters returned with the rest of the troops, and the company began final preparation to consolidate the perimeter.

The cavalrymen were unaware that their landing zone was ringed by bunkers set twenty-five yards or less into the treeline and surrounded by four hundred North Vietnamese soldiers. The enemy troops were silently watching and waiting with automatic weapons, heavy machine guns, mortars, and B40 rockets at the ready. Dozens of snipers were tied into the trees to prevent their falling, even if hit. The North Vietnamese leaders quietly observed the Americans begin organizing search teams to probe the woodline, but held their fire as a single Huey descended into the clearing.

Lieutenant Colonel Hardesty stepped out of his command helicopter, briefly conferred with Captain Fitzsimmons, then returned to the Huey. As the command ship was clearing the treetops, the NVA suddenly opened fire. The landing zone was swept by a devastating hailstorm of bullets, mortar explosions, and rocket detonations. Dead and wounded cavalrymen fell everywhere, and the majority of the company never had a chance. The surviving troopers desperately tried to dig in, but the ground was like rock underneath the parched cracked crust, leaving them completely exposed.

The first B40 rocket burst into a raging grass fire on the field. The troops frantically attempted to beat out the blazing grass with their tunics as they returned fire into the trees, and many were killed or wounded in the effort. Some men were wounded so badly that they were unable to crawl away, and the fire burned them alive as their ammunition pouches discharged from the heat.

Sergeant Allison considered the scene a nightmare where everything was going wrong, and foolish heroism was compounding the slaughter. The artillery forward observer, who had celebrated his twentieth birthday on the eve of the assault, stood up and began calling in artillery fire as everyone shouted, "Get down, Thirty!" (his call sign). He was killed almost instantly. The dead lieutenant observer slumped over the radioman, who struggled to push the body off and use the radio. Finally, the radio operator was able to start directing fire support through the smoke into the forest.

Captain Fitzsimmons's radioman, "Buzz," dropped his radio, grabbed a machine gun, and disappeared into the grass as he moved all over the field firing bursts of return fire. Sergeant Allison furiously grabbed the abandoned radio and tried to stay in contact with battalion, but communications kept fading. Each time he set the radio upright, the North Vietnamese concentrated their fire on the antenna, so Allison laid the backpack radio flat on the ground and put the whip antenna over his shoulder to keep it off the ground. A sniper round slapped dirt in the sergeant's face, but miraculously he wasn't hit. He called for immediate resupply of water, ammunition, and medical evacuation support.

The medical helicopter whirled onto the burning, fire-swept field, but was riddled with machine gun bullets as it landed. The pilot, door gunner, and all the medical aidmen on board were shot, and the co-pilot lifted the stricken helicopter out of the maelstrom at once. Other helicopters darted overhead as their crews tossed out ammunition containers, but they were dropped too high and landed beyond reach. A number of troopers tried to secure the precious cargo, only to be killed or wounded in the process. Men were lying all over the landing zone, crying for water and help, and three medics were killed trying to treat the growing number of casualties.

After five hours of combat, the enemy fire ceased in volume and Sergeant Allison reasoned that the enemy was preparing to overrun the field. He shouted for everyone to gather what ammunition and grenades he could and crawl to his position, thus forming a small perimeter with the thirty-six cavalrymen who were still able to fight.

# Cavalry Screen in III Corps Tactical Zone

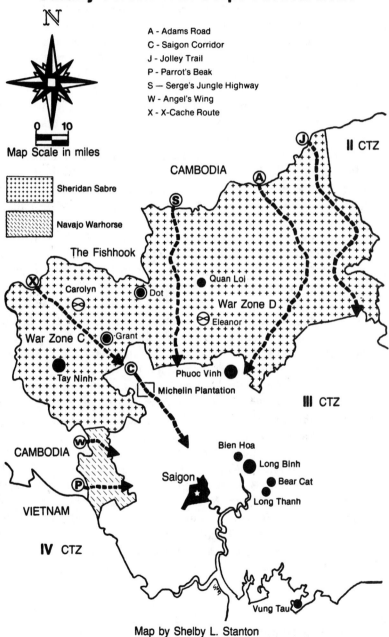

N

A - Adams Road
C - Saigon Corridor
J - Jolley Trail
P - Parrot's Beak
S — Serge's Jungle Highway
W - Angel's Wing
X - X-Cache Route

0    10
Map Scale in miles

Sheridan Sabre

Navajo Warhorse

CAMBODIA

II CTZ

The Fishhook

Carolyn

Dot

Quan Loi

War Zone D

Eleanor

War Zone C

Grant

Tay Ninh

Phuoc Vinh

Michelin Plantation

III CTZ

CAMBODIA

Bien Hoa

Long Binh

Bear Cat

Saigon

Long Thanh

VIETNAM

IV CTZ

Vung Tau

Map by Shelby L. Stanton

However, the North Vietnamese were withdrawing as cavalry reinforcements reached the battlefield to rescue the dehydrated survivors
of Company D. Lieutenant Colonel Hardesty helicoptered onto the
blackened, shattered landing zone. He went over to Sergeant Allison
and patted him on the back, saying, "Fine job you did, Six Mike,"
but his eyes expressed only, "What a hell of a mess."[6]

The decimation of Company D, 2d Battalion, 7th Cavalry, was
a relatively minor encounter in the division's covering operations, but
it demonstrated the high price that a screening force paid to detect
and harass large, advancing enemy formations. In effect, valiant airmobile companies such as Fitzsimmons's were exposing themselves
to North Vietnamese divisions to safeguard the capital, Saigon.

The 1st Cavalry Division was flexible enough to send its battalions hopping over great distances, but they often fragmented into smaller
elements to cover the vast operational area. With a screening mission
to provide timely warning of enemy approach and to report on enemy
movement, these small airmobile forces often landed in unsecured
territory and sometimes suffered reverses. However, the total power
of an airmobile division was greater than the sum of its parts, and
powerful responsive forces could be rapidly shifted to battle the enemy wherever he was found. This capability to change directions and
skirmish along a wide front was effectively impeding and frustrating
enemy attempts to make headway through the war zones.

Colonel Baer's brigade moved into the Saigon corridor to interdict
the movement of the *9th VC Division* from The Angel's Wing on 15
December. Using airmobile and riverine techniques, the brigade slashed
through the Navajo Warhorse area and captured so many munitions
and caches that it was credited with finding a large percentage of the
total amount infiltrated into III CTZ by the enemy division. On 19
January 1969 Colonel Baer reentered War Zone C, leaving only two
companies to monitor Navajo Warhorse. The brigade combed jungles
and ambushed trails in a successful screen which killed forty NVA/
VC a night and uncovered additional material.

Colonel Stansberry's brigade continued its interdictory operations
south of The Fishhook. One of the largest caches was found by its

6. Ltr fm Sfc. John Allison in ref to Div investigation, undtd, frm Eliza-
bethtown, Ky, contained in 1st Cav Div Opn TOAN THANG II files.

attached South Vietnamese 3d Marine Battalion. Containing 250 large rockets, 324 assault rifles, 22 crew-served weapons, and a ton of munitions, the cache could have supplied an entire NVA battalion for a sizable attack. In the meantime Colonel Morton's brigade air assaulted into War Zone D to head off the *5th VC Division*. This mobile screening increased the distance from the border on the western flank, giving the air cavalry reconnaissance squadron more time to detect the enemy approach and use long-range division artillery against it.

The NVA/VC were forced to break their units into smaller components to pass through the screen and to divert combat troops to move additional supplies in order to replace critical material losses. The cavalry continued to batter enemy rear service elements struggling to protect and move their caches, and these support units took the actual brunt of casualties. The main enemy divisions inexorably worked their way forward: the *1st* and *7th NVA Divisions* into the area just north of Michelin Rubber Plantation, and the *5th* and *9th VC Divisions* on both sides of Saigon in The Angel's Wing and southwestern War Zone D, respectively.[7]

The enemy offensive began on 23 February 1969 after the conclusion of the Tet-69 truce, as firefights and rocket or mortar barrages erupted over a wide front. The strength of the *5th VC Division* pushing toward Saigon was steadily eroded. One regiment of the *5th VC Division*, repeatedly hit by ambushes and artillery, aborted its mission and returned to War Zone D. By the time the weakened division attacked the allied gates and bunker line at Bien Hoa airbase, it was stopped cold by the 199th Infantry Brigade. The 1st Infantry Division repelled a regimental assault of the other weakened enemy prong at Dau Tieng and counterattacked through the Michelin Rubber Plantation to finish off the attackers.

In War Zone C the *1st NVA Division* had been bottled up by the 1st Brigade, under the command of Col. Joseph P. Kingston since 3 March 1969. Cavalry operating out of Fire Support Base Grant, occupied by Lt. Col. Peter Gorvard's 2d Battalion of the 12th Cavalry, kept interdicting the enemy division's lines of communication and prevented it from conducting the assigned diversion mission. Shortly after midnight on 8 March 1969, the base was hit by intense rocket

7. 1st Cav Div, *Combat Operations After Action Report*, dtd 2 Sep 69.

and mortar fire and stormed by the *95C Regiment*. The battalion headquarters bunker was destroyed by two 120mm rockets in the opening bombardment, killing Colonel Gorvad and numerous other key personnel.

The massed enemy attack on Fire Support Base Grant was smashed by concentrated defensive fires and airstrikes. Quad .50-caliber machine guns sliced through the onrushing NVA soldiers with four-barreled ribbons of fire. Capt. Bill Capshaw of Battery C, 1st Battalion, 77th Artillery, directed his troops as they manhandled a 105mm howitzer forward to rake the North Vietnamese with Bee Hive rounds. While the main assault was finally destroyed in the perimeter wire, enemy regimental reserves were smothered by artillery concentrations. The shattered remnants fled the battlefield only two hours after the attack commenced.

Two battalions of the *101D Regiment* tried to overrun Fire Support Base Grant in the predawn hours of 11 March 1969, but were quickly repulsed. Fast pursuit by 1st Squadron, 9th Cavalry, helicopters further diminished the retreating enemy. The successful defense of Fire Support Base Grant insured the continuity of the cavalry screen in War Zone C, and Colonel Baer shifted his brigade flag to take over the Navajo Warhorse area. During March the Navajo Warhorse area also flared with action as the cavalry intercepted elements of the *9th VC Division* attempting to drive east into Saigon.[8] The 2d Brigade became responsible for War Zone C, while Colonel Morton's brigade continued hunting expeditions in War Zone D.

With the NVA/VC offensive timetable wrecked and its combat formations in obviously depleted condition, II Field Force Vietnam went over to the offensive in Operation ATLAS WEDGE during mid-March. The 11th Armored Cavalry Regiment fought through the Michelin Rubber Plantation and pushed the *7th NVA Division* out of its staging area. By the end of March 1969, it was apparent that the North Vietnamese threat to Saigon was over. The airmobile division accomplished its screening objectives by impeding the advance of four

---

8. A detailed account of a particularly bitter night firefight by the 1st Cavalry Division in The Angel's Wing sector can be found in the author's *The Rise and Fall of an American Army*, (Novato, Calif.: Presidio Press, 1985), pp. 308–13.

NVA/VC divisions, causing large enemy cache and material losses throughout northern III CTZ, and breaking the core of the projected enemy sweep into Saigon during the enemy post-Tet 1969 spring offensive.

Cavalry screening was largely uneventful during April. The division initiated the MONTANA SCOUT/MONTANA RAIDER series of operations, seeking the NVA/VC forces which were refitting in III CTZ. Colonel Morton's brigade screened War Zone D to locate and intercept the *5th VC Division*. In early May the *9th VC Division* initiated an attack toward Tay Ninh in coordination with the *1st NVA Division*, while the *7th Division* held the Saigon corridor open. With all four enemy divisions once again on the move, the 1st Cavalry Division retracted its mobile screening net to assume an interdictory posture, typified by small patrols and ambushes, across the southern portion of War Zone C.

Maj. Gen. Elvy Benton Roberts brought a wealth of veteran airmobile knowledge and combat paratrooper background when he took command of the 1st Cavalry Division on 5 May 1969. Roberts was born in Manchester, Kentucky, on 21 August 1917. He graduated from West Point in January 1943, then completed infantry, parachute, and airborne school demolitions courses before joining the 501st Parachute Infantry Regiment of the famous 101st Airborne Division at the end of the year. He jumped into Normandy during D-Day, 6 June 1944, and served with the regiment throughout the rest of World War II, participating in five major campaigns, including the parachute assault of Holland and the defense of Bastogne.

After the war, Roberts served on various assignments in the United States, Germany, and Iran, including the command of the 1st Airborne Battle Group, 506th Infantry, at Fort Campbell, Kentucky, from June 1961 through January 1963. At that point Colonel Roberts was assigned as Chief of Staff of the 11th Air Assault Division and became one of the prime developers of the modern airmobile division concept. He brought the 1st Cavalry Division's 1st Airborne Brigade to Vietnam and led it through the central highlands until March 1966, when he was assigned to MACV and promoted to brigadier general that September. Returning to Vietnam as deputy commander of the 9th Infantry Division in June 1968, Roberts moved up to USARV Deputy Chief of Staff for Plans and Operations before taking command of the 1st Cavalry Division. Possessing an intimate knowledge of airmobile application, Major General Roberts acted aggressively and without hesitation in shifting division forces to interdict and destroy enemy elements throughout northern III CTZ.

The day after Roberts assumed command, the 1st Cavalry Division scored one of its hardest-fought screening victories during the battle of Landing Zone Carolyn. Lt. Col. Richard W. Wood's 2d Battalion of the 8th Cavalry had opened LZ Carolyn two weeks earlier in a large open area near the abandoned Prek Klok Special Forces camp as a forward command and firebase inside War Zone C. Two batteries of artillery were located inside the perimeter: Battery B of the 1st Battalion, 30th Artillery (155mm), on the northern side; and Battery A of the 2d Battalion, 19th Artillery (105mm), along the western perimeter. The cavalry operating out of LZ Carolyn quickly became a thorn in the side of enemy forces, engaging NVA/VC forces in sixty-two separate contacts within the period of twenty-four days. The North Vietnamese decided to annihilate the post because of its pressure on X-Cache Trail traffic.

In the early morning darkness of 6 May, the North Vietnamese retaliated with an intensive rocket and mortar barrage, followed by a massive *95th Regiment* pincer ground assault against two sides of the base an hour later. LZ Carolyn's garrison was reduced by the absence of several line companies on patrol, and the withering defensive fires of the battalion's Company C and E were unable to prevent the onrushing battalions from storming through the wire and into the landing zone from both directions. Six perimeter bunkers were overrun, one of the medium howitzers was captured, and the enemy threatened to slice through the center of the base.

The Americans counterattacked with all available personnel, the officers involved being killed at the head of their troops. Artillerymen, supply and signal personnel, and engineers fought and died as emergency infantry reserves. The counterattacks were hurled against both enemy penetrations, but the most violent fighting occurred on the northern side, where a seesaw battle raged for possession of the 155mm howitzer position. During the course of the battle, this weapon exchanged hands three times in hand-to-hand fighting decided at close range with rifles and entrenching tools.

Overhead, rocket-firing AH1G Cobra helicopters rolled in, ignoring heavy flak, and blasted the NVA with rockets and miniguns. Air Force AC47 "Spooky" and AC119 "Shadow" aircraft, supported by fighter-bombers, were employed against the numerous enemy antiaircraft weapons ringing the perimeter. Controlled and uncontrolled fires were raging everywhere, and it seemed that LZ Carolyn was ablaze throughout its entire length. Waves of North Vietnamese infantry charging into the southern lines were met by defending troops who took advantage of the aviation gasoline storage area. They shot holes in the fuel drums and ignited them to create a flaming barrier, which effectively blocked further enemy penetration. In the LZ's opposite sector, a medium howitzer gun pit received three direct hits which touched off a fire in its powder bunker, yet the crew calmly stood by its weapon and employed it throughout the night.

Both 105mm artillery ammunition points were exploded by enemy fire around 3:30 A.M., and shrapnel from more than six hundred disintegrating rounds in the two dumps sprayed the entire landing zone continuously for four hours. LZ Carolyn appeared threatened with total destruction as the thundering conflagration tossed detonating artillery projectiles to shower men and equipment with flying rounds and burning shell fragments.

The defending artillerymen and mortar crews fought in desperation heightened by the loss of communications between most weapons and their fire direction centers (FDC). The initial enemy barrage destroyed communications from the 155mm gun sections to their FDC, forcing crews to individually engage targets on their own volition by leveling tubes full of Bee Hive or high-explosive charges. When telephone lines from the mortar tubes to their FDC were severed, the direction personnel switched to a bullhorn to relay fire commands across the deafening noise of the battlefield. The battalion mortar platoon's four tubes fired fifteen hundred rounds, ranging from critical illumination to searing white phosphorus. In all cases effective fire support was maintained.

Ammunition shortages quickly developed. As on-hand mortar ammunition beside the weapons was exhausted, volunteers dashed through fire-swept open areas to retrieve more rounds from storage bunkers. The destruction of the 105mm ammunition points caused an immediate crisis in the light howitzer pits. The cannoneers were forced to redistribute remaining ammunition by crawling from one gun section to another under a hail of enemy direct fire and spinning shrapnel from the exploding dump. The crews continued rendering direct fire, even though they were often embroiled in defending their own weapons. One light howitzer section was caught in an enemy cross fire between a heavy machine gun and rifles, until the artillerymen managed to turn their lowered muzzle and pump Bee Hive flechettes into the enemy. All automatic weapons fire against the howitzer was instantly silenced. Cavalry counterattacks reestablished the perimeter, and the enemy force began withdrawing, breaking contact at 6:00 A.M.[9]

The NVA/VC forces increased their activity throughout the war zone, but the high point was reached between 12 and 14 May 1969 as Fire Support Bases Grant, Jamie, and Phyllis were hit by ground attacks. Action tapered off almost immediately afterward as the cavalry screen effectively disrupted the flow of enemy logistical traffic needed to sustain the enemy's advance. Now General Roberts airmobiled his division into the attack as he resumed its offensive role, striking enemy formations and their assembly areas throughout central War Zone C. Division forces conducted air assaults throughout the thick jungles in the wake of massed B52 bombing runs. Extensive use was made of large amounts of chemical gas crystal to channel enemy movement and contaminate his supplies.

Division search operations and difficult "bunker busting" tasks continued through the humid summer, reducing the next round of NVA/VC attacks in August to feeble one-battalion thrusts against remote provincial capitals near Cambodia. These attacks could be staged directly across the border from The Fishhook and other adjacent territory without having attacking units run the gauntlet of cavalry interception or relying on forward depots subject to destruction by cavalry patrolling.

The 1st Cavalry Division screen was stretched across northern III CTZ from 15 November 1968, when Operation LIBERTY CANYON ended, until 23 June 1969, the official termination date of the Operation MONTANA SCOUT/MONTANA RAIDER series. During this time the cavalry screening effort cost the lives of 567 troopers killed in action and another 3,555 wounded.[10] In exchange, the di-

9. Hq 2d Bn, 8th Cav, Ltr dtd 1 Jun 69, Subj: Recomm for Awd of the VUA w/spt papers.
10. 1st Cav Div, *Operational Report*, dtd 15 Feb 69, Tab J; and 14th MHD, *The Shield and the Hammer: The 1st Cav Div in War Zone C and Western III Corps*, undtd, p. 28.

vision whittled down the offensive momentum of four NVA/VC divisions in the heart of war zone country and rendered them incapable of inflicting damage on Saigon. For the 1st Cavalry Division, the successful conclusion of this mission represented the airmobile fulfillment of a quintessential cavalry function throughout military history: the cavalry screen.

# CHAPTER 9

# Cavalry Exploitation

## *The Cambodian Invasion*

Maj. Gen. E. B. Roberts's 1st Cavalry Division paired up its brigades with ARVN airborne brigades in late 1969 to assist South Vietnam to develop its Airborne Division into an airmobile strike force. The cavalry conducted extensive joint field exercises to impart technical airmobile doctrine and helicopter expertise to the South Vietnamese units. This posture temporarily reduced division field screening, but by early 1970 the division and its mated Vietnamese airborne brigades were leapfrogging closer to the Cambodian border, giving the Vietnamese practical combat experience in airmobile cavalry techniques.

The cavalry was traveling fast and light to actively interdict the sparse enemy foot, cart, and truck traffic. The advance was preceded by division ranger teams weaving and ambushing their way deep into uncharted territory to scout out the trail networks and bunker complexes for NVA/VC troops and to report rapidly on enemy movements. Behind the rangers the airmobile companies and platoons fanned out through the maze of forest trails, being resupplied twice a week and using temporary firebases closed out every few days. An umbrella of B52 bombers, helicopters, fighter-bombers, and aerial artillery remained overhead.

This dangerous business was being pushed steadily forward in northwestern War Zone C by Col. William V. Ochs, Jr.'s, 1st Brigade and attached 3d ARVN Airborne Brigade. His command consisted of two cavalry battalions, the 2d Battalions of the 7th and 8th Cavalry (later replaced by the 5th Battalion, 7th Cavalry), and the

5th, 9th, and 11th ARVN airborne battalions, all reinforced by the
1st Squadron of the 11th Armored Cavalry Regiment.[1]

Fire Support Base (FSB) Illingworth was among a dozen hasty
forts built by the brigade, but it was placed extremely close to Cambodia in the corner pocket of War Zone C, a rough patch of no-man's-
land that the troops rancorously called the "Dog's Head." Lt. Col.
Michael J. Conrad's 2d Battalion, 8th Cavalry, occupied FSB Illingworth on 18 March 1970. The command post, one line cavalry company, and the support company were placed alongside eleven howitzers and five combat vehicles. The rest of the battalion began scouring
the nearby jungle.

Company A performed the garrison duty until a close-range B40
rocket and machine gun attack cut into the fire support base perimeter
in the evening ten days later, causing thirty-five casualties and the
company's withdrawal to rest and absorb replacements. That same
night in the "Dog's Throat" sector four miles directly south, a massed
NVA attack nearly overran FSB Jay of Lt. Col. Robert Hannas's 2d
Battalion, 7th Cavalry. The garrison of FSB Illingworth were told to
brace for assault next, and Company C became the perimeter company. Since it mustered only thirty-nine troops, the battalion recon
platoon was added so that three officers and seventy-four enlisted men
manned the berm.[2]

FSB Illingworth was a typical late-war forward base on the Cambodian front. The oval-shaped fort contained twenty squad sandbag
bunkers, each containing six or nine men, roofed with steel culvert
sections and three sandbag layers, built into the four-foot-high earth
berm. Foxholes were dug between bunkers. The company placed a
dozen claymore antipersonnel mines in front of each bunker, but only
set two machine guns on the perimeter because of recent losses. Four
armored personnel carriers and one Sheridan light tank backed up the
line, but the Sheridan was inoperative except for its .50-caliber machine gun. This weapon was pulled off and dug in beside the single
quadruple .50-caliber antiaircraft gun on the southwest berm corner.

1. 1st Cav Div, *Operational Report*, dtd 15 May 70.
2. Exact organization of FSB Illingworth was Battalion CP and Companies
C and E of the 2d Bn, 8th Cav; Btry A, 1st Bn, 30th Arty; Btry A, 2d Bn,
32d Arty; Btry B, 1st Bn, 77th Arty; part of Tp A, 1st Sqdn, 11th Arm Cav
Regt.

One 8-inch (another was unserviceable), three 155mm medium, and six 105mm light howitzers were prepared with "killer junior" and other antiinfantry rounds.

No barbed wire was placed around FSB Illingworth because it was not intended as a permanent firebase, but rather one that could be dismantled in a day. Barbed wire was ineffective in slowing enemy sappers unless it was staked down and included tanglefoot, and the battalion did not have sufficient personnel to build elaborate wire barriers nor the airlift needed to backhaul it. For the same reasons, all relating to the temporary nature of the position and its hasty assembly, chemical gas projectors, fougasse flame barrels, and other weapons were not emplaced. The field first sergeant of Company C, Sfc. Charles H. Beauchamp, was distressed about the condition of Company A's previous fighting bunkers, which were not well constructed.

At precisely 2:18 A.M., 1 April 1970, the NVA/VC opened their attack on the fort with a blistering rocket and mortar barrage, knocking out the communications antennas. Groups of NVA troops charged out of the woodline toward the firebase parapets. A heavy pall of choking dust, raised by weapons firing on both sides, dropped visibility to nearly zero and fouled many weapons. The cavalry defenders were unable to see the North Vietnamese infantrymen until they were nearly on top of them. The enemy soldiers, clad in shorts and sandals and, sometimes, shirts, ran forward firing assault rifles and tossing satchel charges, as the cavalry riflemen returned fire with M16s until their weapons jammed (between 2 and 3 magazines) and then threw hand grenades. In seconds the NVA were up and over the berm in a welter of hand-to-hand combat. Sp4 Gordon A. Flessner stabbed his way through several enemy soldiers with a bowie knife, Sp4 Frederick L. Sporar and SSgt. James L. Taylor strangled NVA with their bare hands, and Sp4 Peter C. Lemon (later awarded the Medal of Honor) used his rifle as a club.

The mortar platoon leader, 1Lt. Michael H. Russell, could hear the screaming and firing, but it was impossible to see even muzzle flashes through the cloud of dust enveloping the battle area. He fired his mortars based on sound, but suddenly one mortar tube disintegrated as a satchel charge was heaved into it. Within minutes another crew started shouting and dived behind the blast wall as their mortar was detonated by a sapper. The ammunition stocks in both destroyed mortar pits began burning and exploding intermittently.

The reconnaissance platoon members under 1Lt. Gregory J. Peters made a fighting withdrawal to a secondary defensive line, where they stopped the North Vietnamese who had broken through. The howitzers were starting to fire, although one was destroyed by a direct hit, and the 8-inch ammunition dump was on fire. The situation seemed to improve as the berm was recaptured and cleared of the enemy. Overhead, AC47 "Spooky" aircraft, tactical fighters, and armed helicopters were gaining firepower ascendancy.

Shortly after 3:00 A.M. the fires started to worsen at the 8-inch ammunition point, which had not been dug in. The excessive amount of projectiles, cannisters, and powder bags were heaped together in ammunition carriers and on the ground.[3] The point's controlling artillerymen of the 2d Battalion, 32d Artillery (attached to the division), had witnessed their previous 175mm cannon ammunition dump explode with catastrophic results at FSB St. Barbara and shouted to warn the recon troops and other cavalry to get away.

Lieutenant Peters and his men elected to stay at their positions to prevent another breach of the line. Within ten minutes the entire ammunition dump detonated in a single fiery blast which completely demolished part of the fort, destroyed two full-tracked M548 ammo carriers, ripped apart one 8-inch howitzer, and leveled much of the berm line. Troops were hurled through the air (including Lieutenant Peters, who survived), and flying shrapnel sliced through men and material. All artillery stopped firing as the crews dropped, wounded or stunned by ruptured eardrums. However, the tremendous explosion stopped an enemy company—the NVA fled from the field.

The attack on FSB Illingworth repeated many circumstances at FSB Jay. In both cases the first enemy volley struck down the antenna array and a heavy curtain of dust made observation nearly impossible. Defensive deficiencies inherent in such hasty fortifications abounded. The defending garrison lost twenty-four killed and fifty-four wounded in the action, while seventy-four complete enemy bodies were counted, although doubtless many more were carried away by comrades retreating into Cambodia. In the final analysis it was probably the valor of a few cavalrymen that saved the tiny fort from certain destruction. As Sp4 Richard Whittier, a platoon radioman of Conrad's battalion,

3. 1st Cav Div, *Operational Report*, dtd 15 May 70, p. 49.

stated, "I had never seen so many enemy in the open. . . . It is my profound belief that Illingworth wasn't overrun because these people stayed, probably in the knowledge of certain death and knowing that the 8-inch ammo dump was about to go up. They held their positions."[4]

Prior to 1970 the North Vietnamese were able freely to occupy and use parts of two neutral countries, Laos and Cambodia, adjacent to South Vietnam for massive material and reinforcement routes and division staging bases. MACV was politically restricted from maneuvering against these enemy trail networks and base camps. The NVA/ VC developed increasingly sophisticated sanctuaries close to Vietnam, in which supplies could be stockpiled and armies refurbished with immunity from allied intervention.

The 1st Cavalry Division troopers were understandably frustrated by their inability to pursue North Vietnamese marauders into Cambodian territory, but permission would be forthcoming shortly. The communist military use of Cambodian sanctuaries had become so blatantly menacing by the spring of 1970 that military action against them was urgently required. President Richard M. Nixon wanted the safety of both the Saigon area and the remaining American troops guaranteed as U.S. troop withdrawals accelerated. Once the politically sensitive decision was made to conduct a limited spoiling offensive, the tropical Cambodian environment mandated that action be quickly taken during the brief April–May seasonal transition between the northeast and southwest monsoons.

Detailed MACV combined planning for a multidivision Cambodian attack was initiated on 27 March 1970, a day previous to the FSB Jay attack. Lt. Gen. Michael S. Davison, the commander of II Field Force Vietnam, received instructions from MACV to begin preparations for a drive into The Fishhook area of Cambodia on 24 April. Two days later Major General Roberts was given the task of planning and directing the major II Field Force Vietnam thrust into The Fishhook area to disrupt the suspected enemy headquarters for the Viet Cong Liberation Front and to eradicate his major depots.

The allied spring invasion of Cambodia would be the most dramatic and significant utilization of the division during 1970 and placed

4. 14th MHD, *Combat After Action Interview Report*, dtd 3 Jan 71, p. 15.

a capstone on its service in the Second Indochina War. At this stage of the conflict, the 1st Cavalry Division (Airmobile) was the unquestioned premier attack division of the allied command, and it would spearhead the main Cambodian offensive. The division personnel prepared for revenge after years of command-imposed restraint from challenging the North Vietnamese in foreign base territory.

The 1st Cavalry Division's Cambodian operations exemplified the essence of another historically vital cavalry function: mobile cavalry exploitation. The 1st Cavalry Division was selected as the main exploitation force of the entire Cambodian operation. Military exploitation is a role historically undertaken by cavalry to follow up success in the attack. Cavalry formations exercising this mode of attack rely on two overriding considerations: speed and violence. The attackers bypass pockets of resistance to concentrate on the destruction of the more vulnerable headquarters, combat support, and service support units. They disrupt the enemy's command and control structure and his flow of fuel, ammunition, repair parts, food, and other necessities. This weakens or destroys the enemy defenses and makes it possible for smaller (or less proficient, as was the ARVN) forces to overpower a larger enemy.

The main assault on The Fishhook was coded TOAN THANG (ROCKCRUSHER) 43. The Cambodian Fishhook was a raised hilly area of rugged jungle and swamps which melted into the flat, wet riceland plain to either side. As the rolling terrain faded both east and west into the lowland, the dense patches of jungle became intermixed with light, leafy forests and grassy fields, and finally with upland rice and rubber plantations. Allied intelligence believed that the Communist Supreme Command for the liberation of South Vietnam (COSVN) lurked somewhere in the jungled morass of The Fishhook, defended by the *7th NVA Division*, recently withdrawn from War Zone C, and supported by various artillery and service regiments. Additionally, the *5th VC Division*'s right flank was tied in to the eastern flank of The Fishhook region.

Brig. Gen. Robert M. Shoemaker, the brilliant airmobile tactician and veteran of the 11th Air Assault Division, was given command and control over The Fishhook drive. He arrived as Chief of Staff of the 1st Cavalry Division on 21 April 1969, but the high point of his tenure came on 12 August 1969, when the enemy launched an attack

against Binh Long Province with supporting drives in two other provinces.

On that day Assistant Division Commander-A (Operations), Brigadier General Meszar, was in the Philippines on leave, and division commander Major General Roberts became ill in the afternoon and was medically evacuated to the 3d Field Hospital. This left Assistant Division Commander-B, Brig. Gen. George W. Casey, in technical command, but he had just arrived and relied on Colonel Shoemaker as his right-hand man. Together they directed the 1st Cavalry Division to victory in the repulse and destruction of NVA/VC forces in the August battle for Binh Long Province. Colonel Shoemaker was quickly nominated for star rank in September and elevated to Assistant Division Commander-B (Logistics) of the 1st Cavalry Division on 22 November 1969, being promoted to brigadier general on 1 December 1969.

As General Roberts planned and coordinated the operation, insuring that his officers and their Vietnamese counterparts developed the final plans properly, Task Force Shoemaker began to take shape. Col. Robert C. Kingston's 3d Brigade (1st and 2d Battalions, 7th Cavalry, and 2d Battalion, 5th Cavalry) and the reinforced 3d ARVN Airborne Brigade formed the nucleus of the task force, reinforced by a tank (2d Bn, 34th Armor) and mechanized battalion (2d Bn, 47th Infantry) and the entire 11th Armored Cavalry Regiment under cavalry expert Col. Donn A. Starry.

Task Force Shoemaker's concept of attack in Operation TOAN THANG 43 was to swing directly west into The Fishhook by airmobile assault, establishing three deep penetration airheads as anvils for three hammering columns of armored cavalry and tank battalions to smash against from the south, trapping COSVN between them. One mechanized battalion would seal off the far western approaches to The Fishhook, while the aerial reconnaissance 1st Squadron, 9th Cavalry, intercepted any threat behind the cavalry strike force from the far north.

The 1st Cavalry Division was initially informed that it must be prepared to launch the offensive within seventy-two hours of notification. On 28 April this lead time was shortened to forty-eight hours after permission was received to extend the planning down to brigade level. On 30 April, the original date for initiation of operations, Task

Force Shoemaker was established at Quan Loi as the control head-quarters for the first U.S. cross-border operation. However, President Nixon delayed the attack twenty-four hours, so that U.S. forces actually crossed the border on 1 May 1970.

The allied Cambodian invasion commenced in the predawn darkness, as 6 heavy B52 strategic bomber serials pummeled Cambodia's thick jungle in front of the cavalry's lines. At 6:00 A.M., as the last high-level bombs were exploding through the layers of rain forest, a massive preparatory artillery bombardment thundered across the border. For the next six hours, the 94 long-range cannon and heavy howitzers of II Field Force Vietnam Artillery, placed in direct support of Task Force Shoemaker, boomed incessantly and fired 2,436 shells into preselected targets. Fighter-bombers roared through the morning sky to deliver 48 tactical airstrikes. On the invasion day a total of 5,460 II FFV artillery rounds, 36 strategic B52 bombing strikes, and 185 tactical airstrikes supported the attack.[5]

The South Vietnamese airborne battalions helicoptered into two landing zones, LZ East and LZ Center, which were carved out of thick jungle by detonating Air Force Commando Vault fifteen thousand-pound bombs seven feet off the ground. The scout helicopters of Lt. Col. Clark A. Burnett's 1st Squadron, 9th Cavalry, dashed above the rolling jungle and through drifting plumes of smoke to strafe surprised NVA truck drivers and soldiers unexpectedly caught in the cyclone of the airmobile advance. The Vietnamese 5th Airborne Battalion helicoptered into LZ Center and immediately engaged a North Vietnamese battalion. The twenty-two supporting Cobra gunships furiously raked the NVA lines with rocket volleys and minigun fire, shattering the enemy ranks and sending them fleeing from the aerial onslaught.

Complete tactical surprise was achieved as the stunned NVA/VC elements milled in confusion, then scattered in full retreat, pursued by division armed helicopters and observation craft. More cavalry battalions joined the attack as the cavalry penetration deepened. The Cambodian offensive was politically limited to a depth of twenty miles,

---

5. Maj. Gen. David E. Ott, *Vietnam Studies: Field Artillery* (Washington, D.C.: Dept. of the Army, 1975), p. 212.

but numerous enemy depots and astonishing quantities of weapons, ammunition, vehicles, and foodstuffs were discovered within this zone during the first five days of the operation. At that point in the drive, with more than six hundred enemy soldiers eliminated and the discovery of several large storage and training areas, Task Force Shoemaker was dissolved.

On 5 May 1970 the 1st Cavalry Division headquarters assumed direct control of the Cambodian drive, now consisting of thirteen allied maneuver battalions. The division's 1st and 3d Brigades and 1st ARVN Airborne Brigade drove deeper into the NVA/VC base areas as the 11th Armored Cavalry Regiment sped north to seize Snoul in a series of sharp skirmishes. Col. Carter W. Clarke, Jr.'s, 2d Brigade initiated the division's second cross-border drive, TOAN THANG 45, by air assaulting two battalions into Cambodia northeast of Bu Dop on 6 May. At the outset resistance was light and scattered. An early evening contact on 7 May led to the discovery of a very large ammunition and weapons storage area the next day by Lt. Col. Francis A. Ianni's 2d Battalion, 12th Cavalry. The area was nicknamed "Rock Island East," after a major U.S. arsenal located at Rock Island, Illinois. Supporting engineers opened a road into the massive depot to haul out the vast amount of seized material. Removing the contents of the Rock Island East complex required nine days.

The largest enemy depot was discovered by Troop B of the 1st Squadron, 9th Cavalry, on 4 May 1970. The scoutships detected several field positions and structures in dense jungle, complete with paths matted with bamboo between complexes. The next day elements of Lt. Col. James L. Anderson's 1st Battalion, 5th Cavalry, airmobiled into the area and found 182 large storage bunkers, 18 mess halls, and a training area complete with an animal farm. One of the troopers remarked that the enemy storage complex looked like a small city. The depot, which supported the *7th NVA Division* with provisions and supplies, was promptly nicknamed "The City." Supporting engineers constructed a connecting road into Vietnam to facilitate overland evacuation of the large quantities of new weapons, quartermaster supplies, material, and rice.

Beginning on 6 May 1970, the 1st Cavalry Division commenced its exploitation of the NVA/VC warehouse areas and supply marshaling areas. Air cavalry elements were employed against small vehicle convoys and enemy troop movements, while the cavalrymen continued removing materials from the various caches and logistical complexes. On 11 May 1970 the 5th Battalion of the 7th Cavalry vacated FSB Brown in the TOAN THANG 45 sector, and the attached 5th Battalion of the 12th Infantry moved into the fort. The next night FSB Brown was attacked by a large enemy force, marking one of the first NVA counterattacks.

With the Cambodian invasion well underway, Maj. Gen. George W. Casey took command of the 1st Cavalry Division on 12 May 1970. A former brigade commander and chief of staff of the division from 1966 to 1968, Casey possessed experience as an airmobile wartime leader and comprehended clearly both the unique missions and capabilities of the airmobile division. He was born 9 March 1922 in Maine and graduated from West Point in 1945, served as a paratrooper officer with the 11th Airborne Division until 1948, and earned the Silver Star in heavy combat with the 7th Infantry Division in 1952 during the Korean War.

The 1st Cavalry Division continued to uncover more weapons and food storage areas, but by 29 May every battalion was reporting contact with the enemy. The cache discoveries in the meantime had grown in number faster than the committed units could evacuate or destroy their contents. On 5 June 1970 Major General Casey air assaulted his last remaining maneuver battalion into Cambodia. Aerial cavalry struck lucrative personnel and material targets throughout this period, but weather conditions were rapidly worsening. On 20 June the division started a phased withdrawal from Cambodia as fog and rain increased. B52 bombing runs were used to hinder enemy forces from interfering with the cavalry withdrawal and to destroy the multitude of supply sites found but not fully searched. The last cavalry elements withdrew from Cambodia on 29 June 1970.[6]

The pace of the Cambodian offensive and exploitation can be best judged by following one battalion into Cambodia. The 5th Battalion of the 7th Cavalry under Lt. Col. Maurice O. Edmonds was flown to Bu Dop on 5 May 1970, and the next morning Company B spearheaded the battalion air assault into Cambodia. Contact remained light as the advancing cavalrymen fired on small teams of North Vietnamese evading the area. An air assault by Company A on 7 May, to

6. 1st Cav Div, *1st Cav Div, Operational Report*, dtd 14 Aug 70.

establish Fire Support Base Neal, was challenged by scattered anti-aircraft fire, but the enemy quickly dispersed. The cavalrymen began finding increasing amounts of rice and weapons in their sweeps around FSB Neal. Within ten days combat started to increase as the enemy recovered and tried to defend his larger cache sites. Two days later Company A fought for six hours to advance up one hill and found a hospital complex on the summit.

Late in the afternoon of 23 May, Company B fought past stubborn rearguard resistance on a small hill to find rows of ammunition bunkers. The rising ground was called "Shakey's Hill," in honor of the first man killed on the hill, Pfc. Chris Keffalos of Albuquerque, New Mexico, who was nicknamed "Shakey." Company D was inserted to help empty the multitude of enemy munitions bunkers and tunnels full of mortar rounds, B40 and B41 rockets, recoilless rifle shells, and antiaircraft ammunition. The North Vietnamese tried to salvage part of the stockpile, but avoided further combat. On the morning of 30 May, a platoon from Company D, moving forward to clear a bunker, was engaged by enemy fire. Capt. Glenn Colvin moved the platoon on line and swept into the attack, but the enemy force fled, leaving behind a pistol belt, a small bag of rice, and two Chinese grenades. The month ended as Company C found a motor pool containing ten jeeps, twelve bicycles, and a maintenance shop.

In June ambush activity escalated throughout the battalion sector as Company D continued the back-breaking chore of emptying out the bunkers on Shakey's Hill. They were forced laboriously to haul the boxes of munitions from the ammunition point back uphill, but there was little complaint, as the troops explained. "Better to haul it out of the bunkers and up the damn hill than to have Charlie shoot it at us!" The troops began calling the depot simply "Charlie's Rod and Gun Club."

Their work was not only hard, but it was also extremely dangerous. Cache sites were normally booby-trapped, and the NVA implanted mechanical ambush devices in several of the bunkers at Shakey's Hill. One bunker was rigged with a Chinese grenade pull-string tied to a stack of mortar boxes, with the grenade itself buried deep in flamethrower fuel thickener. Fortunately for the cavalrymen, the moisture had rotted the string, and it simply broke two inches above the grenade when a trooper inadvertently tripped it. In another bunker a blasting cap was set to detonate a mortar round and explode the entire structure, but the trap was detected and disarmed. On 2 June Company D turned over the task of completing the depot clearance to another battalion.

The monsoon rains began in earnest the following day, and daily thunderstorms intensified. The North Vietnamese were also reorganizing, and combat became more frequent. On 7 June FSB Neal started receiving ground probes. Two bodies of 199th Infantrymen reported earlier as missing in action were found by Company C and carried to the 5th Battalion of the 12th Infantry at FSB Myron. In the meantime Company D suffered a small ambush by four enemy soldiers armed with B40 rockets and machine guns while moving into their night defensive positions. Enemy hit-and-run raids increased, and American casualties started to escalate. For example, a single B40 rocket round exploded inside Company B's perimeter on 10 June, wounding three cavalrymen. The company engaged the suspected enemy firing position with defensive fires, artillery, and rocket-firing helicopters, but reported "negative enemy assessment."

The next day Company A reached Hill 315 and found a sixty-ton rice cache. The battalion supply helicopter crashed on the afternoon of 13 June, wounding the pilot. The crew was extracted, but the helicopter was stripped and burned as a total loss by the cavalrymen before they left the area. The battalion continued to probe the general area around FSB Neal, freely giving captured rice to Cambodian natives who approached them riding elephants. After continued light skirmishing and discovery of other scattered caches, the battalion prepared to leave Cambodia. Several more members were seriously wounded by an ammunition supply point fire at FSB Barry (when a trip flare ignited in a box of mixed ammunition), and another battalion supply helicopter crashed. Led by Company B, Lieutenant Colonel Edmonds's battalion helicoptered out of Cambodia at noon on 29 June for a three-day rest at Bien Hoa, outside Saigon.[7]

The Cambodian invasion became the supreme test of the cavalry division's ability to maintain fast-paced communication, but the operation outstripped its signal capacity. For example, Task Force Shoemaker in its jump-off position at Quan Loi was supported by elements of the single division tactical signal battalion. Communications was

7. Hq 1st Bn 5th Cav, *Unit History*, 1970.

barely adequate to support the division equivalent of one cavalry brigade, one Vietnamese airborne brigade, and the armored cavalry regiment. On the final day preparatory to the attack, this force expanded with the addition of a tank battalion and a mechanized battalion, another infantry battalion (5th Battalion, 12th Infantry, from the 199th Infantry Brigade), and the division's 2d Brigade.

Signal difficulties quickly developed as the offensive began, especially among the frequency modulated (FM) radios which were the primary means of communication. The scope and diversity of the offensive overwhelmed FM radio communications, as radio interference, channel duplication, and congested airwaves swamped signal efforts. At least one hundred FM radio nets existed within the task force headquarters, and one signal tower belonging to the 3d Brigade contained more than fifty antennas. The desire for secrecy greatly hampered communication exchange between rapidly moving elements, which tightly guarded their signal operating instructions, cipher keylists, code material, and channel frequencies.

By the fifth day of the Cambodian incursion, when the task force increased to the equivalent of two divisions and reverted to direct 1st Cavalry Division control, communications was a signal nightmare. The overworked divisional 13th Signal Battalion was operating well beyond its intended capacity, and operations were simply "hand to mouth" on an emergency basis. Near-impossible feats of communications were performed by innovative cavalry communications specialists. However, the division suffered from an absence of required signal resources because MACV apparently underestimated communication levels and requirements for such a large maneuver.

Throughout this period enemy action aggravated the adverse communications situation. For example, on 14 June 1970 the North Vietnamese hit Fire Support Base David from three directions, destroying critical forward signal transmissions equipment and severely wounding the brigade signal officer and dozens of other signalmen. Acting Sergeant Goldsworthy, who was in charge of the variable high frequency (VHF) equipment, valiantly maintained communications throughout the battle and earned the Silver Star for gallantry in action.[8]

8. Lt. Gen. Charles R. Meyer, *Vietnam Studies: Division-Level Communications* (Washington, D.C.: Dept. of the Army, 1982), pp. 55–59.

Despite such problems, the Cambodian invasion was an overwhelming material success. While COSVN escaped destruction, the NVA base depots suffered heavy damage and stock depletion. The strategic cavalry exploitation in Cambodia stymied enemy offensive capability and allowed South Vietnam to enjoy a prolonged respite from NVA/VC Cambodian-launched activity into III CTZ for several years afterward. The overall invasion success was verified by the vast quantities of foodstuffs and weapons captured by the allied forces. The NVA/ VC lost enough rice to feed more than twenty-five thousand soldiers for one year, or nearly thirty-eight thousand soldiers on reduced rations for a year. Enough individual weapons were taken to equip fifty-five full-strength Viet Cong infantry battalions, and enough machine guns and other crew-served weapons were seized to outfit thirty-three full-strength Viet Cong infantry battalions.[9]

Comparative statistics show that the 1st Cavalry Division (Airmobile) was responsible for the bulk of exploitive damage inflicted on the NVA/VC in Cambodia. During Operation TOAN THANG 43 (the largest operation involving U.S. forces), the 1st Cavalry Division killed 1,336 enemy, captured 3,009 individual weapons, and took 167 vehicles, compared to 664 enemy dead, 382 individual weapons, and 54 vehicles credited to the 25th Infantry Division. The differences in ammunition stocks is even more revealing. The 1st Cavalry Division seized 1,779,720 rounds of 7.62mm machine gun ammunition and 2,630 grenades, compared to 17,316 MG rounds and 1,040 grenades taken by the 25th Infantry Division, out of a total of 2,211,836 rounds and 4,230 grenades captured by the allies (the ARVN found 414,800 rounds and 560 grenades).[10]

The Cambodian invasion offers a convenient set-piece battle, rare in Vietnam, for mathematically assessing whether the 1st Cavalry Division was employing "unbridled firepower" in the Second Indochina War. The tremendous amount of ordnance utilized to support the division's Cambodian offensive is displayed by category in Table A. During this time the 1st Cavalry Division claimed a total of 2,574

9. MACV, *Command History*, 1970, Volume I, p. C-106.
10. Ibid., pp. C-73, C-74.

## TABLE A

1st Cavalry Division Ammunition Expenditures, Cambodian Offensive
1 May to 30 June 1970[1]

| | |
|---|---|
| Rifle and machine gun ammunition (M16 and M60) | 6,167,645 rounds |
| Mortar ammunition (81mm) | 119,127 rounds |
| Light artillery ammunition (105mm) | 241,294 rounds |
| Medium artillery ammunition (155mm) | 65,028 rounds |
| Aerial rocket artillery ammunition (2.75-inch) | 92,016 rounds |
| C-4 explosive demolition compound | 75,418 pounds |
| Detonation cord | 152,200 feet |
| TNT explosive compound | 1,736 pounds |

1. 1st Cav Div, *Combat After Action Report for the Cambodian Campaign*, Annex B-IV, Logistical Operations in Support of Operations in Cambodia (d) Class V Expenditures, p. B-13.

enemy personnel killed inside Cambodia. Additionally, 31 enemy soldiers were taken prisoner and 18 voluntarily surrendered (Hoi Chanh).[11] The division used an average of 2,396 bullets and 201 shells or rockets for every enemy soldier known to be killed, which reflected the prodigious expenditures of ammunition in Vietnam, even by elite formations.

The 1st Cavalry Division's exploitation mission exacted the highest price of any U.S. formation involved in the Cambodian operations. The division suffered 122 killed in action, 964 wounded, 10 taken prisoner, and 6 missing in action in the territory of Cambodia. This represented nearly half of all U.S. casualties incurred in Cambodia (284 KIA, 2,339 WIA, 29 POW, 13 MIA), despite the fact that nearly three other division equivalents participated: 25th Infantry Division, 3d Brigade of the 9th Infantry Division, 199th Infantry Brigade, 11th Armored Cavalry Regiment, 12th Aviation Group, II Field Force Vietnam Artillery, and various other II Field Force Vietnam units.[12]

11. 1st Cav Div, *Combat After Action Report for Cambodian Campaign*, dtd 15 Feb 71, p. 63-A.
12. MACV, *Command History*, 1970, Volume I, p. C-51.

The division casualty losses during the May–June 1970 period were actually higher, since personnel (such as Major General Casey) were killed inside Vietnam on Cambodia-related missions and there was a considerable degree of incomplete casualty reporting. In fact, this serious problem was addressed in the division operational report of this period and was found to stem from subordinate unit noncompliance with follow-up paperwork after casualties were sustained, as well as missing casualty reports from lack of communication. Medical evacuation helicopters from other aviation units simply whisked patients to the nearest field station or hospital, and the division relied on input from internal units to keep posted.

Disregarding the unknown quantity of missing data, the total division losses for May and June were reported as 157 killed in action, 9 missing, and 1,124 wounded troopers. In addition, according to personnel reports for May and June, the division sustained 32 deaths and 247 injuries from noncombat causes. The division surgeon, again acknowledging incomplete information, reported 1,530 cases of disease (1,167 from malaria or fevers of unknown origin). The increase in serious disease rates was traced to increased exposure because of "the higher number of troops in the field" and their "operations in the hyperendemic malaria areas which were recently NVA sanctuaries,"[13] and seasonal increases associated with the monsoon shift.

Given the certainty that the lightly wounded (about 200 according to the 15th Medical Battalion records) and many ill patients returned to their units, the division still suffered high personnel losses during two months' time. Of course, none of these loss statistics counts the thousands of personnel departing the division on normal end-of-tour rotation or those temporarily absent on R&R (Rest and Recreation). In the latter category alone, 1,937 troops were absent in May and another 1,877 during June, taking them to Hawaii, Sydney, Hong Kong, Bangkok, Toyko, Taipei, and Manila. Perhaps the most telling indicators of actual manpower drain are the replacement reports, which show that the division had to absorb 1,762 replacements in May, 1,955 in June, and 2,101 in July—a total of 5,818 new personnel in one-quarter of a year.[14]

---

13. 1st Cav Div, *Operational Report*, dtd 14 Aug 70, p. 93.
14. Ibid., Tab I (G1 Activities), Tab M (Surgeon Activities).

Another salient aspect of the personnel situation, common to all Army divisions serving in Vietnam, was the tremendous size of the division rear echelon support base compared to line fighting strength. In this regard the 1st Cavalry Division was no exception. A graphic illustration of who was actually bearing the burden of field service and risk exposure is presented by the division's personnel daily summary for the evening of the Cambodian invasion on 1 May 1970 (Table B). On that date both the division assigned strength and numbers deployed in frontline capacity were maximized, because of its offensive stance as well as close command scrutiny by II FFV. On 1 May 1970, the critical opening day of the only major U.S. cross-border attack in the Second Indochina War, the spearhead 1st Cavalry Division was assigned 20,211 personnel, but only 7,822 troops were engaged in firebases and forward combat locations both in Vietnam and Cambodia (as defined by the division itself, and separately categorized on the division report form).

This personnel situation report shows the large overhead which sapped division "foxhole strength" throughout the war. The 1st Cavalry Division, with an assigned level of 20,211, was close to its authorized strength of 20,154,[15] confirming that the division was in fact fielding as many troops as possible for the opening of the Cambodian attack. However, as Table B demonstrates, only a third of this number was actually somewhere close to combat, and nearly 80 percent of this one-third slice is in the cavalry maneuver (infantry) battalions. In fact, the only unit totally committed to the frontline was the division ranger company! Thus, whatever losses occurred in the 1st Cavalry Division must have come out of the thin crust of riflemen or artillerymen actually doing the fighting, with some modification for aviators discussed below.

Table B does not reflect aviation personnel exposed to combat, since helicopters are staged out of helipads, LZs, or airstrips and only spent transitory time over the combat area before returning. However, the division possessed a total of 426 helicopters and 8 fixed-wing aircraft on 1 May 1970,[16] and if we multiply this by three for the average crew of each (assuming that all aircraft are flying), then we can safely estimate that perhaps 1,302 more personnel were routinely

15. Ibid., Tab I-1.
16. 1st Cav Div, *Combat After Action Report*, dtd 6 Jul 70, Annex L-1.

exposed to frontline service on a daily basis. Obviously, their exposure would be of shorter duration than ground troops. The "Blue" riflemen of the 9th Cavalry reconnaissance squadron (about 90 men) should also be added, as these reaction troops on standby were often in the thick of combat. Even counting these additional estimates, the imbalance between rear and frontline allocation remains striking.

The division's Cambodian drive represented the only period when the formation mustered as many troops as possible for a major offensive involving a defined frontline on a conventional axis of advance. This time frame provides one of the few opportunities to compare objectively the ratio between division frontline and support manpower in the Vietnam War. The frontline ratio did not vary appreciably throughout the length of the campaign, but casualties were making inroads on frontline numbers by June, despite constant infusion of replacements. A close scrutiny of daily personnel summaries shows the following division distribution between total assigned strength/personnel at firebases and in forward combat locations: 20,211/ 7,822 (1 May 1970); 20,270/7,386 (15 May 1970); 20,003/6,813 (1 Jun 1970); 19,638/6,952 (15 Jun 1970); 19,417/6,674 (28 Jun 1970). In the final analysis the airmobile riflemen were the most endangered troopers who shouldered the crushing weight of most division losses.

No one realized their sacrifice more than division commander Maj. Gen. George W. Casey, who decided to fly across country into Cam Ranh Bay to visit the wounded Skytroopers in the coastal hospital on the morning of 7 July 1970. The general was proud of these men and the jobs they had done during the Cambodian campaign. Extremely heavy monsoon weather precluded normal flight operations, and his staff urged him to express his written congratulations already prepared for the division. However, Casey knew that some of the most seriously wounded were either dying or were already scheduled for medical evacuation to the United States and Japan. He insisted on giving them a personal report on their success.

The only way to reach Cam Ranh Bay from III CTZ in the monsoon front was by flying on instruments, using the notoriously unreliable DECCA low-level navigation system. DECCA was installed and maintained by the Army, but rarely used because of nonacceptance by the Air Force. Casey accepted the risk. Flying over the storm-laden, rugged mountains of the central highlands, his helicopter entered a thick cloud bank and disappeared. Search operations began

**TABLE B**

1st Cavalry Division Personnel Strengths, 1 May 1970 (Cambodian Incursion)[1]

| Division Organization | Assigned | | | At Firebases and in Forward Combat Locations | | |
|---|---|---|---|---|---|---|
| | Officer | Warrant | Enlisted | Officer | Warrant | Enlisted |
| A. Maneuver Battalions | | | | | | |
| 1st Bn, 5th Cavalry | 41 | 2 | 798 | 29 | 0 | 625 |
| 2d Bn, 5th Cavalry | 44 | 2 | 823 | 34 | 0 | 631 |
| 1st Bn, 7th Cavalry | 39 | 2 | 796 | 26 | 0 | 608 |
| 2d Bn, 7th Cavalry | 39 | 2 | 818 | 26 | 0 | 591 |
| 5th Bn, 7th Cavalry | 42 | 3 | 833 | 30 | 0 | 609 |
| 1st Bn, 8th Cavalry | 39 | 2 | 802 | 36 | 2 | 689 |
| 2d Bn, 8th Cavalry | 42 | 2 | 838 | 36 | 2 | 681 |
| 1st Bn, 12th Cavalry | 40 | 2 | 826 | 36 | 2 | 713 |
| 2d Bn, 12th Cavalry | 42 | 2 | 831 | 38 | 2 | 740 |
| Total in Maneuver Battalions | 368 | 19 | 7,365 | 291 | 8 | 5,887 |

## TABLE B
### (continued)

**B. Division Support**

| | | | | | | |
|---|---|---|---|---|---|---|
| 1st Sqdn, 9th Cavalry (Air) | 63 | 95 | 890 | 3 | 0 | 104 |
| 11th Aviation Group | 214 | 322 | 2,261 | 0 | 0 | 74 |
| Division Headquarters | 109 | 5 | 364 | 0 | 0 | 0 |
| 1st Brigade Headquarters | 27 | 18 | 230 | 0 | 0 | 0 |
| 2d Brigade Headquarters | 40 | 18 | 209 | 0 | 0 | 0 |
| 3d Brigade Headquarters | 34 | 15 | 243 | 0 | 0 | 0 |
| Division Artillery | 273 | 86 | 2,273 | 103 | 1 | 1,002 |
| Support Command | 137 | 51 | 1,707 | 0 | 0 | 0 |
| 8th Engineer Battalion | 38 | 2 | 627 | 11 | 0 | 218 |
| 13th Signal Battalion | 17 | 4 | 386 | 0 | 0 | 16 |
| Company H, 75th Infantry[2] | 4 | 0 | 98 | 4 | 0 | 98 |
| 15th Administration Company | 82 | 9 | 688 | 0 | 0 | 0 |
| 545th Military Police Company | 8 | 2 | 201 | 0 | 0 | 0 |
| Miscellaneous Assigned Units | 13 | 9 | 127 | 0 | 0 | 0 |
| Division Rear | 33 | 1 | 426 | 0 | 0 | 2 |
| Total in Division Support | 1,092 | 637 | 10,730 | 121 | 1 | 1,514 |
| Totals for Division | 1,460 | 656 | 18,095 | 412 | 9 | 7,401 |

1. 1st Cavalry Division Personnel Daily Summary for the 24-Hour Period Ending 011800 May 70, Cav Form 68 Revised.
2. Ranger reconnaissance company.

immediately to comb the cloud-wrapped peaks and triple-canopied jungles. In the late afternoon of 9 July 1970, the wreckage of the general's command helicopter was found. Maj. Gen. George W. Casey and all those aboard had been killed instantly in the crash.

George W. Casey's final testament happened to be the congratulatory letter he drafted on the evening of his departure, 6 July 1970, addressed "To the SKYTROOPERS of the 1st Air Cavalry Division" about their accomplishments in Cambodia. After explaining that the operations exceeded all expectations, citing results and examples of team spirit, he closed by humbly honoring his men and expressing a special tribute to them:

> This is your achievement. This is yet another demonstration that you of the 1st Air Cavalry Division deserve—and have earned again—the accolade of the FIRST TEAM. It is my honor to have served alongside you during this crucial and historic period. Congratulations and best wishes to each of you![17]

Both Major General Casey and Major General Roberts, who planned the operation and led the division during the first two weeks of the cross-border invasion, were among those rare officers who are truly qualified to lead airmobile cavalry divisions. They possessed a combination of the brilliance and professionalism that wins battles, coupled with the deep love and respect for the division troopers who won their devotion. Their leadership ability insured that the 1st Cavalry Division excelled in meeting one of its most important challenges in airmobile development: aerial cavalry exploitation during a strategic offensive.

17. Hq 1st Cav Div AVDACG, Subj: The FIRST TEAM in Cambodia, dtd 6 Jul 70.

# CHAPTER 10

# The First Team

*Division Structure in Vietnam*

In the Vietnam-era United States Army, a division represented the basic combat instrument capable of conducting large-scale independent missions with its own resources and which contained all necessary basic fighting and support components organically assigned. The 1st Cavalry Division (Airmobile) was designed to concentrate firepower and shock action on the battlefield while maintaining a high degree of responsive vertical mobility to maneuver rapidly over large areas. Theoretically "lean and light," wartime demands to sustain airmobile striking power over considerable distances transformed the organization into one similar to infantry divisions, with the addition of an aviation group.

The 1st Cavalry Division was composed of eight (later nine) cavalry ground maneuver battalions of infantry, five battalions of artillery, three assault helicopter battalions, four support-type battalions, one aerial reconnaissance squadron, one engineer battalion, one signal battalion, and a host of independent specialized companies and detachments. All division elements were usually attached to one of six principal intermediary headquarters which the division commander used to control his subordinate units: the 1st, 2d, and 3d Brigades, Division Artillery ("Divarty"); Division Support Command ("Discom"); and the 11th Aviation Group. The division commander and his immediate staff sometimes retained direct control over certain units.

The 1st Cavalry Division was commanded by a major general with an average of 25 years' regular Army service. His immediate retinue included two assistant division commanders (A and B), brigadier generals who respectively directed operations and logistics/

aviation. The division headquarters provided the command, staff planning, and supervision needed to administer and direct the division and all its functions. Division headquarters gradually increased in size during the war until it contained more than five hundred men, including the attached 14th Military History Detachment. The chief of staff, a colonel, presided over the division general staff and division special staff. The general staff, as in other divisions, included the personnel, intelligence, operations/training, logistics, and civil affairs/psychological operations sections serialized as G1, G2, G3, G4, and G5, respectively. The special staff included the surgeon, inspector general, staff judge advocate, chaplain, adjutant general, information office, finance, chemical, provost marshal, and headquarters commandant sections. Each G-section was headed by an assistant chief of staff, a lieutenant colonel, who coordinated certain special staff sections. For instance, sections such as finance, chaplain, inspector general, judge advocate, provost marshal, and the information office were usually under the assistant chief of staff, G1.

The 1st, 2d, and 3d Brigades were the primary subordinate headquarters which normally controlled the nine maneuver cavalry battalions, and thus made up the tactical heart of the division. Commanded by colonels, these brigades flexibly attached cavalry battalions and other units as needed, depending on the task at hand and battlefield situation. Like a miniature division, the brigade contained a headquarters and headquarters company which contained special staffs, sequenced like division's but prefixed by "S" instead of "G." S-sections were often supplemented by subordinated units. For example, the commander of an attached engineer company would also become the brigade engineer. Brigade headquarters were ever-expanding, finally averaging 250 to 300 personnel.

The brigade usually contained three cavalry battalions and one of the division's three light artillery battalions in direct support. This match in turn enabled each cavalry battalion to have one firing battery in direct support. Each brigade also received a "slice" of the total combat support division "pie." In this fashion the engineer and medical battalions lent one company to each brigade, while Division Support Command provided forward supply platoons and other components.

Although brigades freely exchanged cavalry battalions among them, traditional associations developed over the course of the war. Thus, the 1st Brigade usually contained the 1st and 2d Battalions of the "Jumping Mustangs" 8th Cavalry and the 1st Battalion of the "Chargers" 12th Cavalry. The 2d Brigade normally contained the 1st and 2d Battalions of the "Black Knights" 5th Cavalry and the 2d Battalion of the 12th Cavalry. The 3d Brigade contained the 1st, 2d, and later 5th Battalions of the "Garry Owen" 7th Cavalry (which joined the division 20 August 1966 as its ninth maneuver battalion).

The nine maneuver cavalry battalions, organized as infantry, formed the division's fighting edge. These battalions were composed of the hardened infantrymen—riflemen, machine gunners, grenadiers, and mortarmen—who carried the main burden of the war. The battalions were sent to Vietnam as heliborne components with less manpower than infantry battalions in other divisions. In August 1967 DA initiated a phased program of standardization between all line battalions in the war zone, which brought cavalry battalion organization in line with other infantry battalions serving in Vietnam. The 767-man cavalry battalions were boosted to 920-man levels, giving each battalion a headquarters and headquarters company, four rifle companies, and a combat support company.[1]

As in all military formations, manpower tended to dwindle where the fighting was thickest, and battalions were hard-pressed to keep up to strength. Speaking at a MACV conference in Nha Trang on 2 April 1966, Major General Norton bluntly stated, "We haven't been doing well in keeping our strength in platoon leaders, key noncommissioned officers, and riflemen. Companies of 130 men and battalions of 550 men are common, and this strength is too low."[2]

The ordinary squad rifleman was the backbone of the division. He was armed with the lightweight M16, a highly effective jungle fighting weapon capable of spewing out rounds with such velocity that even a shoulder hit could cause fatal heartbeat reversal. Universally referred to as "grunts," riflemen might be airlifted onto the battlefield, but then "humped" through dense jungle, jagged mountains, broken ricefields, or brackish swamps. Commonly dressed in sweat-soaked rip-stop tropical fatiques, with camouflaged helmet covers colorfully inked over with slogans and short calendars, these dismounted

1. Shelby L. Stanton, *Vietnam Order of Battle* (Millwood, N.Y.: Kraus Reprints, 1986), Chapter 3.
2. MACV, *Command History*, 1967, Volume I, pp. 141–42.

cavalrymen displayed the tactical fire and movement expertise which gave the division a near-perfect record of battlefield success.

The riflemen often carried sixty-five pounds of equipment, munitions, and weaponry. These were stuffed into packs, rucksacks, and pouches suspended from front and back straps, wrapped around waists, and passed over shoulders. An individual's combat load consisted of several days' rations, five to six quarts of water in plastic bladders and canteens, two claymore mines, extra mortar rounds, two or three bandoliers of bullets, an entrenching tool, and a machete. Little room remained for personal items, and even a pair of spare socks found interim utility full of C-ration tins suspended from aluminum ruck frames.

Machine gunners carried the M60 "pig" slung from the shoulder by bunji straps, with one starter belt of 7.62mm ammunition locked in the weapon—ready to spit out that most vital burst of either opening or return fire. Other men in the company carried spare belts of more linked ammunition. The twenty-three-pound M60 machine gun was heavy and its auto-gas operation required continual care and cleaning. However, the handful of M60s in a line company represented more than half of its available firepower, and machine gunners occupied an important and privileged position. As a rule, they were excluded from walking point or checking bunkers.

Grenadiers were armed with the light, compact, and dependable 40mm M79 grenade launcher. This weapon allowed the infantrymen to cover the area between the longest reach of a hand grenade and the shortest range of a mortar. The M79 was popular and handy, being both thoroughly reliable and virtually maintenance-free. The soft, muffled thump of its round being discharged contrasted sharply with the loud explosion of impact. Besides its considerable psychological benefit, the explosion produced a shower of shrapnel often used to shake sniper teams out of trees. Although the grenadier carried a heavy load of ammo, about fifty rounds in vest pouches, he was a most welcome companion. A grenadier routinely walked just behind the point man with a buckshot round chambered in his break-open "thump gun." In case of contact, the grenadier snapped his weapon shut and blasted out "a fistful of ball bearings the size of early June peas."[3]

3. Sp5 George Vindedzis, "Grenadier," *The First Team*, Winter 1970, p. 9.

In Vietnam, where a cunning elusive enemy and difficult tropical terrain placed a premium on division scouting, the division soon raised special patrol units. The volunteer infantrymen of these small, six-man long-range patrols were rangers dedicated to finding the enemy under the most dangerous circumstances, in unknown territory far from friendly columns. Their effectiveness was so great that in March 1968 a MACV study of Vietnam-wide Long Range Patrol (LRP) efforts concluded that the division combination of ample helicopter support "facilitated deception techniques for insertion, assured rapid reaction to enemy contact, and provided an immediate responsive extraction capability. The result was that the 1st Cav Div LRP Company had a higher percentage of patrols lasting over 72 hours than any other division or separate brigade except the 4th Inf Div unit."[4]

Division long-range reconnaissance patrols (LRRP) were first officially organized on 2 February 1967, when two patrols of six men each were formed under the jurisdiction of the 191st Military Intelligence Company. That April the LRRPs were placed under the control of the division G2 section, completed the tough Special Forces–run MACV Recondo School, and expanded. Before the end of the year, on 20 December, this division recon element was formalized as the 118-man Company E of the 52d Infantry "Ready Rifles." The company became the basis of Company H, 75th Infantry (Ranger), created by the division in conformity with DA directives placing all ranger-type units throughout the Army in one parent regiment.

The 1st Cavalry Division increased its scouting capability by employing Kit Carson scouts (KCS), the appellation given former NVA/VC who defected to the allies under the Chieu Hoi "open arms" program and assisted in patrolling and intelligence work. The first Kit Carson scouts used by the division in April 1967 were former local Viet Cong familiar with the terrain in Binh Dinh Province. The 191st Military Intelligence Detachment formally initiated the Kit Carson program in February 1968, and that November the division G5 took control after all Kit Carson scouts were placed under the U.S. Army local national direct hire program. The 1st Cavalry Division employed 72 KCS personnel at the end of 1968 and a year later possessed 161 Kit Carson scouts out of 219 spaces allocated.

War dogs also played their part in division operations. The division had three infantry platoons of scout dogs (25th, 34th, and 37th)

4. MACV, *Command History*, 1968, Volume I, p. 244.

normally attached one per brigade, and one combat tracker infantry platoon (62d) attached to the 1st Squadron, 9th Cavalry. Scout dogs were skilled at detecting mechanical ambush devices, tunnel systems, enemy caches, and humans. Tracker dogs were Black Labradors specially trained for scent which followed retreating or evading enemy groups to reestablish contact. Platoons normally consisted of at least three teams, each having a team leader, a dog and his handler, a scout or tracker, and two covering riflemen.

The main reconnaissance arm of the division was its crack 1st Squadron of the 9th Cavalry, the "cav of the cav," which carried out the first stage of the division operating maxim that "aerial reconnaissance found the enemy, gunships fixed him, and airmobile infantry and artillery finished him." Widely considered the finest air scouting unit in the Army, these modern descendants of the all-Black "Buffalo" cavalrymen of the Indian Wars produced most division contacts in Vietnam. The thousand-member squadron had eighty-eight helicopters in three air troops (A–C), each organized into an aero scout "White" platoon, an aero weapons "Red" gunship platoon, and an aero rifle "Blue" platoon. The squadron also contained a ground reconnaissance Troop D, outfitted with gunjeeps and upgunned 3/4-ton vehicles.

Division aircraft totals remained rather constant. Comparing January 1969 aircraft strengths after division 1965 Vietnam arrivals, the only big changes were replacements of Huey-model gunships with improved Cobras and OH13 light observation helicopters with improved OH6A LOH models as follows: 272/193 UH-series Huey utility helicopters; 0/78 AH1G Cobra attack helicopters; 57/47 CH47 Chinook cargo helicopters, 107/86 light observation helicopters, 6/6 OV1 Mohawks, 0/6 O1 Bird Dogs, and O/2 U6 Beaver fixed-wing aircraft.

The bulk of this aerial armada was under the wing of the 11th Aviation Group, which airlifted the division's supplies, equipment, and troops. The group was commanded by a colonel, and was chiefly responsible for assigning support aircraft to operations ranging from combat assault missions to logistical resupply. The group also provided division with its aviation special staff personnel. The permanent integration of an aviation group into the division cemented air-ground working relationships, bolstering airmobile efficiency well beyond divisions with only temporarily attached helicopters.

The group was designed to provide enough internal aircraft capability to simultaneously airlift the assault elements of two airmobile infantry battalions and three light howitzer batteries. To perform this task, the group contained two assault helicopter battalions, one assault support helicopter battalion, one general support aviation company, and usually one heavy helicopter company attached. The group used internal assets to form such special task elements as the An Khe Airfield Command and was bolstered by various other units like the Air Force detachment of the 5th Weather Squadron which gave twelve- and twenty-four-hour forecast service, weather warnings and watch advisories, and flight briefings.

The 227th and 229th Aviation Battalions (Assault Helicopter) contained the 120 Huey lift helicopters which constituted the prime vehicles of airmobility. The UH1D Huey helicopter, later replaced by the UH1H model, was built to lift one infantry squad, but in Vietnam the added necessity for a door gunner and extra armor reduced this capacity to six or eight men. Each battalion was divided into three lift companies (A–C) of 20 Hueys each and a Company D devoted to armed aerial escort. The latter company was composed of 12 armed UH1B Hueys, later exchanged for AH1G Cobras, and shepherded the lift companies, providing suppressive fire on the LZ immediately prior to air assaults.

The 228th Aviation Battalion (Assault Support Helicopter) was the division's heavy lift workhorse battalion and contained all forty-eight divisional CH47 Chinooks, divided sixteen per company. Described by the troops as a "big green school bus with no class," these twin-rotored Chinooks were the prime movers of light artillery crews and their howitzers and ammunition. The Chinooks were also used extensively in logistical resupply and large troop movements, but required inordinate labor to keep them flying; about ten hours of work for each hour of flight time.

The 11th Aviation Company (General Support) provided command and liaison helicopters for division headquarters. This meant that the company cranked up at least seven Hueys daily to ferry around the division commander and his two assistant commanders, the aviation group commander, the division support commander, and the division's chief of staff. The light observation pilots carried liaison officers and transported visitors for the protocol and information offices. The Aerial Target and Surveillance Acquisition (ASTA) Platoon of the company contained three side-looking radar (SLAR) and three infrared-equipped OV1 Mohawk aircraft.

The largest helicopter within the division was the heavy cargo CH54 Flying Crane, which could transport twice as much weight as the Chinook. The priority roles for division Flying Cranes were airlifting medium artillery and recovery of aircraft, followed by heavy cargo lift. Flying Cranes were provided by the attached "Hurricane" 478th Aviation Company, which was replaced in 1969 by the "Skycrane" 273d Aviation Company.

Modern airmobility required rugged infantry scouts who doubled as air traffic controllers, known as pathfinders or "Blackhats" because of their headwear. The group controlled a pathfinder company which dropped or airlanded teams at objectives to determine the best helicopter approach and withdrawal lanes, scout out sites for heliborne forces, and establish landing zones. Division pathfinders were also air traffic controllers, as an average of two hundred helicopters used any new landing zone during its first forty-eight hours of operation.

By the spring of 1968, the 11th Pathfinder Company (Provisional) conducted thirteen combat parachute jumps in Vietnam. These jumps involved the infiltration of small teams into unsecured areas to provide navigational assistance and aircraft guidance in support of airmobile operations. The first was Capt. Richard D. Gillem's four-man-team jump on a moonless night into the trees of a secret VC base area near Kong Nhou Mountain southwest of Pleiku in December of 1965. Another eight-man pathfinder team was raked by VC machine gun fire as it descended on an objective ten miles southeast of Bong Son on the night of 25 January 1967. Afterward, the division changed its jump altitudes from 950 feet to 600 feet to lessen exposure in the air. These jumps accomplished great surprise in Vietnam because the NVA/VC were accustomed to preparatory artillery fires or helicopter noise prior to American movements.[5]

While aviation moved the division, artillery was relied on to provide most of the division's destructive power. The role of Division Artillery (Divarty), commanded by a colonel, was coordinating tube artillery, aerial rocket artillery, and airstrikes with artillery forward observers to provide accurate, fast, and massive firepower. The mobile artillery forward command post facilitated clearance procedures

5. 1st Cavalry Division, *Airborne Operations of the 11th Pathfinder Company (Airborne)*, dtd 5 Apr 68.

and quick fire channels, insuring that prompt artillery support was available to the fast-paced airmobile infantry. Since howitzers in transit could not support maneuver forces, artillery had to be displaced rapidly to minimize loss of fire support. The swift tempo of artillery operations was highlighted during 1966 Operation MASHER/WHITE WING (discussed in Chapter 4), where artillery battery displacements totaled 57 by air and 109 by road in just forty-one days.

The "Blue Max" 2d Battalion of the 20th Artillery was an aerial rocket battalion intended to substitute for the normally missing divisional medium howitzer battalion. The battalion rendered immediate and devastating fire support, especially for units operating beyond the range of ground artillery, and became the usual savior of isolated airmobile elements in trouble. Initially the battalion was equipped with 2.75-inch rockets and antibunker SS-11 missiles mounted on thirty-six UH1B Huey helicopters, but during 1968 transitioned to thirty-six AH1G Cobra helicopters, each with nineteen-tube 2.75-inch rocket launchers and 7.62mm miniguns. Unlike the Hueys, the Cobras were specifically designed for fire support and carried the firepower equivalent to three conventional artillery batteries.

The three direct support 105mm light howitzer battalions were the mainstay of division firepower, providing the bulk of artillery preparations, time-on-target missions, and enemy contact responses. The advantages of uninterrupted working relationships soon solidified specific artillery battalion assignments to certain brigades. The 2d Battalion of the 19th Artillery usually provided direct support to 1st Brigade. The 1st Battalion of the 21st Artillery normally served with the 3d Brigade. The 1st Battalion of the 77th Artillery rendered direct support to 2d Brigade.

The 1st Battalion of the 30th Artillery, a general support 155mm medium howitzer battalion, was assigned to the division as combat theater augmentation. When operational planning precluded medium artillery support because airlift was impossible, Col. John J. Hennessey's Division Support Command fabricated special slings so the 155mm howitzers could be flown forward by Flying Crane helicopters. After February 1966, the division was able to displace the battalion in the same manner as the rest of its artillery.[6]

The "artillery's air wing" was Battery E of the 82d Artillery, which

6. Maj. Gen. David E. Ott, *Vietnam Studies: Field Artillery* (Washington, D.C.: Dept. of the Army, 1975), p. 104.

used an assortment of light fixed-wing O1 Bird Dogs and utility U6 Beavers as well as Huey and light observation helicopters to adjust artillery fire and provide command liaison for Division Artillery. The flying battery conducted visual reconnaissance, registered artillery fire, relayed radio transmissions, and dropped flares and psychological operations ("psyops") leaflets. Most cavalrymen warmly recalled their constant overhead nighttime surveillance of division base camps and firebases, watching the woodlines for mortar flashes.

Armor was generally a scarce commodity in the 1st Cavalry Division. The small assigned mechanized complement, Troop D of the reconnaissance squadron (1st Sqdn/9th Cav) was known collectively as the "Rat Patrol." By the fall of 1970, it contained twenty-seven combat vehicles, ranging from turreted V100 security vehicles with three machine guns to gunjeeps and armor-plated 3/4-ton trucks with field-expedient machine gun pedestals. Rat Patrol platoons were used extensively for convoy escort, protection of road checkpoints, and limited ambush duties.[7]

General Westmoreland denied repeated division requests for tank support during operations in 1966, exemplified by denial of a tank company attachment even after the THAYER area revealed extensive fortified bunkers which offered excellent tank targets. Reasons cited for refusal of this request included the perceived insufficiency of the area roads and the crop damage and other loss to civilian property which might react unfavorably on civil affairs programs.[8] Finally, in 1967, needed armor reinforcement was permitted, and the mechanized 1st Battalion, 50th Infantry, arrived in Qui Nhon for divisional employment in II CTZ, becoming operational on 29 September 1967. The division was later reinforced with the entire 11th Armored Cavalry Regiment for extended periods beginning in 1969, and it invaded Cambodia alongside the division a year later.

The division's "own private construction firm" was the 8th Engineer Battalion, which averaged just over 650 men in Vietnam. The unit was smaller than most division engineer battalions because it lacked the bridging company and its equipment was lighter for airlift purposes. The battalion spent most of its time building firebases, airstrips, and upgrading landing zones. CH54 Flying Cranes normally

7. Sp5 Jerry Norton, "Rat Patrol," *The First Team*, Fall 1970, pp. 23–26.
8. MACV, *Command History*, 1966, Volume I, p. 378.

transported larger construction equipment such as graders and tractor-scrapers disassembled into several loads and also carried the Chinook-liftable dozers. CH47 Chinooks were used by the engineers to lift the critical International-series of dozers and frontloader/backhoes, which could be brought in under Chinooks complete and ready to work. As a result, these machines were essential to most air assaults and did the lion's share of early LZ clearance, artillery position construction, and bunker building.

The communications required to coordinate all these division activities was rendered by the "Voice of Command" 13th Signal Battalion, which averaged about four hundred men. In Vietnam, FM command nets were the lifeline of battle, and the battalion furnished its vital FM communications with airborne FM radio relay in fixed-wing aircraft. The system was expensive to maintain in manpower and material, but necessary to keep fast-moving elements "on the air." The high frequency communications systems were used almost entirely for radio teletypewriter operation and gave maneuver battalions their only means of secure printed communications. At brigade and division levels multichannel secure teletypewriter circuits were used instead. The battalion also included very high frequency (VHF) systems, tactical operations center switchboards, telephone operations, and multichannel trunking and switching systems.

Unfortunately, the far-flung mobile nature of airmobile division operations in Vietnam quickly disclosed the inadequacy of the signal organization provided. Personnel and equipment were simply insufficient to meet the division's need for responsive, sophisticated communications. Numerous complaints were received by DA throughout the war expressing the need for a stronger airmobile signal battalion. During extended operations, the signal battalion's shortfalls became especially pronounced, and only extensive supplementation by the 1st Signal Brigade kept the division communicating. The wide dispersion of the 1st Cavalry Division made it very difficult for the signal battalion to maintain proper supervision and control.[9]

One unique battalion signal mode seeking to partially remedy signal deficiencies was unfortunately of short duration. In 1966 division

9. 1st Cav Div, *Operational Report—Lessons Learned*, dtd 14 Nov 70, p. 37, with commentary by U.S. Army Pacific at p. 54.

commander Maj. Gen. John Norton directed the reintroduction of carrier pigeons with two birds, Ralph and Spuzy, under CWO James S. Steven, Jr. One of Spuzy's first combat missions involved bringing a message capsule to 2d Brigade during Operation THAYER II, where the bird was spotted on the wire by the brigade intelligence officer. He mistakenly identified the pigeon as a probable Viet Cong messenger and summoned a soldier, who shot it dead, ending the experiment ingloriously.[10]

The soldier who shot Spuzy promptly went AWOL (absent without leave) and became another case for the division's 545th Military Police Company. This company of just over two hundred men provided basic police work to the division community of eighteen thousand to twenty-one thousand people spread over an area as large as four thousand square miles. The unit provided the provost marshal section to headquarters; maintained traffic control and convoy protection; entered villages and checked identification; and insured internal security by enforcing military laws through checkpoints and patrols, crime investigation, and custodial control over offenders. The military police also escorted high-priority shipments, guarded military payment currency and sensitive items, and were used as infantry in emergency situations.

The only support task more difficult than policing and providing signal and construction service to such a large and scattered division with more than 450 aircraft was supplying and maintaining it. This was a job of Division Support Command (Discom), commanded by a colonel, which had a supply and service battalion, two maintenance battalions, and a medical battalion, as well as a headquarters company and the Skytrooper Band. The command fulfilled its mobile battlefield role by dividing assets into mobile logistical depots known as Forward Support Elements (FSE). Each directly supported one brigade at distances averaging twenty-five miles. These contained Forward Support Points, which were usually established along roads and stocked by trucks. Flying supplies from such points lessened the strain of logistical airlift.

10. Lt. Gen. Charles R. Myer, *Vietnam Studies: Division-Level Communications* (Washington, D.C.: Dept. of the Army, 1982), p. 45.

The division used an average of 1.6 million pounds of supplies every day in Vietnam. Everything that the Skytroopers ate, wore, built, or shot involved the 15th Supply & Service Battalion. The battalion furnished almost anything in the division that moved or needed moving, or that the division consumed or expended. This diversity of activity was mirrored by the unit's dazzling array of subordinated elements, from "Redhat" riggers hooking cargo slings underneath helicopters to stock controllers filling normally routine requests which always included the bizarre—such as antifreeze and snow chains. The battalion also supplied all foodstuffs. In Vietnam, military-issue rations were only a small part of the soldiers' diet. Most food was imported, mostly from the mainland United States through such firms as International Marketing, but the battalion also supervised procurement of bananas from local plantations, tomatoes from Japan, fresh fruit from Hawaii, and bread from the Long Binh bakery.

Maintaining the 1st Cavalry Division and its complex aviation inventory required two battalions, which divided their workload according to the division maintenance logo: "If it doesn't fly, the 27th Maintenance Battalion handles it; if it does fly, the 15th Transportation Battalion keeps it that way." The smaller 27th Maintenance Battalion had a headquarters and Company A, a main support detachment, and three lettered detachments. These provided a range of automotive, engineer, electronics, and artillery–small arms and instrument maintenance, but also completed jobs involving everything from glass cutting to canvas repair. The battalion additionally supplied most ground repair parts to the division.

The 15th Transportation Battalion (Aircraft Maintenance) had the unenviable reputation of being perhaps the most overworked unit in the division and had more than thirteen hundred personnel assigned. In mid-1969 the battalion was reorganized and streamlined under the decentralized maintenance concept into a headquarters company, two lettered support companies, and nineteen independent forward detachments with individual aviation units. These detachments maintained the aircraft, effected minor repairs, and generally kept the division flying. Heavier jobs were sent to Companies A and B, which contained the flight line chiefs, mechanics, and shopmen who repaired the difficult cases. Company A handled 60 percent of the helicopters, including the troublesome Chinooks, while Company B maintained the others. The battalion avionics section provided service for aircraft electronics systems involving communications, stabilization, and navigation instrumentation. The biggest headache was non-availability of parts, forcing itinerant battalion personnel to expedite critical item deliveries throughout Vietnam.

Division-level medical support was provided by the 15th Medical Battalion. Specifically tailored for airmobile operations, its twelve medical helicopters allowed aeromedical and air crash rescue support over wide areas. The battalion also provided limited ground evacuation of wounded personnel, medical treatment to include emergency surgery, divisional medical supply and medical equipment maintenance, and complete optometry service. A major part of unit efforts was spent working in medical civic action programs (MEDCAPS), visiting hamlets to treat local Vietnamese villagers. The battalion consisted of a headquarters and support company and three lettered companies, which usually operated in direct support of the brigades. Each company contained a clearing aid station platoon, a ground evacuation platoon, and two supporting air ambulance helicopters.

Installations of hoists on division medical evacuation craft allowed the extraction of casualties from triple-canopy jungle and other inaccessible areas, using either forest penetrators or rigid canvas litters with steel ribbing. The 250-foot hoist cables were color coded to mark length of cable extensions, and detonator charges at the top of the hoist cable permitted instant severing of the steel cord from the ship in case the hovering rescue helicopter was forced to quickly exit the area. The dangers involved in hoist missions were demonstrated during the Cambodian incursion of May 1970, when such missions accounted for only 7.6 percent of the total division flights, but accounted for 53 percent of the helicopters hit.[11]

The 15th Administration Company, which comprised the division headquarters rear echelon, was probably one of the largest companies in the Army. Authorized 380 personnel, the company mushroomed to nearly 800 by the time of the Cambodian invasion in May 1970. The company provided personnel for various staff sections throughout the division, such as finance clerks, legal counsels, postal workers,

11. 1st Cavalry Division, *The First Team in Cambodia*, dtd 6 Jul 70, App. L-3.

## 1st Cavalry Division

**20,346 soldiers**

**418 aircraft**

# 1969 Average Monthly Issues

 **Foodstuffs**          **1,005 tons**

 **Rations**          **597,311 meals**

 **Milk**          **944,780 pints**

 **Ice Cream**          **11,430 gallons**

 **Ice**          **2,777 tons**

 **Clothing & Equipment**    **1,082 tons**

 **Barrier Materials**          **749 tons**

 **Fuel**          **4,010,700 gallons**

**Ammunition**          **4,609 tons**

by Shelby L. Stanton

personnel specialists, and information managers, and even the division's 24 chaplains. The company became so large that it created the 1st Personnel Service Battalion (Provisional) out of its own resources, to which it also attached the 41st and 42d Public Information Detachments. The divisional Replacement Training Center was formed on 1 October 1966 to consolidate training of replacements at division level. The center conducted a four-day replacement training course (RTC) and a combat leaders course (CLC) in facilities including booby-trapped pathways and a complete mock fortified village. The center became the basis of the First Team Academy stationed at Bien Hoa after the division moved south in 1968. The academy instituted a division sniper program and graduated its first snipers on 31 July 1969.

Combat intelligence and counterintelligence were handled by the division's 191st Military Intelligence Company and its attached 583d MI Detachment, which also supported the Deputy G2's combat intelligence center in the Division Tactical Operations Center. The company was compartmentalized into sections devoted to enemy order of battle, prisoner interrogation, aerial imagery interpretation, and counterintelligence. The local intelligence service provided by the company's screening of NVA/VC prisoners, detainees, and ralliers (Hoi Chanhs) was often significant; for instance, in July 1969 the debriefing of a Hoi Chanh furnished timely information on enemy attack plans against a fire support base at Quan Loi.

The 184th Chemical Platoon and its attached 26th Chemical Detachment were responsible for all chemical material within the division, and its tasks ranged from delivery of riot gas and use of flame weapons to spraying of insecticides and inspection of protective masks. Chemical weapons included flamethrowers, incendiary fire drums filled with jellied gasoline (fougasse barrels), and persistent gas "Bunker Use Restriction Bombs" (BURBs), invented by division M. Sgt. Jack Watts. Division Chemical also operated the helicopter-mounted "people sniffer" personnel detectors and was extensively engaged in defoliation operations with Agent Orange and other agents, relying primarily on four-hundred-gallon metal tanks fabricated for CH47 helicopters and one-hundred-gallon spray apparatus on UH-series Hueys.

The combination of assigned components made the division quite strong in manpower, not including all the attachments. In a normal stateside mode an airmobile division was authorized 15,818 personnel (as of 31 December 1968). This compared very favorably with the 14,253 total present in a standard infantry division of World War II in June 1944, and with the 14,843 men permitted the 1st Cavalry Division in the Korean conflict in July 1951. In comparison, a modern cavalry division enjoyed a higher allowance of enlisted cavalrymen than the entire U.S. Army of fifteen cavalry regiments at the turn of the century (12,240 in 1902).[12]

The actual strength of the 1st Cavalry Division in Vietnam fluctuated during the war, but always exceeded its standard authorizations by wide margins. The division's assigned strength of 16,732 at the end of December 1965 steadily increased to 17,405 by mid-1966 to over 18,000 during the crucial years of 1967 and 1968 (18,194 on 31 January 1967; 18,309 on 31 January 1968–Tet). During its last two years of full Vietnam service, in 1969 and 1970, the division expanded to more than 20,000 assigned personnel, containing 20,346 at the end of January 1969 and 20,211 on 1 May 1970, the start of the Cambodian offensive.[13]

Comparison of personnel statistics at the end of 1968, chosen as the high point in American Vietnam participation as well as division overseas service, renders a typical summary of manpower allocations. On 31 December 1968 the 1st Cavalry Division was authorized 15,818 men by TOE 67-Test, but was modified upward by MACV combat augmentation to 19,465 men. On that date the division had 20,271 personnel actually assigned. This represented a 28 percent increase in actual division strength over TOE authorization. While warrant officer spaces reflected little variation and the number of pilots remained about even, officers increased 22 percent (1,442 actual compared to 1,179 by TOE) and enlisted strength jumped 30 percent (18,168

12. TOE 7 (adjusted to Jun 44); DA Rpt CSCAP-13-R2, *Strength in Troop Program Sequence by Organization and Type of Personnel*, Sec 1-A (31 Jul 51); TOE 67-T w/Change 1 (adjusted to 31 Dec 68); Hq of the Army General Orders No. 108, *Organization of the Army as directed by the President*, dtd 24 Oct 1902.

13. 1st Cav Div, *Operational Report on Lessons Learned*, dtd 5 May 66, p. 6; Shelby L. Stanton, *Vietnam Order of Battle* (Millwood, N.Y.: Kraus Reprints, 1986), p. 7; 1st Cav Div, *Operational Reports—Lessons Learned*, dtd 15 Feb 69, App. I-1; 1st Cav Div, *Personnel Daily Summary*, dtd 1 May 70.

actual compared to 13,965 by TOE). Not counting aviators, the division officer-enlisted ratio was actually 1:12, compared to 1:15 in Korea and 1:17 in World War II. While increased officer proportions partially mirrored increased technology, the division's Vietnam ratio was still top-heavy.

The division was handicapped throughout the war by the DA-imposed individual rotation system, which required all soldiers to serve only one year in the combat zone. This policy constantly refilled the formation with green troops and caused severe personnel turbulence. The resulting instability was particularly disruptive in late 1966 operations, because most division members were lost in a single block of time as their twelve-month combat tours expired. MACV replacement inexperience at this early juncture of the war could not properly counterbalance such "hump periods." The division lacked leverage over higher command's belated and insufficient infusion policies, and devastating imbalances occurred in such key categories as aviation. As the war continued, the Army adopted better methods of insuring division refill with phased programs.

The enormity of the one-year combat tour problem was illustrated by the numbers involved. From the beginning of 1966 through January 1967, the division absorbed 19,837 new enlisted replacements and lost 16,173 enlisted veterans to outprocessing, injuries, or death.[14] Since officer turnover also exceeded 100 percent the division underwent complete recycling which actually accelerated in later years (after the casualties of Tet-68, for example). However, morale was most threatened in the first "hump crisis," which the division command took stern steps to counteract. Brigadier General Wright, then Assistant Division Commander-A under Major General Norton, was aghast to hear new division troops being referred to as the "Second Team" as the initial "First Team" headed home. Internal command emphasis stamped out such derogatory references, and instilled collective pride of accomplishment as the First Team (actually a World War II term) for all serving members.

Rampant personnel turbulence had the potential of greatly diminishing the combat proficiency of any unit. The 1st Cavalry Division

14. 1st Cavalry Division, *Operational Reports—Lessons Learned*, dtd 5 May 66, p. 6; 15 Aug 66, p. 6; 22 Nov 66, p. 5, and 15 Feb 67, pp. 4, 5.

was fortunate in that pride of heritage and dedicated teamwork provided much wartime stiffening which lessened adverse turnover impact. Both the spirit of the predecessor 11th Air Assault Division and determined sense of mission displayed by the airmobile 1st Cavalry Division forged a strong bond of individual and unit identity. The dash and daring which typified division operations in Vietnam directly resulted from the unusually high confidence and appreciation that division members expressed for their teammates. Soldiers worked hard and competently to earn the trust of their comrades and implicitly felt that the whole division was behind their efforts. While teamwork was the goal of any military organization, the 1st Cavalry Division excelled in creating a special aura of cooperation and teamwork reflected in a favorite motto, "Anyone who isn't engaged is in reserve."

The members of the 1st Cavalry Division were very proud of and identified closely with their large shoulder sleeve insignia containing a black horsehead and diagonal bar on a golden shield. This patch was worn by assigned troops on their uniform's right shoulder sleeve, and wartime division service was signified by its wear on the left. Veterans returning for additional duty could display their patches "sandwiched." The insignia was designed in response to an official directive after the War Department authorized the division's establishment in September 1921. The message outlined the design criteria: that it bind men together in a common devotion, be an easily recognizable sign by which men could reassemble after battle, and be a symbol of inspiration to division members.

The resulting patch was designed by Mrs. Ben Dorcy, the wife of the 7th Cavalry Regiment's commanding colonel. She used the bright yellow inner liner of one of her husband's old dress capes as the cloth on which the design was first drawn. The choice of the horse's head was made by the Dorcys after they observed a mounted trooper ride by their home on a beautiful shining black thoroughbred. The shape of the patch represented the shield carried by knights in battle, and the bar, or slash, represented a scaling ladder used to breach castle walls. (On 7 January 1969 Mrs. Dorcy wrote the division a letter suggesting that the ladder also represented the Chinook-dropped Jacob's ladders of the Vietnam period.) Because of economic concerns, the Army specified that only two colors be used, and Mrs. Dorcy chose blue and yellow, the traditional colors of the cavalry. Over time the blue was changed to black. The patch was purposely oversize compared to other division insignia, according to Mrs. Dorcy, because "the patch had to be large enough to be seen through the dust and sand at Fort Bliss." The 1st Cavalry Division shoulder sleeve patch insignia remains the largest in the Army.

The First Team mystique was evident at all levels, from its Army-wide reputation of success to individual deeds of selfless team spirit known only within the division. At the higher level the division quickly gained an unsurpassed record of operational skill at finding and defeating NVA/VC forces. There were accounts of lightning airmobile assaults so sudden that the Viet Cong were caught firing unarmed mortar shells, the shipping plugs still inserted, at cavalrymen spilling out of their helicopters. While MACV expressed open delight at the uncanny willingness of division elements to search out and knock heads with the enemy, division members were more impressed with the unflinching reliability of their fellow soldiers.

Maj. Gen. George I. Forsythe, who commanded the division from August 1968 until April 1969, recounted an incident which exemplified the internal First Team spirit. The last platoon of the 1st Battalion, 12th Cavalry, was being picked up from a typical jungle landing zone. The platoon radio-telephone operator (RTO) had already been ordered aboard one of the helicopters lifting out. Suddenly four NVA machine guns in the treeline raked the LZ, and the pilots pulled pitch to clear the area. The young RTO took only an instant to realize his platoon was being left without radio communications; grabbed his radio backboard from the helicopter cabin floor; and, forty feet from the ground, jumped out. He broke both legs, but crawled back through the fire-swept elephant grass, enabling his lieutenant to call in gunships. When his actions were later rewarded with the Silver Star, he stated that his dedication to the team had been an automatic response.[15]

The 1st Cavalry Division encouraged high morale in every way possible. Communications call signs were not changed because over time they became trusted bywords. The division was intensely proud of its field living conditions and did not relish other commands with air-conditioned bunkers and velvet curtains over mapboards. The

15. USAMHI, *Senior Officers Oral History Program*, Lt. Gen. George I. Forsythe Interview, p. 448.

division helicoptered slingloads of freshly laundered fatigues into remote sectors to give troops clean clothes regardless of size or markings and dismissed complaints from higher headquarters about mixed-up or missing name tags. While this emphasis on morale undoubtedly reinforced division standards, the 1st Cavalry Division also enjoyed many real advantages over other American formations in Vietnam.

The MACV commanders, Generals Westmoreland and Abrams, displayed unabashed admiration for the division. This favoritism was reflected in May 1967 when MACV force requirements were adjusted to place the 1st Cavalry Division in the role of a special exploiting force designed to penetrate and neutralize major NVA/VC base areas. All other MACV divisions except the 1st Infantry Division (the other exploiting force) were linked to specific provinces. In September 1967, in view of increased NVA activity in northern I CTZ, General Westmoreland revised the force structure of MACV to establish the 1st Cavalry Division as the sole "countrywide offensive force." These heightened responsibilities were invariably matched by special MACV command emphasis. In addition to priority on equipment, informal guidance was issued to the 22d and, later, 90th Replacement Battalions so that the division received the pick of nonparatrooper arrivals. This MACV effort lavished the division with high-quality personnel and equipment to insure levels of performance excellence.[16]

It is important to remember, however, that although the 1st Cavalry Division appeared magnificently endowed with aviation and personnel assets, the reality of Southeast Asian warfare greatly diminished its airmobile strike capability. Vietnam's higher air density and the combat necessity to add the weight of armor, emergency supplies, and larger armament systems onto helicopters greatly reduced aircraft power. Even if all its aircraft were flying, the division normally worked with one-third less lift capacity than that projected by the airmobile developers at Fort Benning.

Insufficient numbers of mission-ready aircraft further eroded airmobile potential. During 1966 aircraft availability averaged only 68 percent for UH-series Hueys, 63 percent for CH54 Sky Cranes, and a mere 43 percent for CH47 Chinooks, attributed mostly to lack of

16. MACV, *Command History*, 1967, Volume I, pp. 144–45, 152.

spare parts beyond effective MACV influence. By late 1968 the mission readiness of Huey helicopters had dropped to 60 percent and Chinooks to 40 percent. Instead of the practically unlimited aerial response that most people believed the airmobile division possessed, the 1st Cavalry Division was continually forced to modify its tactical operations with great economy and innovation.[17]

17. 1st Cav Div, *Operational Reports on Lessons Learned*, dtd 5 May 66, App. 4-9; dtd 15 Aug 66, App. 4-8; dtd 22 Nov 66, App. 5-4; dtd 15 Feb 67, p. 75; dtd 15 Feb 69, p. 68.

# CHAPTER 11

# The Skytroopers

## *Division Performance in Vietnam*

More than 150,000 troops served in the 1st Cavalry Division during eighty-two months of combat in the Second Indochina War.[1] These division personnel were primarily responsible for the wartime development of the airmobile concept and for the aerial cavalry's success or failure as a viable military instrument. How these troops fought and behaved is an essential aspect of division operations in Vietnam and an integral ingredient of the mobile cavalry's capability.

The hallmark of ground maneuver which dominated Army tactics in Vietnam was the fire support base, often referred to simply as firebase. Conceptually, the fire support base functioned simply to provide a secure but mobile artillery position capable of rendering fire support to infantry operating in areas beyond the normal range of their main base camp cannon and howitzers. This concept afforded infantry a greater degree of flexibility without sacrificing artillery protection. However, firebases quickly became targets for enemy counterattacks and bombardments, and increased defensive measures were undertaken. More sophistication meant less mobility. Over the course of the war, firebases developed to the point where ground maneuver was

---

1. 1st Cavalry Division service credited as commencing in Vietnam in September 1965 and ending with the withdrawal of its 3d Brigade in June 1972; personnel total taken from 1st Cav Div Vietnam Departure Ceremony brochure dtd 26 Mar 71, p. 5. Considering that the separate 3d Brigade remained in Vietnam another fifteen months, the totals of personnel were doubtless much higher.

hampered because of their size, elaborate construction, demand on supply and protective resources, and troop reluctance to leave their comforts and safety, a condition called "firebase psychosis."

The 1st Cavalry Division (Airmobile), as the most tactically mobile formation in Vietnam, gave priority to rapid firebase deployment and construction. In order adequately to cover its large areas of operation, the division was constantly opening, closing, and reopening firebases throughout the war. The first division firebase was designated as Bill, built during October 1965 in Pleiku Province. However, by 1969 they had blossomed from jungle clearings with unsophisticated defenses into formidable semipermanent fortresses.

The typical cavalry fire support base was a defensive area roughly 250 yards in diameter with an 800-yard perimeter, which contained howitzers and enough equipment and supplies to support the infantry with artillery fire around the clock. The firebase also supplied logistics, communications, medical, and rest facilities for the cavalrymen within its area. The division's 8th Engineer Battalion was responsible for initiating firebase construction. The engineer line companies, assigned one to a brigade, cleared the initial area, performed demolitions work, established water points, and provided the supervisory expertise, equipment, and manpower to build sophisticated fieldworks.

Once the fire support base site was selected, usually by aerial photographic reconnaissance at division level, the brigade and battalion responsible for its sector began detailed construction planning. Terrain and weather information were used to determine its size, shape, and required facilities. Construction priorities were then issued, hopefully in a timely fashion. It was proven repeatedly that minutes spent in coordinated planning by all concerned units saved hours in actual construction time. The normal order of construction was: temporary helicopter pad for delivery of supplies, howitzer positions, perimeter berm, artillery fire direction center (FDC), infantry tactical operations center (TOC, the command post), ammunition supply point, "VIP" helicopter pad, garbage sump, defensive wire barrier, and, finally, medium artillery positions if applicable.

The division prepared basic firebase kits, each designed for a battalion-level fire support base and its supporting six light howitzers, which contained all the necessary materials for construction. Nails, spikes, metal culverts, chain-link fence rolls, tar paper, sandbags, pickets, and lumber were all prepalletized or arranged in slingloads for rapid helicopter delivery. The firebase kit required about twenty-five CH47 Chinook cargo helicopter sorties to deliver to the field. The amount of equipment needed to clear the area of the firebase varied depending upon terrain. In dense jungle large Air Force bombs were used to demolish enough vegetation to blast out a landing zone. The more common bomb of this type was the 750-pound "Daisy Cutter" that detonated about ten feet above the ground, effectively destroying all foliage for ten feet around and knocking down trees over a considerably larger radius. The 10,000-pound "Instant LZ" opened up larger swaths of demolished jungle, while late-war 15,000-pound "Commando Vault" bombs offered the most destructive power. Napalm was a useful supplement if tropical forests were clogged with bamboo or additional thick jungle growth.

The air assault to secure and establish the firebase site was the riskiest part of the construction task. If the site was not large enough to accommodate the landing of a single helicopter, combat engineers with axes and explosives rappelled from a helicopter hovering fifty to one hundred feet above the ground. They were escorted by small parties of volunteer infantry which provided security while the engineers cleared an area large enough for the CH47 Chinook and CH54 Flying Crane cargo helicopters. Using demolitions and chain saws, the assault engineers could clear a landing zone for the larger helicopters within three hours. Of course, in most instances the selection of open fields demanded only a small amount of advance clearing.

The foremost task of any firebase construction effort was to produce a tenable tactical position by nightfall on the first day, with overhead cover for every man. This "tactical phase" was a time of heavy helicopter traffic bringing in more engineers and their equipment, the infantry and artillerymen, ammunition, barrier and bunker materials, rations, fuel, water, and howitzers and other weapons. As soon as the perimeter trace was cut out, defensive positions were started.

The normal construction site required the use of one engineer platoon under the direction of a "project engineer" with two medium D6B dozers, two Case light dozers, and one backhoe. As engineers worked with explosive charges, bangalore torpedoes, and chain saws to expand the perimeter, the first vehicular machines were being flown to the area. The invaluable light dozers could be airlifted in one piece underneath Chinooks and were the first equipment in. They were used to clear fields of small trees and stumps and to level artillery positions. The backhoe dug emplacements for the TOC, FDC, medical bunker, and perimeter bunker. Heavy dozers were lifted in two pieces, the blades and tracks by Chinook and the tractor body by Flying Crane. Once hauled in, the dozer had to be assembled, which required at least thirty minutes (more if the pilot did not set the machine down on its tracks); then it was immediately put to work pushing up earth to create a four-foot berm completely around the perimeter.

As engineer dozers and backhoes carved out the main firebase defenses, the infantry and artillerymen began emplacing wire entanglements, digging perimeter fighting holes, and emplacing perimeter bunkers in backhoe excavations. "Quick Fix" combat bunkers were simply five-foot-by-eight-foot shoulder-high holes covered with lumber or natural timber and sandbags. Standard perimeter bunkers provided better protection because they were covered by wooden stringers and steel mat decking. The simplest fighting positions were the two-man foxholes, each covered by three sections of sixty-inch metal culverts and topped by sandbags. In the meantime, once the first strand of tactical wire was emplaced, the artillerymen returned to build ammo storage bunkers and parapets around their weapons.

The final defensive phase of construction began when the Chinooks had delivered enough kit material to permit the engineers to build the main infantry TOC, artillery FDC, and medical bunker. These were built using large dimensional timbers, precut to anticipated firebase requirements. The main bunkers were started at the end of the first day or the beginning of the second day and finished by the end of the fourth day. Construction time was often shortened by employing reusable TOC and FDC bunker modules. Bunker modules were composed of two CONEX containers emplaced facing each other, with the overhead gap between them covered by steel matting. Two modules (four containers) sufficed for a battalion command center. Using these containers allowed an operational TOC/FDC complex to be completed within eight hours, including pushing earth fill around the sides and sandbagging the tops.

The infantry and artillerymen continued improving the wire barriers with tanglefoot and a second perimeter strand. Individual sleeping positions were built using metal seventy-two-inch half-culvert sections. The improvement of firebases was a never-ending job, as all structures were continually reinforced, surface drainage improved, and fields-of-fire constantly maintained by additional clearance. One squad of engineers was normally kept on any fire support base.

The life span of a fire support base depended on the tactical situation in its area. Since firebases were normally established to give a battalion and its direct support howitzer battery a pivot of operations to patrol the immediate vicinity, the firebase was closed when the battalion relocated. When the decision was made to close out a firebase, the brigade engineer usually provided one platoon to assist the infantry company tasked with dismantling it. Structural removal was aimed at salvaging the timbers, culverts, steel matting, and chain-link fencing in order to reconstitute division firebase kits, but holes were filled and berms leveled at command discretion.[2]

The 1st Cavalry Division's fire support bases were another example of adopting traditional frontier cavalry forts to the Vietnam environment, fusing airmobility to enhance the process. The advent of helicopter support and better material resources allowed these forts to be established more quickly and more often and projected cavalry battalions into hostile territory with greater assured safety. Once emplaced, however, they effectively limited cavalry movement to the radius of their guns. More substantial firebases of a semipermanent nature mushroomed into major camps with recreation areas, snack shops, mess halls, and elaborate living facilities, which actively hindered field operations because of their large garrison requirements.

The infantry which swept through the trackless, arboreal wilderness within range of fire support bases, usually found the NVA/VC entrenched in well-constructed, mutually supporting bunker positions. One outgoing battalion intelligence officer briefed his replacement on enemy fortifications within his area of operations by merely flattening his hands against the tactical wall map and saying, "Place your hand anywhere on the map and you've got a thousand bunkers in the palm of your hand." The myriad NVA/VC infiltration and supply trails were randomly connected to base camps of various sizes which were guarded by bunker complexes.

Reduction of fortified positions in World War II and Korea was a matter of deliberate attack against a deliberate defense. Elimination

---

2. 1st Cav Div Document, Subj: The Construction of a Fire Base in the 1st Cav Div, 7-69, dtd 10 Oct 69.

of sophisticated enemy defense lines was accomplished by using heavy concentrations of naval gunfire, artillery, and aerial bombing, followed by mixed teams of infantry, armor, and engineers to destroy successive enemy positions. After the initial fire support preparation, artillery was fired as the assault teams approached in order to drive the enemy soldiers out of lightly protected supporting positions and back into their larger shelters. Then tanks, tank destroyers, and assault guns fired armor-defeating rounds at the bunker embrasures to suppress enemy defensive fires. Under the cover of these armored vehicles, infantry and engineers moved up and used flamethrowers, rocket launchers, and explosives to eliminate the enemy defensive works. This method required large ground forces well versed in demolition techniques.

In Vietnam the 1st Cavalry Division encountered enemy bunkers in sudden clashes, usually when enemy machine gun and rocket crews occupying perfectly camouflaged bunkers opened fire on advancing infantry at close quarters. The bunkers were built in mutually supporting arrangements in dense bamboo groves or thick jungle undergrowth and constructed from locally available material. Although the division encountered some concrete bunkers, these were the exception. NVA/VC fortifications were not designed for deliberate defense, but only to disorganize and delay the attackers until withdrawal could be effected. The enemy bunkers and spider holes ringed base camps which contained living quarters, workshops, logistical depots, rest areas, and other facilities. The base camps were constructed in a circular pattern for all-around defense until prompt evacuation of supplies could be effected.

The bunkers themselves were so well camouflaged that they remained undetected until the enemy initiated fire on the unsuspecting cavalrymen. Usually, the advancing troopers were allowed to approach within five or ten feet of bunkers before the enemy positions cut loose with devastating cross fires. When the battle started, the cavalry was often mired in confused fighting, with a number of casualties.

Immediate retreat was required to save the seriously wounded, but intensely accurate automatic weapons fire ripped into troops trying to reach and drag their comrades out of the hail of enemy bullets. Leading platoons were often able to pull back only by using helicopter-dropped bangalore torpedoes. Once delivered, these exploded enough vegetation to allow accurate counterfire with machine guns and light antitank weapons. Positions were marked with smoke and white phosphorus to create smoke screens, which both covered the withdrawal and enabled aircraft to spot the forward edge of the battlefield.

One of the best ways to break close contact was by dropping chemical gas canister clusters out of helicopters. The troops donned gas masks as the command and control helicopter raced low overhead, and crew members kicked riot gas bomblets directly on top of the enemy positions. The 1st Battalion, 12th Cavalry, experienced several hard bunker contests, but reported that the enemy was never able to place effective fire on friendly troops after the gas was dropped.

At the outset of the action, the enemy usually not only blocked further infantry advance, but forced a tactical retreat. However, the enemy situation was extremely precarious. The cavalry had located his positions, and by breaking contact the troops could call in airstrikes and artillery to pound the base camp and prevent successful evacuation. Sometimes cavalry units were fortunate enough to know their exact positions and were able to bring accurate artillery fire on the rear and flanks of bunker complexes within minutes. Aerial scout helicopter teams often sealed off exits by calling in artillery and aerial rockets while they strafed escape routes. Physically blocking routes of egress with additional infantry was not preferred because of fire support coordination difficulties and the chance of encountering more bunkers in masking positions.

The "bunker busting" phase of the battle commenced as the Air Force dropped 500- and 750-pound bombs to clear the jungle canopy and to blast large holes in the foliage. The explosive power of direct bomb hits crushed many field positions and drove dazed enemy troops into the impact areas. After enough of the overhead canopy was blown away, aerial observers and forward air controllers could direct precision fires on the bunkers and installations within the base camp. The enemy bunkers were usually so solid that only 17-pound helicopter rockets and heavy bombs were effective against them. Light 105mm howitzer fire was ineffective against bunkers, while medium 155mm artillery fire could achieve only a low rate of destruction. The heavy 8-inch howitzer was both accurate and destructive, but the time and ammunition expenditures required made it impractical to use this weapon against a cluster of only sixty bunkers.

Artillery and aircraft saturated the target area with a cloud of riot gas to force the enemy out of remaining defensive positions. After giving time for the gas to take effect, cluster bomb units, light and medium artillery barrages, and aerial rockets were used to annihilate enemy soldiers in the open. In one instance, where the 1st Battalion, 77th Artillery, employed "firecracker" munitions mixed with quick-fused high explosives in this manner, the helicopter pilot adjusting artillery fire described the target as looking like an anthill that had been kicked.

When the ground commander estimated that the bunker complex was adequately "softened up," he directed that supporting firepower be shifted to cover enemy withdrawal and reinforcement routes. The cavalry troops then proceeded back into the area to finish the bunkers at rifle point. If heavy enemy return fire was encountered, another retreat was ordered and the preparatory fires resumed. Artillery and tactical airstrikes were applied until the enemy defenses were sufficiently weakened to allow the infantry to get into the bunker complex and mop up individual pockets of resistance. In this final phase of bunker destruction, the cavalrymen relied on .50-caliber machine guns, M72 light antitank weapons, 90mm recoilless rifles, and lightweight XM191 multishot flame projectors (FLASH). Regular flamethrowers were used infrequently because of their weight and refilling problems. The 1st Cavalry Division rarely used tanks because of mine hazards and poor avenues of approach. Tanks could not crash through dense jungle for long distances without considerable drain on the vehicles and crews.[3]

The whole complexion of fighting fortifications in Vietnam was totally different from previous conventional conflicts. Instead of a deliberately planned attack to get within range of enemy fieldworks, the infantry was subjected to an unexpected clash at very short ranges. Instead of a deliberate defense, the enemy tried to stay in action only long enough to permit his base garrison to escape with supplies. Instead of using artillery and bombers to fix the enemy in place and infantry-armor-engineer assault groups to destroy him, the cavalry used infantry to fix enemy defenses and artillery and airpower to destroy him. These tactical differences partially reflected area warfare attrition versus linear warfare territorial advance, but both placed an equally high premium on courage, tactical expertise, and calm leadership.

3. 1st Cav Div, *Bunker Busting: Attack on Fortified Areas*, dtd 18 Jan 71.

"Bunker busting" became the norm of offensive cavalry combat after 1968, and this style of fighting proved to be one of the most difficult tests of combat fortitude in Vietnam. Throughout the mobile and fragmented war in Vietnam, a premium was placed on intelligence gathering to locate elusive enemy forces, base areas, and trail networks. The 1st Cavalry Division's long-range patrol (LRP) company, later designated as ranger infantry, provided much of this dangerous work. Each patrol platoon was commanded by a lieutenant, who had eight six-man teams under him. Each team was authorized a staff sergeant team leader, a sergeant assistant team leader, a front scout, a rear scout, a radioman, and a medic. However, most teams were led by buck sergeants or Specialists 4th Class during the war. All long-range patrol members were volunteers, and the majority were parachutists.

Each long-range patrol mission was unique, and the experience of one patrol of Company E, 52d Infantry, on 17 August 1968 is presented as an example of the dangers and accomplishments of this elite force. On that day SSgt. Stephen Tefft was told that his LRP Team 32 would be inserted in the southern portion of Enemy Base Area 101, a jungled mountain area of I CTZ. Staff Sergeant Tefft and his assistant team leader, Sgt. George Kennedy, were taken on a helicopter reconnaissance over their area of operations that afternoon. They familiarized themselves with the prominent terrain features that could be used later as reference points should they become disoriented or have need of an emergency extraction pickup zone. Upon their return to the team's rear base location, Tefft called his men together and gave them the patrol order.

In a small patrol, operating deep in enemy territory, it was necessary that all team members clearly understood their mission, the terrain, and the enemy situation. Since the mission entailed a two-day patrol, no rucksacks were carried. All ammunition and basic necessities were placed in pouches on their combat harnasses or in their bedrolls, which consisted of half a poncho per man. Full rubber ponchos reflected too much light and made too much noise, but the half-poncho was lightweight and kept the upper part of the body warm. Also, if the team was hit at night, a man could quickly discard the poncho half and be ready for action. Only two dehydrated LRP ration meals were carried per man, and since the weather was cool no need existed for water beyond the five quarts that each man carried.

The insertion was scheduled for 6:30 P.M. the next evening, so Sergeant Tefft gave his men time off until noon the following day. This helped to counterbalance the high tension they would face during the patrol. On the afternoon of 18 August, the team assembled again. This time they were dressed in camouflaged fatigues and bush hats, and their faces were streaked and darkened by charcoal sticks. They were briefed once more, then they rehearsed immediate action and contact drills for the rest of the day. These were automatic procedures used in case of sudden contact with the enemy and were practiced over and over until performance became instinctive. Since the patrol was so small, they faced superior numbers in virtually any expected encounter. Survival depended on teamwork and the instant, coordinated reaction of the entire patrol.

At 6:30 P.M. the team was aboard the helicopter, part of a three-troopship formation with two gunships flying escort, en route to its landing zone. The insertion was made in an old bomb crater in the middle of triple-canopy jungle at last light. The lift helicopters approached the landing zone in file with the patrol in the first troopship. The control helicopter was second, and an empty helicopter was last in file. The first helicopter sat down quickly, and the team dashed out, while the other two helicopters continued to fly at low level overhead. At precisely the right moment, the team helicopter lifted off to become third in file. By executing a number of hops in this fashion, the NVA/VC remained unaware of the exact drop-off point for any patrol.

Everything was quiet on the ground, and the team quickly left the bomb crater and moved one hundred yards directly south into the jungle, where they made their initial communications check with the long-range patrol control headquarters. It was becoming very dark as the patrol moved a little farther and discovered a trail. The front scout, Sp4 Clare Michlin, checked the pathway for signs of recent use. The front scout fulfilled both point and tracking duties, looking for signs such as recently broken brush or discarded material. After determining that the trail was probably cold, the team moved away from the path and up a small hill. They set out claymore mines and prepared an overnight position. Usually, after 9:00 P.M. Sergeant Tefft kept one man awake, on half-hour shifts, but on occasion, depending on the enemy situation, the whole patrol stayed awake.

Early the next morning the team moved farther south and traveled down the hill into a valley. At 8:00 A.M. they tried another communications check, but could not establish radio communication because of the low ground. Finally, they made contact with a friendly station which acted as relay. The team continued its cautious movement through the jungle until 11:00 A.M., when they sat down for "Pak time." This interval lasted until 2:00 P.M. and was observed to conform patrol movement to enemy travel habits. The NVA/VC frequently took a midday break during these hours.

At 7:00 P.M. that evening, the patrol trekked south into a gully containing a stream. The men refilled their canteens and then silently listened for any sounds of possible enemy presence. After waiting for a while and hearing nothing unusual, the patrol continued. About two-hundred years downstream they found a trail which ended at the bank, and Staff Sergeant Tefft believed that this might be an enemy water point. The patrol moved up the trail, but had proceeded only a few feet when they saw a group of twenty North Vietnamese soldiers walking directly toward them. Before the team could jump off the trail, the enemy opened fire with automatic rifles.

The patrol responded automatically with their reaction drill. Specialist Michlin, the point man closest to the enemy group, threw a white phosphorous grenade in front of the North Vietnamese soldiers, who were also taking evasive action. The patrol quickly maneuvered back to the stream, the men giving covering fire to each other as they bounded backward. This leapfrogging retreat soon placed the rear scout closest to the advancing enemy troops, and he also tossed a white phosphorous grenade in an attempt to discourage pursuit. The patrol was equipped with claymore mines and time-capsule fuses, which it usually carried for emergencies when contact had to be broken, but the charges had a fifteen-minute delay period. The enemy was too close.

The team ran across the stream and clambered up a steep slope into a treeline along an upland rice paddy where they reassembled into a hasty perimeter. Sp4 Plisch frantically called for aerial support on his radio. Since they had been spotted, Staff Sergeant Tefft decided to try for an emergency extraction under the covering fire of helicopter gunships. During Plisch's radio transmissions for help, the other team members saw another eight enemy soldiers moving across a clearing to surround them. They fired on this new NVA element with silencer-equipped M16 rifles. The enemy squad, unsure of the exact location of return fire, stopped forward movement and became pinned down.

A Cobra gunship and a scout helicopter from the 1st Squadron, 9th Cavalry, were quickly overhead. The Cobra was diverted from another mission, and its low ammunition and fuel status allowed the pilot to make only one firing pass. The light observation helicopter remained at the scene, firing its M60 defiantly in support and guiding the team to a suitable pickup point. The team used fire and movement tactics to relocate for extraction. Two more Cobra gunships and a second light helicopter appeared within minutes, and their rockets and miniguns caused the North Vietnamese to retreat. A Huey troopship quickly swooped down, and when it was three feet off the ground, the team jumped aboard. Although their primary mission, reconnoitering for enemy movement, was compromised, the patrol was credited with finding the enemy and directing aerial rocket fire on his positions.

The long-range patrol members received no extra pay or privileges for their work. Their satisfaction came from pride of comradeship and the special contribution they made to the effectiveness of the First Team. Throughout the Vietnam War the rifle scouts of the 9th Cavalry, battalion and brigade recon forces, and the long-range/ranger infantry of the division patrol company served the 1st Cavalry Division with confidence and valor. Their exploits more than made up for their small numbers, because they operated over a wide area to find the NVA/VC, report on his movements, disrupt his activities, and pioneer areas for large-scale action by the airmobile battalions.[4]

While the combat performance of elite and line battalion components of the 1st Cavalry Division was beyond reproach, the general personal conduct of all personnel within the division was quite high. Accurate assessments of such intangibles as morale and esprit de corps are probably impossible, but quantitative evaluation can be made in determining troop discipline and obedience to orders. Division troop performance in these areas is examined by surveying general crime rates, grenade incidents ("fragging"), and war crimes in Vietnam.

The personnel of the division demonstrated exemplary behavior

4. 1st Cav Div AVDAMH Doc, Subj: Long Range Patrols of the 1st Air Cav Div, dtd 26 Dec 68.

compared to other formations stationed in Vietnam. The USARV provost marshal quarterly summary reports for all major Army commands confirm the high esteem in which the division was held. Two sample quarters are statistically cited here, as they represent the final three-month figures for 1969 and 1970, the most troubled period of American troop service when all units were still incountry and before strengths were eroded by major withdrawals.

During the period of October through December 1969, the 1st Cavalry Division had only 37 persons confined in the USARV Long Binh stockade, a rate of 1.85 per thousand, and the lowest of any division or equivalent command. In crimes against persons and property, where there was a 7.2 percent rise in other division crime rates to include murder, manslaughter, and rape, the 1st Cavalry Division's most serious crimes from October through December 1969 were six aggravated assaults, eleven simple assaults, one robbery, and twelve larcenies (most under fifty dollars). One year later, during the period of October through December 1970, the 1st Cavalry Division had 96 persons in the USARV prisoner population at Long Binh, a rate of 4.68 per thousand, which resulted largely from increased division crackdowns on drug offenders. The true measure of division troop behavior again focuses on serious crimes against persons and property, which at this point in the war had escalated to alarming levels throughout USARV. However, the 1st Cavalry Division had only one case of murder, twenty simple assaults, and fifteen petty larcenies. These statistics are astonishingly low, even for a peacetime garrison division in Europe or the United States, and a tribute to the leadership and men of the division.[5]

In Vietnam, "fragging" was a slang expression originally referring to the use of a fragmentation grenade to kill or injure another person, usually as a measure taken against unpopular officers or sergeants. However, a great deal of fragging was directed toward fellow enlisted men as a result of grievances and drug trafficking. Common Army usage expanded the meaning of the term to encompass the use of other varied explosive devices. The crux of the problem in Vietnam was found in control and leadership at the company and battalion

---

5. USARV, *Command Progress Reports*, 2d Qtr FY-69, pp. 60.02, 60.08; 2d Qtr FY-70, pp. 70.05, 70.08.

level. Most commanders and senior sergeants were rarely able to see their entire unit at one time, because of widespread base camp elements and dispersed units in the field.

Fragging incidents rose sharply throughout Army divisions and separate brigades in 1970, which represented the peak year for this type of criminal activity. A close scrutiny of fraggings and shootings during the second half of the year gives a good picture of how the 1st Cavalry Division compared in troop discontent. During these six months, the division had only five incidents of grenade fraggings and twenty-two cases of shootings. At the same time there was a total of thirty-eight grenade fraggings and ninety-seven shootings among the five Army divisions and five separate combat brigades from July through December 1970 (with two brigades departing country during this period). Again, the 1st Cavalry Division has a conspicuously low rate of grenade incidents, despite having the highest number of assigned personnel and the largest area of operations with scattered firebases in Vietnam.[6]

The 1st Cavalry Division was also remarkably free from the taint of war crime accusation during its service in Vietnam. This fact reflects great credit upon an organization that waged a very difficult war in the midst of an often hostile civilian population.

There were only three main allegations of improper wartime activity brought against units of the 1st Cavalry Division in Vietnam. The first complaint stemmed from the alleged mistreatment of a Viet Cong prisoner following the appearance of an Associated Press photograph in the 30 December 1965 issues of *The Chicago Daily News* and *Milwaukee Journal*. The photo showed a seemingly nonchalant cavalry major looking on while "a Vietnamese Popular Forces militiaman kicks a Viet Cong prisoner in the head at an interrogation point . . . after being captured by U.S. troops of the 1st Cavalry (Air Mobile) Division." The Army ordered a full investigation with the following results.

The 1st Cavalry Division received a report in December 1965 that some VC were hiding in caves in the Binh Khe district. The Binh Khe district chief appointed one of his policemen as a guide for a

6. DCS P&A DF TO C/OS Dept. of the Army, fm Maj. Woodbeck AVHDP-MMW, DF, Subj: Grenade Incidents, dtd 14 Mar 71, w/supporting papers.

search expedition by the 1st Squadron, 9th Cavalry. No caves were found, but a VC suspect was captured by Troop C of the squadron and evacuated to the landing zone for immediate interrogation by the 3d Brigade intelligence officer (a major) prior to evacuation as a prisoner of war. About the same time that the helicopter arrived with the major and AP photographer Mr. Huet, the Binh Khe policeman saw the prisoner and recognized him as a fellow villager. The policeman accused him of being a known Viet Cong responsible for trouble in the hamlet and ran over and kicked him before the cavalrymen could react. The major rushed over and immediately stopped the civilian policeman from kicking the prone VC suspect.

Mr. Huet later stated that he had already had his camera focused; otherwise, he would have been unable to take the picture, since the incident happened so quickly. He also agreed that the photo was misleading because the major was about to rush over to stop the mistreatment. Unfortunately, the major seemed to be permitting, or merely observing, the kicking at the instant the shutter clicked. The photograph was that of an isolated incident whereby a civilian guide was inadvertently allowed to get close enough to a village adversary to vent his rage upon him. The situation was quickly remedied, but not before a chance photograph gave a completely erroneous impression of the incident. The 1st Cavalry Division, which prided itself on according prisoners proper treatment, ironically became associated with harsh retribution by a national press eager for dramatic photographs.[7]

The next untoward division incident, the "Brooks Incident," did not arise until 18 May 1971, when a "hunter-killer" team of three helicopters from Troop A, 1st Squadron, 9th Cavalry, performed a visual reconnaissance mission over a small Cambodian village. The scoutship crew observed a number of motorcycles and bicycles with packs near the hamlet, which they suspected was an enemy convoy. The villagers were signaled from the air to open the packs, and machine gun fire was used to force the inhabitants into the open after the instructions were ignored. On another pass over the area, the pilot of the observation helicopter heard gunfire behind his craft and notified the Cobra gunship that he was taking fire. The mission commander in the third helicopter saw automatic weapon muzzle flashes

7. MACJI Ltr Serial No. 3844 1st Ind, Subj: Complaint, Alleged Mistreatment of a Viet Cong Prisoner, dtd 1 Mar 66, w/ investig papers.

from a dike one hundred yards south of the village and so advised the Cobra pilot. The attack helicopter rocketed the dike and adjacent buildings, while the gunner aboard the scoutship sprayed the rest of the village. An ARVN platoon led by cavalry Capt. Arnold H. Brooks was airmobiled into the contact area under the cover of gunship support fires (this was a technical violation of standing orders not to enter Cambodia at the time). The South Vietnamese raced into the village with weapons blazing, gunning down several people, including children, then looted the hamlet. The platoon was not fired on, did not search for enemy positions, and did not treat any of the wounded civilians. The Vietnamese troops left the area, taking large quantities of tobacco, poultry, radios, and other booty, while Captain Brooks helped himself to a motorcycle which he later presented to Lt. Col. Carl C. Putnam, the squadron commander, as a war trophy. Several days later Lieutenant Colonel Putnam decided to investigate.

The Army concluded that the 9th Cavalry had engaged in excessive bombardment and pillage of a Cambodian village and had violated several rules of engagement. Letters of reprimand were issued to Lieutenant Colonel Putnam and others, but court-martial charges against Captain Brooks were dismissed at Fort Knox, Kentucky, on 21 April 1972. Division members felt that the cavalry actions were appropriate, that the South Vietnamese were responsible for the actual problems, and that the investigation was unfair. Air cavalrymen functioned in a very dangerous flight pattern. A "low bird" light observation helicopter was flown at slow speed as a carrot to make the enemy reveal his location. The "high bird," an armed helicopter, circled the bait scoutship to render immediate protective response. To stay alive, these aviators had to react instantly with deadly effective firepower. This incident transpired in a "hot area" full of enemy traffic, where it was common NVA/VC practice to use motorcycles and bicycles for transporting war materials and supplies.[8]

The final war crime incident involving a 1st Cavalry Division unit was commonly known as the "Woodcutters Incident," since it allegedly involved the murder of two Vietnamese woodcutters. On 7 Jan-

8. CG Third Regional Assistance Cmd Ltr AVDACG, Subj: Report of Investigation: Firing Incident in Cambodia, dtd 12 Dec 71, and related paperwork; DA Investigation summary #219, dtd 1 May 72.

uary 1972 a Mr. Nguyen Xuan Tuyet from Binh Son hamlet near the village of Long An reported that three days earlier an unidentified helicopter fired upon some woodcutters in his district, hitting two of them. He stated that the helicopter then landed, at which time Army soldiers got out and finished the woodcutters off with pistols, took their chain saw and bicycle, and departed. MACV immediately initiated a full investigation.

The investigation revealed that the Vietnamese were actually killed in a ground action by Ranger Team 73 of Company H, 75th Infantry (Ranger) of the 3d Brigade, 1st Cavalry Division, and that no helicopter weapons were fired during that mission. The ranger team was in a special strike zone on a reconnaissance patrol when two armed Vietnamese were spotted sitting beside a pile of brush. Both were immediately ambushed and killed. The rangers stripped the bodies of clothing, an AK47 assault rifle, two grenades, and some small tools, but no identification was found on either. The rangers found a bicycle twenty-five yards away and placed it aboard their helicopter. A small, inoperative chain saw was sighted but not taken.

The Vietnamese officials were using a pass system for woodcutters in the area. The Vietnamese in the hamlet insisted that the victims had such passes and reiterated that the victims were merely innocent woodcutters. However, the hamlet was rated as 70 percent VC sympathetic in the latest MACV Hamlet Evaluation System rating report. The MACV investigation concluded that there was insufficient evidence to refute the ranger team's testimony, but concluded that they violated the laws of war by taking the bicycle. This result was so ludicrous, however, that after the brigade commander "took appropriate action to preclude recurrence of such an act as the taking of the bicycle," the Army dismissed the complaint.[9]

The excellent combat and personal performance of the 1st Cavalry Division troopers during its long service in Vietnam reflects very favorably on a formation which experienced great personal turbulence and heavy action. The remarkable ability of this highly mobile division to retain its characteristic élan and combat spirit is especially noteworthy in the final war years, when the rest of the Army had entered a marked state of decline in morale, fighting efficiency, and individual behavior.

9. DA Investigation Summary #214, dtd 7 Aug 72.

# CHAPTER 12

# The Total Battlefield

*From Airmobility to Armor*

After the summer of 1970, when contingents of the 1st Cavalry Division returned from Cambodia to Vietnamese soil, the American withdrawal from Southeast Asia began escalating sharply. Pentagon war plans were revised to hasten the extrication of remaining U.S. ground forces and to turn the war's conduct over entirely to the South Vietnamese regime. Partially in deference to these larger plans, Maj. Gen. George W. Putnam, Jr., was selected to command the 1st Cavalry Division in the wake of Major General Casey's tragic death on 7 July. At that time Major General Putnam was in charge of the 1st Aviation Brigade, which was heavily engaged in direct support of ARVN operations against Cambodia and thoroughly familiar with both airmobile doctrine and Vietnamese requirements.

George W. Putnam, Jr., was born in Fort Fairfield, Maine, on 5 May 1920 and was commissioned in the field artillery from officer candidate school during May 1942. During World War II, he was a gunnery instructor and battalion operations officer, arriving in Europe early in 1945. He transferred to the Regular Army in August 1946, served in the occupation forces of Japan, and became aviator-qualified ten years later. Appointed to the crucial airmobility development Howze Board, Colonel Putnam served as executive to the Secretariat, which was the administrative workhorse of the board. He was Deputy Director of Army Aviation until May 1965, when he was named the Assistant Commandant of the Army Aviation School at Fort Rucker, Alabama. His next assignment took him to Vietnam, where he served successively as the 1st Cavalry Division artillery commander, acting assistant division commander, and division chief of staff. In 1968

General Putnam became the Director of Officer Personnel in the Pentagon and returned to Vietnam in January 1970 as the commanding officer of the 1st Aviation Brigade and the chief aviation officer of USARV.

Major General Putnam was anxious to implement one important concept of the Howze Board that had not been tested because of lack of funding and the events of the Vietnam War, the Air Cavalry Combat Brigade (ACCB). The Howze Board's final report of 21 June 1962 had specified that the ACCB was one of the most original and decisive combat tools of projected airmobile force structuring. The air cavalry combat brigade was to be predominantly an offensive machine in the true spirit of swiftly mobile cavalry, designed to "seek out and destroy the enemy and carry out traditional cavalry missions." Two or more attack helicopter squadrons were to be grouped under a tactical headquarters to form a brigade in the Howze Board scheme.[1]

The 1st Cavalry Division was given a new operational area to fill the gap created by redeploying American units such as the 199th Infantry Brigade after the Cambodian incursion. The division was tasked to cover an immense region of 4,536 square miles east of Saigon, spanning the width of the entire country from the Cambodian border through War Zone D all the way to the South China Sea. This increased territorial responsibility presented Major General Putnam with the need to stretch air cavalry assets and a reason to create his de facto air cavalry combat brigade. In August 1970 he directed a divisional aircraft productivity analysis which found that the attack Cobra gunship platoons escorting the aviation lift battalions were not being used correctly and that many light observation helicopters could be freed from general support duties.

Based on the findings of this internal aircraft resource investigation, the assault weapons companies (Company D) were withdrawn from both the 227th and 229th Aviation Battalions beginning on 1 September and transferred to the control of the 1st Squadron, 9th Cavalry, as lettered air cavalry troops. Combined with a sudden infusion

1. U.S. Army Combat Developments Command Combat Arms Group, *The Origins, Deliberations, and Recommendations of the U.S. Army Tactical Mobility Requirements Board,* Fort Leavenworth, Kansas, April 1969, p. 51.

of light observation helicopters garnered from other division elements, the 9th Cavalry's aerial reconnaissance squadron (with air Troops A, B, and C) blossomed overnight into a reinforced five-troop (A, B, C, E, F) search-and-attack cavalry squadron. Several squadron scout helicopters were even outfitted with miniguns. While this represented a powerful helicopter squadron, it constituted only half of any projected air cavalry combat brigade.[2]

On 26 October 1970 Putnam secured the 3d Squadron of the 17th Cavalry, an independent aerial reconnaissance unit from his former 1st Aviation Brigade, and attached it to the division. This squadron was bolstered by an additional air cavalry Troop E (Provisional), created by temporarily redesignating the separate 334th Aviation Company on 5 December. The reinforced 1st Squadron of the 9th Cavalry and 3d Squadron of the 17th Cavalry under division control gave Major General Putnam the two search-and-attack helicopter squadrons needed to form a provisional ACCB. The air cavalry combat brigade's effectiveness was increased by assigning two elite airmobile ground reconnaissance companies to help locate enemy forces and material: Troop D of the 9th Cavalry's 1st Squadron and ranger Company H, 75th Infantry, with the 62d Infantry Platoon (Combat Tracker) thrown in for good measure. Finally, the division's sole aerial rocket artillery battalion, the Cobra-equipped "Blue Max" 2d Battalion of the 20th Artillery, was placed in direct support. The 9th Air Cavalry Brigade (Combat) was officially announced as a reality by division General Orders on 5 December 1970.

The 9th Cavalry Brigade had a rather brief and confusing existence and was mostly scattered in support of various divisional and ARVN parachutist or ranger elements. Each air cavalry troop was assigned a zone of responsibility coinciding with a division or ARVN airborne brigade sector. During the month of December alone, it restructured its task organization three times and conducted only one independent operation.

On 29 December 1970 the brigade received a warning order to locate and free allied prisoners supposedly located in the Razorback vicinity of War Zone C. ACCB Task Force Nevins arrived at the

2. 1st Cav Div, *Operational Report*, dtd 14 Nov 70, p. 21.

abandoned Special Forces Camp Dau Tieng airstrip and on the morning of 31 December established a forward operating base with refueling and rearming points. Task Force Nevins consisted of one infantry battalion and two air cavalry troops. Although the mission started with heavy action, a promising sign that the NVA/VC were guarding something worth defending, the operation was abruptly terminated that afternoon because MACV insisted on strictly observing the holiday cease-fire. All elements of Task Force Nevins were pulled back from Dau Tieng airstrip by 7:30 that evening.[3]

The provisional air cavalry combat brigade was sent into Cambodia to support four ARVN task forces along the Kampong Cham–Snoul front on 22 February 1971. Two days later it was augmented further by the addition of the air cavalry troop from the 11th Armored Cavalry Regiment. Adverse modifications to normal air cavalry maneuver were immediately imposed because of the stringent rules of engagement concerning Cambodian operations. The results were generally unsatisfactory. Tortuous clearances for fire support rendered the ACCB incapable of responding effectively with the prompt, devastating firepower it was designed to deliver. ARVN airmobile ground forces called "Browns" replaced the experienced U.S. infantry "Blues" employed by the brigade as quick reaction forces, since American combatants were not allowed on the ground. The "Browns" not only lacked rudimentary knowledge of helicopter tactics, but often were not responsive to American control.

The exact date of disbandment of the 9th Cavalry Brigade is hard to pinpoint. The ACCB was actually whittled away over a period of months as components left to reinforce the Laotian battlefront during Operation LAM SON 719, rejoin parent units, or depart Vietnam. The provisional brigade's final report gives its own closure as 15 February, but the quarterly division operation report (mentioning the unauthorized ACCB under the guise of the 1/9 Cav TF) claims reassignment to the 12th Aviation Group of 1st Aviation Brigade on 10 April 1971. General Putnam's air cavalry force was inside Cambodia with at least six troops and an aerial rocket artillery battery at the beginning of April.

The experimental air cavalry combat brigade was created as an

---

3. 1st Cav Div, *Operational Report*, dtd 13 May 71, p. 36.

ad hoc enterprise to field-test Howze Board findings under combat conditions. Its mission in Vietnam as stated was to: (1) perform reconnaissance and security for the division or its major subordinated elements, (2) engage in combat "as an economy-of-force unit," and (3) provide a limited air and ground antitank capability. Additionally, the brigade was tasked to receive and employ other combat units, such as the composite infantry and rocket artillery battalion later assigned. The brigade was to serve as a senior command and control headquarters for a specific area of operations.[4]

The ACCB concept as outlined above was actually tailored to European- and Middle Eastern–style warfare and could not be adequately demonstrated in Vietnam or Cambodia because of political constraints in the form of unique rules of engagement. General Putnam had the right idea, to create a true cavalry force by taking the gunships out of the lift battalions and giving their escort mission to the aerial artillery battalion. His ACCB harmonized with enlightened Howze Board recommendations about creating special corps cavalry reserves, but was still too advanced to be grasped adequately by the Army. In the Vietnam theater the experiment was stifled. He merely proved that the ACCB initiated 67 percent of all division actions against hostile forces during the period of its existence, that an infantry battalion would be a useful adjunct to the air cavalry combat brigade, and that further testing was needed. Even the contact initiation statistic was suspect, since it was only slightly better than the performance of the aerial reconnaissance squadron used as intended, but the ACCB possessed twice the aerial capacity. Again, the most serious and vexing problem was the lack of qualified maintenance personnel to keep the air cavalry combat brigade flying.

Further experimentation with lingering Howze Board ideas or tactical innovations was given lower priority after 20 December 1970, when the men of the 1st Cavalry Division (Airmobile) were notified of divisional selection as part of the sixth redeployment increment from Vietnam, coded KEYSTONE ROBIN CHARLIE. From the beginning of 1971 until the main division withdrawal at the end of April, the division staff was occupied primarily with planning, coordinating,

4. 9th Cav Bde (Prov) ADVARS-3, *Combat After Action Report*, dtd 23 Mar 71, with attached ltr dtd 24 Oct 70.

and implementing retrograde procedures. Fortunately, NVA/VC activity within the region actually decreased during this period, enabling the division to phase out smoothly with minimal enemy interference. Small roving platoon and squad-size airmobile cavalry forces were able to patrol their defensive sectors without difficulty.

Composite or split artillery batteries were used to provide adequate coverage, but these configurations were disadvantageous since they increased helicopter support requirements and logistical problems. The lack of meaningful North Vietnamese confrontations enabled the 1st Cavalry Division to boast of using strike infantry flexibly outside the range of tube artillery, armed only instead with Huey-transportable 81mm mortars as close defense. This was largely a hollow doctrinal improvement because the intensity of the "big battle years" in Vietnam (for the American Army, from 1966 to 1968) relegated support weapons like 81mm medium mortars to either idle storage or supplementary support in base camps. The intensity of the Ia Drang Valley campaign of late 1965 offered early demonstrable proof of mortar insufficiency compared to heavier artillery. Only the lowered level of NVA/VC combat, coupled with the lack of continuous frontline experience institutionalized by the Army rotation system, allowed the 1st Cavalry Division to rely on and claim the advantages of mortar substitution.

Beginning in February, the division's operational area was reduced as more Vietnamese territorial forces were summoned to perform guardianship over roads and hamlets and line ARVN units were moved into former cavalry firebases. The 1st Cavalry Division continued to function with high esprit throughout this difficult withdrawal period. For example, the 1st Battalion of the 5th Cavalry fought fifteen skirmishes with the North Vietnamese during its last nine days in the field, with every member of the battalion keenly aware of the exact day scheduled for extraction from the jungle. The two-battalion 2d Brigade, charged with interdiction of NVA/VC supply channels between Cambodia and War Zone D, completed its disengagement by turning over Fire Support Base Buttons to the South Vietnamese on 11 March 1971. The 1st Brigade with four battalions scoured War Zone D until 24 March, when it commenced stand-down. These events left the three-battalion 3d Brigade, slated to remain as a separate entity in Vietnam after the rest of the division departed, with defense of the central region just east of Bien Hoa and Saigon, protecting the most crucial military installations from rocket barrage.[5]

On 29 April 1971 the 1st Cavalry Division (Airmobile) furled its guidons and left Vietnam for Fort Hood, Texas. Sixteen days previously, former Assistant Division Commander-A, Brig. Gen. Jonathan R. Burton, took over the separate 3d Brigade "Garry Owen" Task Force. His separate brigade was assigned a very large area encompassing thirty-five hundred square miles and defensive responsibility for the eastern approaches toward vital Saigon and Long Binh. As a result, the brigade was reconstituted with seven recycled battalions as well as sixteen additional companies and platoons. The brigade contained four infantry battalions (2/5 Cav, 1/7 Cav, 2/8 Cav, 1/12 Cav), one reinforced artillery battalion (1/21 Arty), one composite 229th Aviation Battalion, and the 215th Support Battalion. The eight separate companies or batteries included rangers (Co H/75 Inf), aerial rocket artillery (F/79 Arty), howitzers (Prov F/26 Arty), aviation target acquisition (F/77 Arty), signal (525th), engineers (501st), military intelligence (191st), and aviation (362d). The 362d Aviation Company was effectively converted into an air cav reconnaissance troop to supplement the brigade's intrinsic Troop F, 9th Cavalry. The brigade's platoons and detachments, ranging from chemical to military police, gave the task force all the trappings of a miniature division. This formidable cavalry contingent had an assigned strength of 7,632 men at the end of 1971.

General Burton had two concurrent main concerns, finding the enemy and personnel management within the brigade. The NVA/VC routinely avoided confrontation with the cavalry, and increased emphasis was placed on remaining abreast of enemy activity. The brigade's two air cavalry troops gained the most information on enemy dispositions and discovered new base camps or resupply routes. Air cavalry missions were accomplished normally by using OH6A scout "white bird" in a visual reconnaissance role to draw fire under the covering support of an AH1G Cobra "red bird," which also provided suppressive fire, navigational control, and a communications

---

5. 1st Cav Div, *KEYSTONE ROBIN CHARLIE After Action Report*, dtd 15 Apr 71, Appendix 3 to Annex C.

link to higher headquarters. Together, these "pink team" combinations rendered 44 percent of all credited brigade kills from April through December 1971.[6]

The outstanding success of the ranger company was attributed to its extensive training, as well as individual ranger team knowledge that the entire brigade stood ready to react rapidly in case of adverse hostile contact. The strength of Company H, 75th Infantry (Ranger), had been reduced to conform with 3d Brigade size, but Burton doubled the number of teams from four to eight based on its battlefield performance. All ranger volunteers were trained by the company staff, and the rigorous training standards washed out three-fourths of all candidates each training cycle. Qualified rangers became skilled in rappelling and the use of McQuire rigs, which were Special Forces–developed hoisting devices for penetration of difficult tropical terrain. Brigade ranger teams were inserted into enemy-dominated territory on missions of five-day duration primarily to gather intelligence, but their skill at ambush accounted for approximately 30 percent of all brigade kills from April through December.[7]

The brigade's internal military intelligence posture was enhanced by close coordination between the Vietnamese Counterintelligence Service and the dreaded Military Security Service (MSS) beginning in September 1971. When four MSS agents were added to the brigade, it marked the first time that MSS personnel were assigned to a U.S. combat unit in Vietnam. Several female MSS agents were hired in a drug-suppression role. General Burton implemented a strong drug abuse intervention program centered around the special Brigade Drug Rehabilitation Center. From 1 May to 31 October, 633 brigade personnel underwent detoxification and treatment at the center. Unannounced urinalysis testing was conducted frequently, and often identified drug users were sent to the Drug Abuser Holding Center (DAHC) for administrative and judicial action.[8]

Troop welfare was also maintained through positive rewards, primarily by the introduction of a rifle company rotation program. The

6. DAAG-PAP-A (M), *Senior Officer Debriefing Report: BG Jonathan R. Burton,* dtd 3 May 72, p. 7.
7. Ibid., pp. 6–7.
8. Ibid., p. 13.

infantry companies operated independently to cover the wide expanse of the brigade's area of responsibility, but each remained within the artillery fan of at least one firebase. The general pattern kept companies in the field for fifteen days, where they received helicopter resupply of ammunition, rations, and water every three or four days. If the landing zone conditions permitted, a hot meal and ice cream, change of clothing, mail, and other comfort items were delivered. When the company completed its fifteen-day field duty, it was rotated to a fire support base to provide security for another five days. During this time, the company was refitted, underwent bunker assault and marksmanship training, and took care of personnel affairs. Every forty-five days, on a rotational basis, each rifle company and recon platoon was sent to the First Team R&R Center, opened at the beach resort of Vung Tau in March 1971, for three days of rest and recreation. The troops were given considerable latitude to unwind after six weeks in the field. The maintenance of the center was a drain on brigade material, personnel, and monetary assets, but the high effect on morale was considered worthwhile.

Brig. Gen. James F. Hamlet, another former Assistant Division Commander-A, took over the separate 3d Brigade on 14 December 1971. The formation was infused with a rash of transferred soldiers from other redeploying divisions, such as the 101st Airborne (Airmobile), at the rate of five hundred a week. Regardless of "bush time," these new arrivals were sent through the brigade Combat Training Center. The cavalry brigade continued its fourfold mission of defending the Saigon–Long Binh military complex, training Vietnamese territorial forces, remaining ready to move into other military regions as a security fire brigade, and preparing to execute various late-war contingency plans.[9]

The separate 3d Brigade was still involved occasionally in heavy combat, despite continuing readjustment of operational areas to bring it closer into the defensive arc of the Bien Hoa–Long Binh–Saigon rocket belt (that area within range of NVA rocket attacks). The brigade's former forward operating base at FOB Mace, beside Nui Chua Chan, was closed, and a new rearmament and refueling facility was

9. 3d Bde (Sep) 1st Cav Div, *Operational Report*, dtd 1 May 72, p. 1 (Mission) and Tab I-1 (Brigade Strength Report).

opened at Xuan Loc airfield. On 3 January 1972 the 2d Battalion of the 5th Cavalry was displaced to FSB Charger in conjunction with this rearward move. A platoon of Company C was attacked by elements of the *33d NVA Regiment* using a hasty U-shaped ambush. The company maneuvered to link up with its trapped platoon and to attack the ambush site from another direction. The North Vietnamese fled the field after a fierce two-hour skirmish, during which the airmobile cavalry reaction force, gunships, and medical evacuation helicopters all suffered heavy return fire.

On 1 April 1972 the generally slow pace of the war in Military Region 3 suddenly changed. Three NVA divisions attacked from the Cambodian Fishhook vicinity after staging a diversionary assault north of Tay Ninh. The enemy quickly overran Loc Ninh and besieged An Loc. The 3d Brigade ground troops were not members of this fighting force, but the two brigade air troops (F/9 Cav and D/229 Avn Bn) and the aerial rocket artillery battery (F/79 Arty) were involved in constant combat to stem the North Vietnamese advance. Despite intense antiaircraft fire from 23mm, 37mm, and even some 85mm AA guns, the brigade's AH1G Cobra gunships destroyed twenty-nine trucks and five tanks and damaged a sixth.

Attempts to rescue American advisors at Loc Ninh were unsuccessful, but several advisors were lifted by brigade helicopters from the Cam Lo Bridge after being cut off and surrounded for three days. The brigade aviators also evacuated ARVN soldiers and civilians from Bu Dop and Song Be, helped repulse an NVA attack against the Nui Ba Den radio relay site, and supported several South Vietnamese counterattacks into An Loc.[10]

The American withdrawal from Vietnam continued unabated even though such renewed NVA/VC onslaughts threatened to destroy the Saigon government without continued U.S. military presence. The 3d Brigade (Separate) of the 1st Cavalry Division was redeployed from South Vietnam as part of Increment XII KEYSTONE PHEASANT on 26 June 1972 and returned to rejoin the rest of the 1st Cavalry Division at Fort Hood, Texas. The division had been located there since its own KEYSTONE ROBIN CHARLIE arrival the previous year.

10. 3d Bde 1st Cav Div, *Operational Report*, dtd 1 May 72.

# 1st Cavalry Division Presence in Vietnam

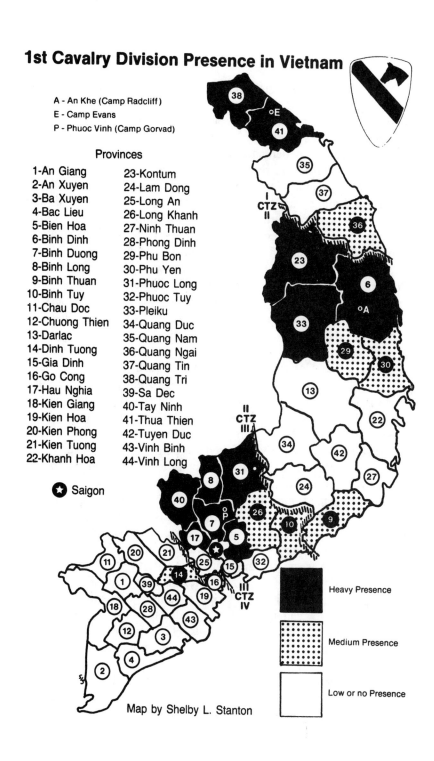

A - An Khe (Camp Radcliff)
E - Camp Evans
P - Phuoc Vinh (Camp Gorvad)

### Provinces

1-An Giang
2-An Xuyen
3-Ba Xuyen
4-Bac Lieu
5-Bien Hoa
6-Binh Dinh
7-Binh Duong
8-Binh Long
9-Binh Thuan
10-Binh Tuy
11-Chau Doc
12-Chuong Thien
13-Darlac
14-Dinh Tuong
15-Gia Dinh
16-Go Cong
17-Hau Nghia
18-Kien Giang
19-Kien Hoa
20-Kien Phong
21-Kien Tuong
22-Khanh Hoa

23-Kontum
24-Lam Dong
25-Long An
26-Long Khanh
27-Ninh Thuan
28-Phong Dinh
29-Phu Bon
30-Phu Yen
31-Phuoc Long
32-Phuoc Tuy
33-Pleiku
34-Quang Duc
35-Quang Nam
36-Quang Ngai
37-Quang Tin
38-Quang Tri
39-Sa Dec
40-Tay Ninh
41-Thua Thien
42-Tuyen Duc
43-Vinh Binh
44-Vinh Long

★ Saigon

Heavy Presence

Medium Presence

Low or no Presence

Map by Shelby L. Stanton

The United States military posture was extremely poor. The most difficult Army task was reconforming its forces to meet national defense priorities, especially the protection of North America and Europe in case of major conflict. This risk had been neglected during the limited war in Indochina, and a long-overdue major reorientation of Army structure was required. New tactical organizations were mandated, but public dissatisfaction with the war had drastically reduced the Army's size and budget. The seemingly radical Modern Volunteer Army Program with no draft was implemented with great difficulty past 13 October 1970, and large quantities of war material were still being siphoned off to Vietnam and other allies.

Lt. Gen. Harry W. O. Kinnard was now in charge of the Army Combat Developments Command, and he still wanted to properly test the air cavalry combat brigade. This organization remained a personal favorite from the Howze Board deliberations, which he considered one step further down the tactical development road than the air assault division. The ACCBs envisioned by the Howze Board were homogeneous forces of air cavalry squadrons, each backed up by aerial rocket artillery, that would be capable of performing the Army's cavalry mission (except the armored cavalry regimental ground mission). An ACCB would contain everything required—firing helicopters, scout helicopters, and lift helicopters—to provide each corps with its own small, self-contained army. While the ACCB was not intended to be a powerful group of shooting helicopters to block Soviet armor, it still provided a swiftly mobile and balanced unit that could dominate hundreds of square miles of Iranian desert or Russian Pripyat marshland. Properly balanced and commanded, the brigade could harass and destroy widespread enemy forces by using scouts to find enemy mechanized and infantry forces, airmobile infantry to furnish ambushes and local security, and gunships to attack selected targets.

On 23 November 1970 Army Chief of Staff General Westmoreland approved the creation of a "triple capability" division combining armor, airmobile, and air cavalry brigades to test possible high-intensity-warfare structural modifications. He programmed the 1st Cavalry Division to be the vehicle for this project upon its arrival at Fort Hood, Texas, from Vietnam. On 5 May 1971 the cavalry division was reorganized accordingly as the experimental Triple Capability (TRICAP) Division. It used the personnel and equipment of the 1st Armored Division, which in turn sent its flag to Germany.

The potential of the TRICAP and allied ACCB enterprise was suffocated from the start by Army bureaucratic imcompetence. The test division was placed at Fort Hood, an entrenched armor post full of officers convinced that tanks would dominate future battlefields and that aircraft were only supplementary to tracked steel. Furthermore, both TRICAP and ACCB were buried in an institutional morass under the unlikely direction of Project MASSTER (Mobile Army Sensor Systems Test, Evaluation, and Review).

Project MASSTER was established in 1969 to manage the development of surveillance, target acquisition, and night observation (STANO) equipment and doctrine. The task apparently engendered so little respect that the Army's Vice Chief of Staff was forced to direct that "CONARC, USACDC (Combat Developments Command), USAMC (Material Command), and USASA (Security Agency) establish visible STANO offices within their headquarters to serve as points of contact for the coordination of STANO matters in intercommand and Department of the Army Staff–command activities."[11] Nestled at Fort Hood since 1 October 1969, MASSTER provided an already funded but suitably vague bureaucratic instrument available to incorporate TRICAP.

The method that produced the highly successful 11th Air Assault and airmobile 1st Cavalry Divisions had been the appointment of a young brigadier "tiger" with open directives and wide latitude to report back with results. In this case, however, the Army followed its usual nonprogressive path of testing and analysis, reports and more reports. TRICAP was incorporated into the unwieldy MASSTER management structure, which was expanded to oversee sensor and night surveillance equipment development, the integrated battlefield control system (IBCS), and, last, TRICAP/ACCB. On 25 June 1971 the MASSTER acronym was conveniently retained by changing the organizational title to Modern Army Selected Systems Test, Evaluation, and Review. The revised MASSTER charter was published on 2 September, designating the commanding general of III Corps and Fort Hood to be the commanding general of MASSTER as an additional duty.[12]

---

11. USCONARC, *Annual Historical Summary: FY 71*, p. 121–22.
12. III Corps and Fort Hood GO 275, dtd 25 Jun 71, and CONARC, *Annual Historical Summary*, dtd 15 Jul 72, p. 122.

The charter's objectives were so hopelessly diversified as to be almost ludicrous. MASSTER (nicknamed the "Mass Management Structure") was charged—in this exact order—with testing to improve the Army's combat intelligence/reconnaissance and STANO capabilities, improving the Army's tactical command and control capability within the IBCS framework, evaluating the air cavalry combat brigade and the TRICAP division concept, and supporting the development of other selected concepts, organizations, and material systems which might be assigned for evaluation.

Confusion reigned supreme. The serious shortage of helicopters initially prevented the air cavalry combat brigade from either conforming to the organization envisioned by the Army Combat Developments Command or commencing meaningful training. Although one air cavalry squadron was present, the other envisioned attack helicopter squadron was instead a battalion of medium tanks.

Even more detrimental to evaluation of either ACCB or the TRICAP testing was the fact that the resource-starved Army suddenly decided to redress emergency war plans for Europe. The Army ordered the entire TRICAP/ACCB test package to be made potentially available as a combat-ready division. During the same month that the 1st Cavalry Division was redesignated as TRICAP, instructions were received to fashion the new structure to facilitate quick conversion into a standard armored division which, by using reserve components, could replace the already-departed armored division at Fort Hood. So many variations on the possible employment of the 1st Cavalry Division began appearing that frustrated staff officers, drafting long-range stationing alternatives for Army units, simply labeled it the "Experimental Division"—with no particular numbering, title, or imagined composition—under Fort Hood entries.[13]

The 1st Cavalry Division, with its 3d Brigade still separated in Vietnam, lost most of its airmobility under TRICAP. A 4th Brigade was formed, and the armored commanders at Fort Hood brought over their tanks and armored personnel carriers. The Johnny-come-lately battalion to Vietnam (5th Bn, 7th Cav) was inactivated, and the howitzer battalion picked up overseas (1st Bn, 30th Arty) sent to Fort

13. CONARC/ARSTRIKE, *Annual Historical Summary—FY 1971*, dtd 15 Jul 72, Table 8.

Sill, Oklahoma. This left the 1st Cavalry Division (TRICAP) with four mechanized cavalry battalions from each of its traditional regiments (1st Bn, 5th Cav; 2d Bn, 7th Cav; 1st Bn, 8th Cav; 2d Bn, 12th Cav); two aviation units newly formed at Fort Hood (170th Avn Co and 230th Avn Bn, later retitled as the 227th to preserve Vietnam heritage); three tank battalions transferred from the armored division (1st and 2d Bns, 13th Armor, and 1st Bn, 81st Armor); three artillery battalions (the 1st Bn, 6th Arty, and 3d Bn, 19th Arty, arrived from the armored division; the 1st Bn, 77th Arty, remained; and both 2d Bn, 19th Arty, and 2d Bn, 20th Arty, were inactivated); and one cavalry reconnaissance squadron (4th Sqdn, 9th Cav, previously the armored division's 3d Sqdn, 1st Cav, which became the 1st Sqdn, 9th Cav, when the latter returned from Vietnam on 28 June 1971). The support structure was revised as well.[14]

Numerous MASSTER tests were undertaken during the year. As predicted by the airmobile pessimists, battalion organizational and tactical development models were jointly tested with such things as STANO border surveillance/anti-infiltration devices, unattended ground sensors, and battle information control centers. An attack helicopter squadron was finally activated for both TRICAP and ACCB testing at the end of February 1972, when the 4th Squadron, 9th Cavalry, was reformed at Fort Hood. The unit was raised by folding down the 170th Aviation Company and inactivating Company C, 2d Battalion, 13th Armor, on temporary duty supporting tests at Hunter-Liggett Military Reservation in California, and bringing back its personnel and equipment. Only the personal intervention of Lt. Gen. George P. Seneff, Jr., now the III Corps commander, forced the Army to rescind the attack helicopter title and authorize reorganization of the unit as an air cavalry squadron on 22 March 1972.[15]

---

14. The 1st Cavalry Division (TRICAP) support base contained the 8th Engineer Bn, 13th Signal Bn, 15th Medical Bn, 15th Supply & Transport Bn, 27th Maint Bn, 315th Support Bn, 545th MP Co, 15th Admin Co, 15th Finance Co, and 15th Data Processing Unit. Note the loss of the 15th Trans Bn and 15th Supply & Service Bn, but the addition of two new battalions (15th S&T Bn, 315th Spt Bn) in their places. Source of 1st Cav Div reorganization from DA Msg 091810Z Apr 71, Subj: Reorg and Inactiv of Armored Div; and DA Msg 091930Z Mar 71, Subj: Reorg to TRICAP Div.

15. ODCSFOR, *Semi-Annual Hist Report, January–June 1972*, p. 4.

While air cavalry proponents became more frustrated over the miring of TRICAP and ACCB in the bureaucratic quagmire at Fort Hood, the 101st Airborne Division (Airmobile) was completely reorganized and rebuilt at Fort Campbell, Kentucky, during 1972. The 101st Airborne Division was the second airmobile division raised by the Army for Vietnam duty. On 4 October 1974 the division dropped its parenthetical airmobile identifier in exchange for air assault and became the Army's second air assault formation. Although the "unique capability of its air assault resources" was not recognized as an official part of its mission statement until 31 August 1977, the division's modern rendezvous with destiny was clear. On that date the division's 477 helicopters and 16,600 well-trained light infantrymen and women, replete with their silver air assault badges, placed the 101st Airborne Division (Air Assault) in the dynamic future of airmobility forfeited by the 1st Cavalry Division.[16]

TRICAP and ACCB failed because their real purpose was simply to justify as many troops in the force structure as possible, while revitalizing the old Howze Board dream of an air cavalry combat brigade in the early 1970s. The resulting division mix consisted of an infantry brigade, an armor brigade, and an air cavalry brigade, each of which was too vastly different to form an integrated whole.[17]

The overriding demand to conform scant Army resources to projected war plans forced the experimental division into an emergency armored division mode for European contingencies. This was perhaps a foreseeable result of placing cavalry units in the backyard of heavy armor advocates at Fort Hood. Light and swift air cavalry could not be nurtured in such an environment. Finally, the experiment was doomed by its subjugation to the bureaucratic MASSTER beast. Throughout the rest of the decade, the triplex surveillance-cavalry-target acquisition relationship was solidified by the Armor and Military Intelligence Centers. By 1 August 1980 this latter development inevitably transformed the 1st Cavalry into a heavy armored division with a target servicing air cavalry attack brigade.

Airmobile firepower relied not on tanks linked to target-seeking

---

16. 101st Abn Div, *1975 Historical Summary*, p. 31; *Fiscal 1977 Historical Summary*, pp. 9, 12.
17. USAMHI, Seneff Debriefing.

aircraft, but on fusing manpower, weapons, and aerial transport with cavalry doctrine. Air assault integrates attack, transport, and observation aircraft with the fighting elements of a division. By maintaining intrinsic helicopter and other aircraft resources, the air assault division insures the continuous availability of proficient aviation responsive to its unique tactical requirements. Even an air assault aviation cadre subjected to heavy battle loss and fatigue on a nuclear battlefield will sustain this advantage. While the 1st Cavalry Division performed this role, it was officially termed airmobile. The 101st Airborne Division (Air Assault) now wears the crown, and in many historical respects this is proper, given the original preferences of General Howze and other paratroopers who formulated modern Army airmobility principles. As long as the 101st represents a lean, light infantry organization, the forward thinking and spirit that General Kinnard considered essential for dashing airmobile operations will be preserved.

The Army's cavalry normally consisted of either ground or aerial reconnaissance units. Armored cavalry was used much like standard armor in Vietnam. It was in the air that cavalry played such a unique role. The 1st Cavalry Division, endowed with the great mobility and flexible response offered by its organic aircraft, was the first organization to combine light infantry and artillery howitzer forces with vertical assault, aerial firepower, and air reconnaissance capabilities in combat. Deployed to Vietnam as early as was practical, the division quickly demonstrated its skill and determination in finding and eliminating the enemy through air assault and clearing operations. Unleashed throughout the country as MACV's premier fighting formation to locate and destroy the elusive NVA/VC, the First Team insured battlefield domination with a dazzling array of cavalry techniques ranging from sustained pursuit and cavalry raids to screening and cavalry exploitation.

Unfortunately, the United States Army ultimately failed to grasp the permanent bond between fast raiding and other cavalry techniques with modern airmobile and air assault doctrine. The fusion of the Vietnam-era 1st Cavalry Division with helicopter mobility and firepower forged a powerful war machine, naturally attuned to optimum performance of military tasks in the rich tradition of American light cavalry. By allowing the 1st Cavalry Division to be retreaded into a conventional armored division, the United States Army forsook the original foresight of Lieutenant General Gavin, the prophet of airmobility.

General Gavin's vision of modern aerial cavalry freed the Army from the tyranny of terrain and sent Skytroopers over the cloud-banked rim of Southeast Asia to battle the enemy from the air. His plea still echoes through the vaults of the Pentagon, the grassy fields of Fort Benning, the concrete helicopter pads of Fort Rucker, and the overgrown foxholes of the lush Ia Drang Valley with a resounding, "Cavalry, and I don't mean horses! I mean helicopters and light aircraft to lift soldiers armed with automatic weapons and hand-carried light antitank weapons, and also lightweight reconnaissance vehicles, mounting antitank weapons the equal of or better than the Russian [tanks]. . . . If ever in the history of our armed forces there was a need for a cavalry arm—airlifted in light planes, helicopters, and assault-type aircraft—this was it!" The legacy of the 1st Cavalry Division remains, and the need still exists.

# 1st Cavalry Division (Airmobile)
## *Assigned Units*

## Command

Headquarters & Headquarters Company, 1st Cavalry Division
Headquarters & Headquarters Company, 1st Brigade
Headquarters & Headquarters Company, 2d Brigade
Headquarters & Headquarters Company, 3d Brigade
Headquarters & Headquarters Company and Band, Support
  Command
Headquarters & Headquarters Company, Rear (Provisional)

## Infantry

1st Battalion, 5th  Cavalry
2d  Battalion, 5th  Cavalry
1st Battalion, 7th  Cavalry
2d  Battalion, 7th  Cavalry
5th Battalion, 7th  Cavalry
1st Battalion, 8th  Cavalry
2d  Battalion, 8th  Cavalry
1st Battalion, 12th Cavalry
2d  Battalion, 12th Cavalry

## Aviation

Headquarters & Headquarters Company, 11th Aviation Group
227th Aviation Battalion (Assault Helicopter)
228th Aviation Battalion (Assault Support Helicopter)
229th Aviation Battalion (Assault Helicopter)

11th Aviation Company (General Support)
Air Traffic Control Platoon (Provisional)

**Division Artillery**

2d Battalion, 19th Artillery (105mm Howitzer)
2d Battalion, 20th Artillery (Aerial Rocket)
1st Battalion, 21st Artillery (105mm Howitzer)
1st Battalion, 30th Artillery (155mm Howitzer)[1]
1st Battalion, 77th Artillery (105mm Howitzer)
Battery E, 82d Artillery (Aviation)

**Division Reconnaissance**

1st Squadron, 9th Cavalry (Aerial Reconnaissance)
11th Pathfinder Company/Platoon (Provisional)
Company E, 52d Infantry (Long Range Patrol)[2]
Company H, 75th Infantry (Ranger)[2]

**Division Support**

1st Forward Service Support Element
2d Forward Service Support Element
3d Forward Service Support Element
8th Engineer Battalion
13th Signal Battalion
15th Medical Battalion
15th Supply & Service Battalion
15th Transportation Battalion (Aircraft Maintenance & Supply)
27th Maintenance Battalion
15th Administrative Company
371st Army Security Agency Company
545th Military Police Company

1. The 1st Battalion, 30th Artillery, was attached to division 1 Jul 66 and assigned 1 Jun 68–6 Apr 71.
2. Company E of the 52d Infantry was formed as the long-range patrol company of the division on 20 Dec 67; on 1 Feb 69 it was inactivated and its assets were used to create Company H, 75th Infantry (Ranger).

1st Personnel Services Battalion (Provisional)[3]
An Khe Airfield Command (Provisional)[4]
Replacement Training School/FIRST TEAM Academy
(Provisional)[5]
U.S. Army Special Security Detachment

## Attached Units

### Armored Cavalry and Infantry

| | |
|---|---|
| 1st Battalion, 50th Infantry (Mechanized) | 22 Sep 67–15 Mar 68 |
| 11th Armored Cavalry Regiment, elements | 12 Apr 69–April 71 |
| 25th Infantry Platoon (Scout Dog) | 20 June 66–20 Mar 71 |
| 34th Infantry Platoon (Scout Dog) | 21 Nov 66–20 Aug 72 |
| 37th Infantry Platoon (Scout Dog) | 15 Nov 69–7 Mar 71 |
| 54th Infantry Detachment (Ground Radar) | 27 May 66–17 Jan 68 |
| 62d Infantry Platoon (Combat Tracker) | 15 Feb 68–15 Aug 72 |

### Aviation

| | |
|---|---|
| 3d Squadron, 17th Cavalry (Air) | 26 Oct 70–April 71 |
| Troop F, 3d Squadron, 4th Cavalry | April 71 |
| Air Cavalry Troop, 11th Arm Cavalry | 24 Feb 71–Mar 71 |
| 17th Aviation Company (Fixed-Wing CV-2) | 15 Sep 65–1 Jan 67 |
| 53d Aviation Detachment (Provisional) | 1 Sep 66–30 Oct 66 |
| 273d Aviation Company (Heavy Helicopter) | Nov 68–Mar 71 |
| 334th Aviation Company (Aerial Weapons) on temporary duty as Troop E (Prov), 3d Sqdn, 17th Cavalry | 5 Dec 70–17 Jan 71 |
| 478th Aviation Company (Heavy Helicopter) | Mar 66–28 Feb 69 |

3. The provisional 1st Personnel Services Battalion was formed by the division on 26 Jan 68 and was disestablished on 1 Jul 69, when it became a company in size.
4. The An Khe Airfield Command was created by internal division resources on 15 Dec 65 and was under division control until Oct 67.
5. The Replacement Training School, later termed the FIRST TEAM Academy, was a provisional organization formed on 1 Oct 66, lasting until the division left Vietnam.

## Aircraft Maintenance Transportation Detachments

| | |
|---|---|
| 1st Squadron, 9th Cavalry | 98th, 151st, 166th, 545th |
| 2d Battalion, 20th Artillery | 80th, 171st, 329th |
| Battery E, 82d Artillery | 564th |
| 11th Aviation Company | 150th |
| 227th Aviation Battalion | 166th, 390th, 394th, 400th |
| 228th Aviation Battalion | 51st, 165th, 255th |
| 229th Aviation Battalion | 391st, 392d, 393d, 571st |
| 3d Squadron, 17th Cavalry | 369th, 575th, 576th |
| 273d Aviation Company | 652d |
| 478th Aviation Company | 382d |

## Artillery

| | |
|---|---|
| Btry A, 5th Bn, 2d Artillery (40mm) | Jan 69–Mar 71 |
| 6th Bn, 14th Artillery (175mm Gun) | 29 Oct 65–1 Feb 66 |
| 2d Bn, 17th Artillery (105mm Howitzer) | 25 Oct 65–1966 |
| 3d Bn, 18th Artillery (8-inch Howitzer) | 26 Oct 65–1 Oct 66 |
| Btry B, 29th Artillery (Searchlight) | 23 Oct 65–6 Oct 66 |
| 268th Artillery Detachment (Radar) | 14 Apr 69–2 Jan 71 |
| 273d Artillery Detachment (Radar) | 5 May 69–15 Apr 71 |

## Support

| | |
|---|---|
| 14th Military History Detachment | 27 Dec 65–20 Mar 72 |
| 26th Chemical Platoon (CBR Center) | 16 Oct 65–26 Mar 72 |
| 41st Public Information Detachment | 21 Mar 67–30 Jun 71 |
| 42d Public Information Detachment | 21 Mar 67–29 Apr 71 |
| 184th Chemical Platoon (Direct Support) | 16 Oct 65–1 Mar 71 |
| 191st Military Intelligence Company | 25 Aug 65–29 Mar 71 |
| 583d Military Intelligence Detachment (Interrogation) | 20 Jul 67–16 Feb 70 |
| American Red Cross Female Contingent | |

## Air Force Weather Squadron Detachments

| | |
|---|---|
| 5th Weather Squadron, Dets 24 and 31 | Dec 66–Mar 71 |
| 30th Weather Squadron elements | Oct 65–Nov 66 |

# 1st Cavalry Division (Airmobile) Formation*

| Division Unit | Source |
|---|---|
| Headquarters & Headquarters Company, 1st Cavalry Division (Airmobile) | Headquarters & Headquarters Company, 11th Air Assault Division (Test) |
| **HHC, 1st Brigade** | **HHC, 1st Brigade, 11th Air Assault Division** |
| 1st Battalion (Airborne), 8th Cavalry | 1st Battalion (Airborne), 188th Infantry |
| 2d Battalion (Airborne), 8th Cavalry | 1st Battalion (Airborne), 511th Infantry |
| 1st Battalion (Airborne), 12th Cavalry | 1st Battalion (Airborne), 187th Infantry |
| **HHC, 2d Brigade** | **HHC, 2d Brigade, 2d Infantry Division** |
| 1st Battalion, 5th Cavalry | 1st Battalion, 38th Infantry |
| 2d Battalion, 5th Cavalry | 2d Battalion, 38th Infantry |
| 2d Battalion, 12th Cavalry | 1st Battalion, 23d Infantry |

* Source: Hq 11th AAD AJVGT Ltr dtd 30 Jun 65, Subj: Reorganization of Units, w/Incl 1, and USARPAC GO 325, dtd 22 Nov 65 (inactivation and activation of aviation units).

| _Division Unit_ | _Source_ |
|---|---|
| **HHC, 3d Brigade** | **HHC, 3d Brigade, 2d Infantry Division** |
| 1st Battalion, 7th Cavalry | 2d Battalion, 23d Infantry |
| 2d Battalion, 7th Cavalry | 2d Battalion, 9th Infantry |
| 5th Battalion, 7th Cavalry** | 1st Battalion, 11th Infantry** |
| **HHB, Division Artillery** | **HHB, 11th Air Assault Division Artillery** |
| 2d Battalion, 19th Artillery (105mm) | 6th Battalion, 81st Artillery (105mm) |
| 2d Battalion, 20th Artillery (Aer Rocket) | 3d Battalion, 377th Artillery (Aer Rocket) |
| 1st Battalion, 21st Artillery (105mm) | 5th Battalion, 38th Artillery (105mm) |
| 1st Battalion, 77th Artillery (105mm) | 1st Battalion, 15th Artillery (105mm) |
| **HHC & Band, Support Command** | **HHC & Band, 11th Air Assault Division Spt Cmd** |
| 8th Engineer Battalion | 127th Engineer Battalion |
| 13th Signal Battalion | 511th Signal Battalion |
| 15th Medical Battalion | 11th Medical Battalion |
| 15th Supply & Service Battalion | 408th Supply & Service Battalion |
| 15th Transportation Battalion | 611th Aircraft Maintenance & Supply Battalion |
| 27th Maintenance Battalion | 711th Maintenance Battalion |
| 15th Administrative Company | 11th Administrative Company |
| 15th Supply & Service Battalion Aerial Equipment Support Company (Airborne) | 165th Aerial Equipment Support Detachment |

** 5th Battalion, 7th Cavalry, was activated 1 April 1966 at Fort Carson, Colorado, and joined the 1st Cavalry Division in Vietnam. Source of unit derived from _Army Times_, dtd 25 May 1966, "Carson Greets Airmobile Unit."

| Division Unit | Source |
|---|---|
| 545th Military Police Company | 11th Military Police Company |
| 191st Military Intelligence Detachment | 11th Millitary Intelligence Detachment |
| 371st Army Security Agency Company | Company C, 313th Army Security Agency Battalion |
| **HHC, 11th Aviation Group (Airmobile)** | **HHC, 11th Aviation Group (Test)** |
| HHC, 227th Aviation Battalion | HHC, 227th Aviation Battalion |
| Company A, 227th Aviation Battalion | Company A, 227th Aviation Battalion |
| Company B, 227th Aviation Battalion | Aviation Company, 6th Special Forces Group |
| Company C, 227th Aviation Battalion | Aviation Company, 7th Special Forces Group |
| Company D, 227th Aviation Battalion | 110th Aviation Company (Aerial Weapons) |
| HHC, 228th Aviation Battalion | HHC, 228th Aviation Battalion |
| Company A, 228th Aviation Battalion | 132d Aviation Company (Assault Support Hel) |
| Company B, 228th Aviation Battalion | 133d Aviation Company (Assault Support Hel) |
| Company C, 228th Aviation Battalion | 202d Aviation Company (Assault Support Hel) |
| HHC, 229th Aviation Battalion | HHC, 229th Aviation Battalion |
| Company A, 229th Aviation Battalion | Company A, 4th Aviation Battalion |
| Company B, 229th Aviation Battalion | Company A, 5th Aviation Battalion |
| Company C, 229th Aviation Battalion | 194th Aviation Company (Assault Helicopter) |
| Company D, 229th Aviation Battalion | 131st Aviation Company (Aerial Weapons) |
| 11th Aviation Company | 11th Aviation Company (General Support) |
| 1st Squadron, 9th Cavalry | 3d Squadron, 17th Cavalry |

# SOURCES AND BIBLIOGRAPHY

The research for this book was primarily based on division documents prepared during the Vietnam conflict, especially the quarterly operational reports, as supplemented by higher command histories issued on an annual basis. The internal division combat after action reports issued at the conclusion of most operations were very useful, as were the wartime division magazine issues of the *The First Team*. Annual historical summaries of the U.S. Continental Army Command and the reports of various Army testing boards provided much information on the stateside service of both the 11th Air Assault and 1st Cavalry Divisions before and after Vietnam service. One important postwar source was the senior officer oral history program conducted by the Oral History Branch, U.S. Army History Institute, Carlisle Barracks, Pennsylvania. The author also interviewed key participants with the 1st Cavalry Division during the Vietnam era, and made extensive utilization of the materials assembled for his earlier *Vietnam Order of Battle* project.

The following is a listing of the more readily available resources, although many reports and articles not listed below are cited for reader convenience in text footnotes.

*The Air Cavalry Division*, Vietnam: 1st Cavalry Division, 1969.

1st Cavalry Division, *Quarterly Command Report*, dtd 1 Dec 65, OACSFOR-OT-RD 650110.

1st Cavalry Division, *Quarterly Command Report*, dtd 10 Jan 66, OACSFOR-OT-RD 650109.

1st Cavalry Division, *Operational Report*, dtd 5 May 66, OACSFOR-OT-RD 660119.

1st Cavalry Division, *Operational Report*, dtd 15 Aug 66, OACSFOR-OT-RD 660292.

1st Cavalry Division, *Operational Report*, dtd 22 Nov 66, OACSFOR-OT-RD 660505.

1st Cavalry Division, *Operational Report*, dtd 15 Feb 67, OACSFOR-OT-RD 670226.

1st Cavalry Division, *Operational Report*, dtd 23 May 67, OACSFOR-OT-RD 670473.

1st Cavalry Division, *Operational Report*, dtd 15 Aug 67, OACSFOR-OT-RD 670798.

1st Cavalry Division, *Operational Report*, dtd 15 Nov 67, OACSFOR-OT-RD 674236.

1st Cavalry Division, *Operational Report*, dtd 17 Mar 68, OACSFOR-OT-RD 681288.

1st Cavalry Division, *Operational Report*, dtd 13 Jun 68, OACSFOR-OT-RD 682337.

1st Cavalry Division, *Operational Report*, dtd 20 Aug 68, OACSFOR-OT-RD 683305.

1st Cavalry Division, *Operational Report*, dtd 6 Dec 68, OACSFOR-OT-UT 684268.

1st Cavalry Division, *Operational Report*, dtd 15 Feb 69, OACSFOR-OT-UT 691115.

1st Cavalry Division, *Operational Report*, dtd 15 Apr 69, OACSFOR-OT-UT 692094.

1st Cavalry Division, *Operational Report*, dtd 15 Aug 69, OACSFOR-OT-UT 693030.

1st Cavalry Division, *Operational Report*, dtd 15 Nov 69, OACSFOR-OT-UT 694007.

1st Cavalry Division, *Operational Report*, dtd 15 Feb 70, OACSFOR-OT-UT 701072.

1st Cavalry Division, *Operational Report*, dtd 15 May 70, OACSFOR-OT-UT 702040.

1st Cavalry Division, *Operational Report*, dtd 14 Aug 70, OACSFOR-OT-UT 703016.

1st Cavalry Division, *Operational Report*, dtd 14 Nov 70, OACSFOR-OT-UT 704030.

1st Cavalry Division, *Keystone Robin Charlie Redeployment Report*, dtd 15 Apr 71, OACSFOR-OT-UT 71XOO6.

3d Brigade (Separate), *Operational Report*, dtd 13 Nov 71.

3d Brigade (Separate), *Operational Report*, dtd 1 May 72.

3d Brigade (Separate), *Operational Report*, dtd 20 Jun 72.

14th Military History Detachment, *The First Team in Cambodia*, dtd 15 Feb 71.

14th Military History Detachment, *The Construction of a Fire Base in the 1st Cavalry Division*, dtd 10 Oct 69.

14th Military History Detachment, *Bunker Busting: Attack on Fortified Areas*, dtd 18 Jan 71.

Albright, John, John A. Cash, and Allan W. Sandsrum, *Seven Firefights in Vietnam*, Washington, D.C.: U.S. Government Printing Office, 1970.

Bergerson, Frederic A., *The Army Gets an Air Force*, Baltimore and London: The Johns Hopkins University Press, 1980.

Brennan, Matthew, *Brennan's War*, Novato, California: Presidio Press, 1985.

Coleman, J. D., *Memories of the First Team in Vietnam*, 1st Cavalry Division Information Office: Vietnam, 1969.

Enthovan, Alain C. and K. Wayne Smith, *How Much is Enough: Shaping the Defense Program, 1961–1969*, New York: Harper & Row, 1961.

Fehrenbach, T. R., *This Kind of War*, New York: Macmillan Company, 1963.

Gavin, Maj. Gen. James M., "Cavalry and I Don't Mean Horses!", *Armor*, Volume LXIII, No. 3.

Hymoff, Edward, *The First Air Cavalry Division: Vietnam*, New York: M. W. Ladd Publishing Co., 1966.

Kinnard, Douglas, *The War Managers*, University of New England Press, 1977.

Marshall, S.L.A., *Battles in the Monsoon*, New York: Morrow, 1967.

———, *Bird: The Christmastide Battle*, New York: Cowles Book Co., 1968. 1968.

Mason, Robert, *Chickenhawk*, New York: Viking Press, 1978.

Ney, Virgil, *Evolution of the U.S. Army Division, 1939–1968*, CORG Memorandum M-365, Fort Belvoir, Virginia: U.S. Army Combat Developments Command, 1969.

Palmer, Gen. Bruce, Jr., *The 25-year War: America's Military Role In Vietnam*, University Press of Kentucky, 1984.

Palmer, Brig. Gen. Dave R., *Summons of the Trumpet*, Novato, California: Presidio Press, 1978.

Sharp, Adm. U.S.G. and Gen. W. C. Westmoreland, *Report on the War in Vietnam (as of 30 Jun 68)*, Washington, D.C.: U.S. Government Printing Office, 1968.

Stanton, Shelby L., *The Rise and Fall of an American Army*, Novato, California: Presidio Press, 1985.

Summers, Col. Harry G., *Vietnam War Almanac*, New York: Facts on File Publications, 1985.

Tolson, Lt. Gen. John J., *Vietnam Studies: Airmobility, 1961–1971*, Washington, D.C.: Department of the Army, 1973.

U.S. Army Training and Doctrine Command, *A History of Army 86*, Volumes I and II, Fort Monroe, Virginia: TRADOC Historical Monograph Series.

U.S. Army Combat Developments Command, *The Origins, Deliberations, and Recommendations of the U.S. Army Tactical Mobility Requirements Board*, Fort Leavenworth, Kansas, 1969.

Westmoreland, Gen. William C., *A Soldier Reports*, New York: Doubleday & Company, 1976.

# INDEX